TRUMP'S AMERICA

TRUMP'S AMERICA

THE TRUTH ABOUT OUR NATION'S GREAT COMEBACK

NEWT GINGRICH

CENTER
STREET®

NEW YORK   NASHVILLE

Center Street
Hachette Book Group
1290 Avenue of the Americas, New York, NY 10104
centerstreet.com
twitter.com/centerstreet

Originally published in hardcover in June 2018
First Trade Paperback Edition: February 2019

Center Street is a division of Hachette Book Group, Inc. The Center Street name
and logo are trademarks of Hachette Book Group, Inc.

The publisher is not responsible for websites (or their content) that are not owned
by the publisher.

The Hachette Speakers Bureau provides a wide range of authors for speaking
events. To find out more, go to www.HachetteSpeakersBureau.com
or call (866) 376-6591.

Library of Congress Cataloging-in-Publication Data has been applied for.

ISBNs: 978-1-5460-7707-7 (trade paperback), 978-1-5460-7705-3 (ebook)

Printed in the United States of America

LSC-C

4 2020

This book is dedicated to the United States
Ambassador to the Holy See, my wife Callista;
our invaluable and irreplaceable associate,
Bess Kelly; and to my grandchildren, Maggie
and Robert Cushman, who will inherit
the America that is evolving.

CONTENTS

PART ONE

THE GREAT COMEBACK

America is deeply divided along a political-cultural fault line. One side wants to see America return to prosperity, strength, and its traditional values. The other wants to fundamentally change America into a different nation that rejects many of its founding principles. Trump's America is not just a name for the people who elected him—it describes this former group that supports the aspirant vision of America that President Trump and his supporters want us to revive. This section aims to explain the American comeback that's underway.

CHAPTER ONE

THE FIGHT FOR TRUMP'S AMERICA

America is in the midst of a cultural-political civil war—a fight over our very identity as a people.

For decades, this conflict has been fought quietly in city halls, classrooms, school boards, courtrooms, town squares, and state houses across the country. However, the election of President Trump has clarified the battle lines in this struggle and elevated these individual fights into a united national conflict.

On one side of this conflict is a factional anti-Trump coalition—a strange amalgam of radicals, liberals, globalists, establishment elites from both parties, and blatantly anti-American groups loosely held together by their hostility to and disdain for the president. On the other side is Trump's America—the millions of hardworking people who are united by respect for our foundational freedoms, traditional values, and history of limited commonsense governance.

Before the president rallied Trump's America and gave us a national voice, the various groups that would eventually form the anti-Trump coalition were winning on their own. For decades, they have meticulously undermined our traditions through politics and courts, entertainment and news media, and liberal schools and curriculum to quietly impose new worldviews on everyday Americans that are counter to our historic principles.

However, the tide turned after the 2016 presidential elections.

Here's the truth the mainstream media is hiding from you: Today, Trump's America is winning.

Under President Trump, America is experiencing a great comeback. After nearly a decade of recession and tepid job creation, our economy is booming. In addition, ISIS has been effectively destroyed, illegal immigration is down, our military is being rebuilt, and our veterans are getting the health care and support they deserve. The administration is achieving success across a variety of sectors daily.

Perhaps more important than these successes, however, is the reinvigoration of America's patriotic sense of self, which the rise of Donald Trump has awakened. Our country is being reconnected to our founding principles, the values that made America the greatest country in the world, and in doing so, is coming to understand just how destructive the last few decades of elite leadership have been to our freedom, prosperity, and safety.

Of course, the anti-Trump coalition is in complete denial about America's comeback under Trump. For them, it is incomprehensible that someone like President Trump, and the tens of millions of so-called deplorables who fervently support him, could be on the verge of reclaiming America.

Because the news media is fully a part of the anti-Trump coalition, its members will not accurately report what is happening in America under President Trump.

This is a major reason why I wrote this book.

Trump's America: The Truth About America's Great Comeback

is intended as a resource for Americans who want the truth about the significant accomplishments President Trump has achieved in his first year-and-a-half in office.

It is also an attempt to describe the nature of the cultural-political conflict we are in and vividly explain the differences in values and principles between Trump's America and those who oppose us.

THE ANTI-TRUMP COALITION

At the center of the fight I'm describing is ultimately one question: Is America an exceptional country? Or more specifically, is America's historic prosperity and power due to our nation's unique founding principles, and is it our duty as a people to uphold those ideals?

My daughter, Jackie Cushman, touched on this notion in a column she wrote in July 2009.[1] She observed that in 2008, President Obama promised us "change we could believe in," and it turned out he wanted to change what we believed.

Jackie's insight points out one of the few common-yet-tenuous threads that bind the members of the anti-Trump coalition together. In various ways, they all want to redefine America, and they would all be happier if the members of Trump's America were once again ignored and forgotten.

This anti-Trump coalition encompasses an incredibly broad group of people. It includes, of course, Democrats of all stripes—from the most moderate to the most radically liberal. It includes activists who protest for niche sexual and gender issues. It includes race-focused activist groups such as Black Lives Matter and La Raza. It also includes violent radical groups, such as Antifa that oppose the American system in general.

Most of the reporters, anchors, producers, and editors of the mainstream media are active, enthusiastic members or cheerleaders of the anti-Trump coalition, as are the ivory tower academics at our elite universities and the legions serving in our government bureaucracies.

This branch of the anti-Trump coalition favors group rights over individual rights and prefers a strong dictatorial bureaucracy that imposes boundaries to freedom upon everyday Americans. They think the consent of the governed is the consent of the ignorant and the deplorable.

Many of these people believe traditional America is an immoral, brutal regime, which tramples on human rights and inflicts its evil upon the world. They say that the American dream does not exist—and it is in fact a racist social construction.

This branch of the anti-Trump coalition believes that some ideas should be censored, religions are oppressive, hateful, dangerous institutions—and only the government can safely guide people to live appropriately.

Ultimately, they say America is not exceptional and should be more like other countries, rather than try to live up to its founding ideals. However, these members are confused. To render America unexceptional is to eliminate the essence of America. In their effort to renounce American exceptionalism, they are in fact seeking to create a new post-American society.

This part of the anti-Trump coalition is made up of groups that typically align with the Left. However, there is another important wing of the anti-Trump coalition: the orderly institutionalists.

This branch includes so-called never Trumpers in the Republican Party. Like many bureaucrats, who are mostly apolitical, these conservatives are part of an orderly sect that simply wants the world to be neat, tidy, and predictable. They value institutional process more highly than achievement gained by risk.

They are the types of institutionalists who bitterly opposed

Barry Goldwater, Ronald Reagan, Jack Kemp, myself, and other Republicans who violated the norm.

This risk-averse group includes much of the national security establishment, which fully adheres to the "new world order" that President George H.W. Bush described on September 11, 1990, before a Joint Session of Congress.

This speech is an important marker for this group because President Bush's concept was not an expressly American order, nor was it a traditional American-British order. It was a "world order."

As such, these orderly institutionalists support the Paris Accord, the Trans-Pacific Partnership, and other international agreements regardless of how Americans are hurt in the name of maintaining the world order. For them, American exceptionalism is a campaign phrase, not a practical doctrine.

These people bitterly oppose President Trump for two main reasons: First, President Trump clearly rejects their global order policies on trade and foreign relations. More importantly, members of this group hate Trump because he explicitly points out and repudiates their failures.

By the time President H.W. Bush's son was in the Oval Office, the so-called new world order had degenerated into a series of wars. Trump was the first major Republican candidate to publicly acknowledge that the global market-focused, peace-through-payment approach of the new world order had utterly failed and stuck Americans with tremendous costs—in blood and in resources.

This is why the orderly institutionalist branch of the then-forming anti-Trump coalition balked at candidate Trump's "Make America Great Again" slogan. It was a callback to Ronald Reagan's similar campaign slogan from 1980. Implicit in the "Make America Great Again" theme is the belief that our country has lost what had made it great and that politicians, bureaucrats, and other elite leaders are to blame.

To many Americans, it was an uplifting, optimistic campaign call. However, for the institutional establishment it was a declaration of war against all the forces that led America through decades of failure.

So, the entire anti-Trump coalition presents a much more complicated paradigm than the typical Right-Left, conservative-liberal, or Republican-Democrat dynamic. This is why we saw a host of very different Republicans, a self-avowed socialist, and the matriarch of the Democratic establishment all declare him enemy No. 1 in 2016.

From a distance, and certainly in the daily news, it appears that Trump is constantly facing a political coalition that seems insurmountable. The anti-Trump coalition takes comfort in this. Its members reassure themselves that his administration cannot withstand the onslaught much longer.

However, this 30,000-foot-view misses something important: Some in this varied coalition of radicals, liberals, conservatives, and elites oppose Trump because they disagree with his vision for America, some oppose his personality, and some simply oppose America.

They are not actually united on anything except their dislike for the president. Their battle cry is "resistance" because, as a coalition, they could never possibly offer a coherent shared vision for the future.

This is their greatest weakness.

TRUMP'S AMERICA

To be sure, Trump's America is also a diverse group, with many different opinions and backgrounds. However, we are united by our national creed and our shared belief in the American dream.

At the beating heart of Trump's America is the patriotic belief in America's exceptional nature.

Those who are part of Trump's America know that in our nation, the people are sovereign and are the source of power for our government—not vice versa. Despite centuries of other civilizations modernizing and becoming more democratic, this is still a unique, exceptional trait of America.

We believe that America, on balance, is morally good. We are a people of deep faith with an unsurpassed record of charity and fairness at home and across the globe. We are the nation that twice liberated Europe, contained the Soviet empire, freed Kuwait, and has championed human rights.

As President Trump said in his first address to the United Nations on September 19, 2017:

> It is an eternal credit to the American character that even after we and our allies emerged victorious from the bloodiest war in history, we did not seek territorial expansion, or attempt to oppose and impose our way of life on others. Instead, we helped build institutions such as this one to defend the sovereignty, security, and prosperity for all.

We believe citizens from any background can work hard, pursue their dreams, and achieve success and prosperity for themselves and their families.

Furthermore, in Trump's America we uphold—with conviction—the understanding that individuals can speak, worship, and live as they please and, so long as those actions do not infringe upon the fundamental rights of others, do so without threat of consequences from the government.

These are all bedrock beliefs that traditionally make America exceptional.

On an everyday level, Trump's America stands for the flag and the national anthem. We like patriotic movies. We believe our young men and women in uniform—both police and military—are heroic for risking their lives to protect us. We believe in the value of a hard day's work and abhor political correctness as a threat to freedom of faith and speech.

Furthermore, in contrast to the elite "citizen of the world" attitude, the people of Trump's America intuit that if America is strong, then our families will have better futures.

This is the feeling that President Trump's "Make America Great Again" slogan so perfectly captures. Trump's America is deeply unhappy with the direction the governing and cultural elite have taken America over the past several decades. We want change and we hope for a better future. We want a fighting administration, and we expect the Left to smear it and attack it. Each smear, each allegation, each biased news story is more proof that President Trump stands for real change.

We are Trump's America because President Trump has unified us by acting as a reversion—a course correction—toward the traditional belief that America is an exceptional country that should act in accordance with historic American principles.

The belief of Trump's America in American exceptionalism is at the heart of the political-cultural civil war because it defines virtually every Trump administration policy and it is driving our country's great comeback.

THE TRUMP PATH TO EXCEPTIONALISM

In his own life, President Trump has witnessed American exceptionalism at work. At a relatively young age, he achieved economic success and gained national recognition. He has wonderful children and grandchildren. He owns his own golf courses, so he can play when he likes. And he won a remarkable race for the presidency.

For Trump, America *is* an exceptional country.

His natural bias is to think highly of the Founding Fathers and the other leaders who gave us this remarkable system of freedom and to praise their achievements.

This pro-Americanism, which upholds the Constitution, follows the vision of our Founders, sees the flag as the symbol of a free nation, and agrees with President Abraham Lincoln that America is "the last best hope of mankind," is horrifying to many people in the anti-Trump coalition.

Trump's greatest strength has been his ability to understand that clearly confronting an unacceptable reality and articulating its failure with passion and conviction can change history. This single insight has guided his campaigning and his governing.

As a businessman, Trump amassed billions by seeing opportunities others missed. He also built large projects by persisting through obstacles and selling people on a vision of success they had not imagined. As president, he has brought the same kind of brute force clarity to politics and government.

When Trump has strategic insight about fixing broken government systems, he is not intimidated by initial rejection, failure, or opposition. He simply redoubles his efforts and looks for new avenues of communication or paths to success. This pattern of stubbornly sticking to an idea and finding new ways to market it is precisely what he did through a half century of success in business.

This ability to address longtime problems without the inhibitions, or the self-censorship to which other so-called sophisticated people feel required to submit, has already made his presidency historic.

Tax reform had not been passed in 30 years because it is difficult and requires a lot of work. Similarly, politicians have campaigned on immigration reform and border security for decades and then comfortably placed these issues on the backburner for "more pressing" issues once elected. Past presidents have done the same about shrinking government and cutting regulations. President Trump is not letting up on any of these challenges.

Consistently, President Trump has approached situations with common sense, ignored the elites—including some on his own staff and government—and followed his instincts. This approach, combined with his knack for using vivid, direct language, has infuriated the anti-Trump coalition over and over.

It is this pattern of looking at reality and applying common sense which has made Trump and his presidency so threatening to his opponents. The values of Trump's America are antithetical to the values of the anti-Trump coalition.

Trump believes patriotism and sovereignty are vital to our survival as a nation. He believes Americans should be proud of our flag, national anthem, history, culture, and military.

Many in the anti-Trump coalition say patriotism and sovereignty are words for belligerence and warmongering. They regard our national traditions as backward, bigoted, and ignorant.

Ultimately Trump's America and the post-American society that the anti-Trump coalition represents are incapable of coexisting. One will simply defeat the other. There is no room for compromise. Trump has understood this perfectly since day one.

The outcome of the struggle will determine America's future for a generation or more.

LEARNING FROM THE PAST

If Trump's America is to win, we must understand how a radical, fringe ideology became the dominant outlook of the political and economic establishment—and why the presidency of Donald Trump represents a turning point in the fight against it.

The brand of radicalism that fuels the left-wing branch of the anti-Trump coalition has been growing for half a century.

Its advocates knew they could never impose their values on America under our traditional system, so they started to undermine it.

At first, their efforts were subtle.

It started in the 1960s, when liberal academics began to critique traditional American ideals. Within a few years, this insidious academic approach was replaced by more open, radical repudiations of traditional America.

At the time, the Left was a radical offshoot of American politics—a minority fringe group that was sympathetic to Euro-Asian communist and socialist movements. The effort to infiltrate academia was effectively the start of the Left's training and recruitment strategy. After more than 40 years, that strategy has been a clear success.

Countless cohorts of young American college students attended courses in which professors promoted secularism, liberal social mores, and a twisted version of history, which casts traditional America as the villain in nearly every era of its existence.

Many of those students then went on to earn postgraduate degrees and ultimately make careers in academia, wherein they continue propagandizing left-wing ideals to their pupils while demonizing traditional American viewpoints. As traditional American values became identified with racism and sexism in the universities, people with traditional American values were pushed out of academia. This cycle produced an increasingly radical and shrill feedback loop that made our schools rapidly more left-leaning.

Meanwhile, those of us who believe in traditional America continued to send our children to these schools and supported these institutions with monetary gifts. I frequently tell conservative groups that we are crazy for paying liberal colleges who train our children and grandchildren to despise us.

It was from this foundation in academia that the left-wing branch of today's anti-Trump coalition grew.

As other newly indoctrinated students moved on to legal, political, media, and economic professions, the beliefs of the Left became the norm in elite circles.

As the late U.S. Supreme Court Justice Antonin Scalia brilliantly wrote in a series of opinions, the courts moved from interpreting the Constitution to inventing a new American Constitution based on radical values, which increasingly repudiate the thinking and writing of the Founding Fathers.

Parallel to the transformation of our courts, American bureaucracies grew in size and power. They were increasingly led by liberals looking to impose the "correct" policies on a nation of voters they consider too ignorant to adopt sound policies voluntarily.

After all, as Hillary Clinton warned in 2016, millions of Americans who were "deplorables" could not be expected to make wise decisions. The social elites believe they preside over a country of inadequately educated, culturally reactionary, and hopelessly selfish people. The elites aim to sacrifice the misguided populace's values, interests, prosperity, and futures to create a supposedly better country. To many in the socially elite echelons of the anti-Trump coalition, traditional America is racist, misogynistic, homophobic, oppressive, anti-female, militaristic, and violent.

Those in the orderly institutionalist wing of the anti-Trump coalition took a multifaceted approach working around the will of these "deplorable" voters without verbalizing it.

Increasingly, America became submerged in international agreements, which force our country to answer to foreign bureaucracies. Some in this group recruited powerful corporate leaders and popular celebrities to help coerce the ostensibly backward and inadequate general population into "doing the right thing." As a result, an elite cultural environment was culti-vated in which thinking the wrong thoughts could lead to pub-lic condemnation, ostracism, isolation, and even firing.

The news media joined the entertainment industry (which it now emulates) to become the enthusiastic cheerleaders for this new, improved America—and the voracious critics of our tradi-tional model.

However, the deep flaws in their post-American nightmare have started to show.

Under the leadership of the orderly institutionalists, 6,948 young Americans have been killed and more than 52,000 wounded in our wars in the Middle East. These conflicts have cost $7.6 tril-lion. Under President Obama, success was seemingly impossible, and we were faced with either defeat or war without end.

We have seen poor children suffer because expensive, union-ized inner city schools have collapsed under their own dysfunc-tion. We have seen the rise of zones of intense violence in big cities such as Baltimore, Chicago, and St. Louis. We watched a decaying economy cause millions of Americans to be forced out of the middle class. The anti-Trump coalition's contempt for small-town America has led to real bitterness. Millions of Americans who once had good jobs in manufacturing feel they have been abandoned by the national leadership.

These hardworking Americans watched their jobs disap-pear as our nation's leaders entered trade deals that favored other countries over America. Meanwhile, these Americans were repeatedly told by Obama that the economy was steadily improving.

In fact, the Obama years' failure to grow economically deepened the anger felt by people who might have tolerated an overbearing government if it delivered. However, being lectured by leaders who were clearly failing was simply unacceptable and increasingly enraging.

The breaking point may have been the explosion of illegal immigration, which led millions of Americans to believe that their government had abandoned their economic and cultural interests in favor of foreigners who broke the law.

Over time, this rise of social, political, and economic ideologies, which rejected the notion of American exceptionalism and were counter to historic American principles, led to a series of political movements aimed at returning our country to its founding principles.

In fact, you can track the rise of Trump's America through Goldwater, Reagan, the Contract with America, and the Tea Party. Trump's America is the response to the rising left-wing forces that want to replace America with something else.

IN A FIGHT OVER IDENTITY, ONLY ONE SIDE CAN WIN

The essence of this cultural-political civil war is a fight over America's identity.

Normal political conflict within the same American identity tends to lead to compromise and finding common ground. If opposing political parties are operating within a broad consensus on what America stands for, there is room for negotiated settlements.

Today, however, there is no broad agreement, no common ground, and no consensus about who we are. This makes compromise nearly impossible.

We have experienced similar periods of identity conflicts in the past.

During the American Revolution, the Founding Fathers were going to win or be hung as traitors to the British Crown.

President Lincoln got slightly less than 40 percent of the vote in a country so bitterly divided it drifted into a civil war. Southerners believed they were fighting for the survival of their civilization, and Northerners believed they were fighting for the survival of the Constitution and the Union. These two sides were mutually exclusive. Those, like General George B. McClellan, who kept looking for peace through compromise, misunderstood the nature of the struggle.

Both Winston Churchill's and Ronald Reagan's great insights into the nature of Nazi and Soviet ideology, respectively, allowed them to see clearly what the foreign policy elite of their times could not: There could be no compromise. Evil had to be defeated.

These types of conflicts do not necessarily involve bloodshed, but they do provoke intense feelings that lead to bitterly fought elections.

The election of 1800 was a fierce fight over the relationship our budding nation would have with Great Britain and our commitment to Republican principles. This was most vividly seen in the controversy over the Alien and Sedition Acts. These were four laws that were broadly aimed at making it more difficult for immigrants to become naturalized in early America and to make it illegal to lie while criticizing the government. The laws were supported by the Federalist Party, which had been fighting an undeclared war with France under President John Adams. Jefferson and his fellow Democratic-Republicans saw the acts as a means for the Federalists to suppress free speech and centralize power. Ultimately, this fight became so intense it led to Jefferson completely wiping out the Federalist Party.

The election of 1896 was a deep identity struggle between the urban industrialism of President William McKinley and the rural populism of William Jennings Bryan. Bryan was a charismatic, ideological rural populist and had essentially waged a war on the urban industry. McKinley, on the other hand, realized that industry and prosperity was vital to the survival of our nation. The fight was so intense that the GOP remains to this day the party of business and jobs while the populist rhetoric of Elizabeth Warren can be traced directly to the Bryan campaign.

Today, President Trump's election and presidency represent the emergence of a political-cultural identity fight, which will define American politics for the foreseeable future.

As in identity fights of the past, there can be no compromise in the battle between Trump's America and the anti-Trump coalition. One side will win, and one side will lose.

CHAPTER TWO

THE COMEBACK OF "ONE NATION"

A key component of America's great comeback under President Donald Trump is his efforts to reunify the country around a common set of values—to make us "one nation" again. The issue where this can most clearly be seen is immigration.

This statement may come as a surprise because it is the opposite of the media's narrative, which insists that what President Trump is trying to do in immigration is divisive.

This disconnect is because the elite media is part of the anti-Trump coalition, and Donald Trump is rolling back the disastrous immigration regime its members have imposed on the country for the past 40 years. That's why every new proposal or statement from President Trump about our immigration system is greeted with howls of outrage from the anti-Trump coalition.

A perfect example of this phenomenon was in August 2017, when the president announced his support for the Reforming American Immigration for a Strong Economy (RAISE) Act, which would reduce the level of legal immigration from the historic highs of the last 40 years and institute a merit-based system for accepting immigrants.

During a press briefing with White House Senior Policy Advisor Stephen Miller to discuss the bill, CNN's Jim Acosta asserted that Trump's support for the bill was "not in keeping with American tradition when it comes to immigration."

Acosta argued that prioritizing English-speaking immigrants, and those with skills useful for the U.S. economy was an attempt to "change what it means to be an immigrant coming into this country." He also asserted that prioritizing English-speaking immigrants would mean all immigrants would come from Britain and Australia—not so subtlety accusing President Trump of racism.

Miller quickly pointed out Acosta's complete ignorance of both civics and history, noting that current naturalization law requires new citizens to be proficient in English. He also expressed astonishment that Acosta thought only people from Britain and Australia spoke English. Indeed, an estimated 1.5 billion people speak English throughout the world. It is the official language of more than 60 countries. In fact, recent estimates suggest that India, with its more than 1 billion people, has more English speakers than any country in the world, including the United States.[1]

Miller also correctly pointed out that immigration to the United States has historically ebbed and flowed. Large periods of high immigration have been followed by significant slowdowns—either to give the new immigrants a chance to assimilate, or in response to changing economic conditions.

So, contrary to the arguments of Acosta and the anti-Trump coalition, there is no requirement of the American creed that says immigration rates must remain high or that we must not prioritize those immigrants who have the skills needed to succeed.

Later, in January 2018, during the president's State of the

Union Address, Trump expanded on his immigration policy and laid out a Republican framework for immigration, which Democrats should have accepted.

The framework calls for offering a legal status and an eventual pathway to citizenship that's based on merit to more than 1.8 million people who were brought to the United States illegally as children. It also calls for fully funding border security—including the southern border wall. The framework would also replace the current, aimless, lottery system for granting visas with one that is based on an immigrant's skills, education, and ability to make a living. Finally, it would place limitations on the family members which immigrants can sponsor to follow them to the United States to include only nuclear family members.

The anti-Trump coalition's refusal to accept this deal, at least at the time I am writing this book, shows just how hollow their rhetoric is. They claim they are sticking up for the well-being of people here illegally who are otherwise law-abiding and have been in America for a long time. So, they should have welcomed this framework. It would help three times the number of so-called dreamers that President Obama's Deferred Action for Childhood Arrivals program did, and it would promote merit-based immigration, for which Chuck Schumer, Bernie Sanders, and even Barack Obama have advocated in the past.[2] However, every single Democrat and several Republicans voted against his proposal in the Senate, attacking the idea of prioritizing immigrants that will integrate and succeed as un-American.

THE MELTING POT

It is true that a key component of American exceptionalism is the idea that anyone of any ethnicity can become an American. But the anti-Trump coalition forgets that the American model puts the obligation on the immigrant to do what it takes to succeed.

Most societies in history have been relatively homogenous ethnically. Diversity was considered a weakness because it led to division, causing societies to come apart.

By contrast, while our country started ethnically homogenous, we developed a way of thinking which was unique about what it meant to be an American.

Americans came to be defined by their common values, not by their country of origin.

We opened our country to talent from anywhere under one condition: that immigrants abandon their old identity in favor of a new American one. In other words, they had to assimilate to become American.

Assimilation meant, among other things, learning English, participating in civil society, and being self-sufficient. Meanwhile, other aspects of the immigrant's native culture—art, music, food—would enrich American society.

Because of the success of this historically unique approach, America became known as the "melting pot." As our country grew increasingly multiethnic throughout its first two centuries thanks to immigration, we still maintained a common culture around which to identify. This allowed America to enjoy the advantages of the entrepreneurial drive and energy of immigrants while avoiding the ethnic strife we have seen in other countries throughout history.

Throughout those centuries, the melting pot has been the cultural system that produced luminism, abstract expressionism, jazz, the blues, rock and roll, baseball, American football, objective news, Broadway, Hollywood, worldwide television broadcasting, hamburgers, hot dogs, macaroni and cheese, and many other inventions, which have roots in other cultures yet are uniquely American.

On a far more serious note, the notions that all men are

created equal, that government should answer to its people, and that humans have natural, inalienable rights endowed by God rather than government were not born in America. They came from other parts of the world, were absorbed by our forefathers, enshrined in our founding documents, and became the core American principles that unite us.

It is also worth noting that our nation's civil rights movements succeeded thanks to the same principles. Civil rights leaders insisted that African Americans have the right to join the common American civic culture rather than be separated from it through segregation and racism.

If we are all children of God, Reverend Dr. Martin Luther King Jr. argued, then we are all endowed by our Creator with the same rights, and it is a violation of the meaning of America to deny people those rights.

Earlier, Susan B. Anthony had made similar arguments to help women gain the right to vote.

Sadly, many in the anti-Trump coalition have rejected this historic American approach.

Because its members reject American exceptionalism, the anti-Trump coalition doesn't think immigrants should assimilate to America; they think America should devolve into segments defined by immigrants and intellectuals.

Because they reject assimilation, many in the anti-Trump coalition do not believe immigrants should be required to learn English; they insist on multilingual public education, ballots, and government accommodations.

Because they favor wealth redistribution and big government instead of personal responsibility and economic growth, many in the anti-Trump coalition are eager to expand welfare and other government benefits. So, its adherents favor visa lotteries and extended family ties over skills and education as the determining factor for who can immigrate. And they are eager to encourage more illegal immigration, creating sanctuary cities and states even if it means protecting dangerous criminals from deportation. The poorer neighborhoods, where gangs like MS-13 run rampant, may suffer but the elites feel self-righteous in their gated communities.

Because many in the anti-Trump coalition see unchecked immigration as a vehicle for political power, they don't care about the impact of adding millions of unskilled laborers to the workforce has on wages. In fact, some in corporate America benefit from it.

Because many in the anti-Trump coalition think that American society is inherently racist, they don't think that different ethnic groups should be expected to embrace a common, American culture. They view the melting pot as a form of arrogant cultural supremacy and prefer America to be "multicultural."

Because they think that America is a source of evil in this world, members of the anti-Trump coalition view immigration and race relations not as vehicles to make America strong, but instead as fault lines of potential division to make America weaker and therefore less dangerous.

In fact, the anti-Trump coalition is attacking the very idea that the United States is one, indivisible nation.

While this effort to partition our country helps some people get elected to public office or earn acclaim and tenure in Ivy League circles, it threatens our unity and weakens us as a nation.

REASSERTING THE TRADITIONAL AMERICAN MODEL

Contrary to the elite media narrative, Donald Trump has never been anti-immigrant. His mother came from Scotland. He has been married twice to first-generation immigrants. He has employed many immigrants in his various properties around the world.

However, Trump does believe the American immigration system should be designed to strengthen America. He believes in assimilation, in learning English, and in self-sufficiency. He does not believe we owe the world open borders and a massive transfer of wealth for anyone who shows up.

So, while Trump does support growing and expanding our American culture through immigration, he wants to do so in a measured, intelligent way. That means reinstating policies based on melting-pot assimilation that promotes American ideals.

Over the past one and a half years, President Trump has put the full weight of his administration behind a series of reforms aimed at reasserting the traditional American model of the melting pot in our immigration system.

The merit-based system of the previously mentioned RAISE Act would prioritize immigrants based on their ability to assimilate and contribute to the economy.

While nuclear family members would still be given the same status they have today, the bill would then introduce a point system based on several factors, including education, job prospects, and proficiency in English.

First, prioritizing those with needed skills is a long-overdue reform in an age of increasing automation, where the number of jobs available for those without effective learning is dwindling.

It is perfectly in keeping with American history that our immigration levels adjust with economic reality. The Brookings Institute (a liberal think tank) noted in May 2012 that the ability to change our immigration policy in response to our national economic needs "remains an important economic policy issue, both in the short term and for our country's long-term growth strategy."[3]

Brookings also noted that there was enormous debate over how immigration impacts wages for low-skilled workers and cited a 2008 study that showed "the influx of immigrant workers from 1990 to 2006 reduced the wages of low-skilled workers by 4.7 percent."

The elite, highly educated, well-paid members of the anti-Trump coalition may roll their eyes at a 4.7 percent wage reduction. However, for relatively poor workers with only a high school education, that's a big deal. For someone who makes $20,000 per year, a 4.7 percent salary increase would be almost an additional $1,000 in their pocket. That extra $83 per month might be the difference between being able to pay rent, buy food, or get treatment for an illness or injury.

Workers like the one in this example, who have had their wages reduced (or have been laid off) due to unchecked immigration, fall squarely into the category of "forgotten Americans," who Donald Trump pledged to help during his campaign. As president, he is working to deliver on that promise.

ASSIMILATION IS NECESSARY

In addition to the prioritization of immigrants with needed skills, the insistence on assimilation is an explicit corrective to the anti-Trump coalition's rejection of the traditional American model over the past 30 years.

Consider these statements from historic American leaders and how closely they track with what Donald Trump is doing.

On January 12, 1802, Founding Father Alexander Hamilton (himself an immigrant) wrote an essay in the *New York Evening Post* in support of strong naturalization requirements. In the essay, Hamilton wrote:

The safety of a republic depends essentially on the energy of a common National sentiment; on a uniformity of principles and habits; on the exemption of the citizens from foreign bias, and prejudice; and on that love of country which will almost invariably be found to be closely connected with birth, education and family.... Some reasonable term ought to be allowed to enable aliens to get rid of foreign and acquire American attachments; to learn the principles and imbibe the spirit of our government; and to admit of at least a probability of their feeling a real interest in our affairs.[4]

In the essay, Hamilton was proposing a five-year residency requirement for naturalization to replace the 14-year requirement under the Naturalization Act of 1798 (and in opposition to an open-border approach being proposed in the newspaper—some things never change). It's important to note that Hamilton's purpose for this requirement was for the incoming immigrant to "get rid of foreign and acquire American attachments." Hamilton went on to warn:

To admit foreigners indiscriminately to the rights of citizens, the moment they put foot in our country, as recommended in the Message, would be nothing less, than to admit the Grecian Horse into the Citadel of our Liberty and Sovereignty.

After reading Hamilton's warning, President Trump's calls to thoroughly vet refugees and immigrants coming from war-torn countries and to end widely abused chain migration policies seem rather uncontroversial, don't they?

We see evidence of this conscious effort to preserve the melting pot more than 90 years after Hamilton's essay, when future president Teddy Roosevelt gave his "True Americanism" speech in 1894. In it, Roosevelt said:

We freely extend the hand of welcome and of good-fellowship to every man, no matter what his creed or birthplace, who comes here honestly intent on becoming a good United States citizen like the rest of us; but we have a right, and it is our duty, to demand that he shall indeed become so and shall not confuse the issues with which we are struggling by introducing among us Old World quarrels and prejudices.

Now, compare Roosevelt's words with President Trump's weekly address from December 2017:

It is time to create a merit-based immigration system that makes sense for a modern economy—selecting new arrivals based on their ability to support themselves financially and to make positive contributions to U.S. society. Base it on love of our country. We want people that come in, that can love our country.

Clearly, Trump's positions on immigration policy are not some radical new take—as media and the Washington elite assert. President Trump is working to return the United States to the system that was supported by Hamilton, Roosevelt, and many other eminent American leaders.

THE SALAD BOWL

Ultimately, the melting pot helped make America the "shining city upon a hill" that Ronald Reagan spoke of throughout his presidency. We became this shining city because we have successfully attracted tens of millions of people who believed in American exceptionalism and wanted to join our culture.

However, for many Americans today—many of whom are Trump supporters—it has been a generation since our nation fit the romantic symbol of the shining city. This is in part because, around the 1970s, we began to move away from the core American idea that we are—and must be—one nation.

Despite warnings from our past leaders and more than two centuries of success as a nation, in the 1960s academic and political elites started working to replace the melting pot with what they call "the salad bowl" of multiculturalism. By the 1970s they had made progress.

The idea of the salad bowl is that various racial, ethnic, or religious groups in America represent various distinct ingredients, which provide their individual, unique flavors. We are all Americans because we are all in the same bowl, covered by the same dressing. That's the concept.

On its face, this theory seems guided by an innocent motive—to celebrate everyone's unique heritage and respect the cultures from which we came. However, it actually presents a radically different model for America—the opposite of E Pluribus Unum. As liberal historian Arthur Schlesinger Jr. said in a 1992 article titled "The Disuniting of America" (which shared a title with a book he wrote the previous year), multiculturalism "belittles *unum* and glorifies *pluribus*."[5]

Schlesinger, who was a lifelong Democrat and an advisor to President John F. Kennedy, warned that multiculturalism engendered a philosophy that "America is not a nation of individuals at all but a nation of groups." The diminishing of individual rights in favor of group rights creates a tribal system of factions constantly vying for power. It is the opposite of the individual-focused rights enumerated in the Bill of Rights and Constitution.

Even back in 1992, Schlesinger predicted the current cultural strife in America:

What happens when people of different ethnic origins, speaking different languages and professing different religions, settle in the same geographical locality and live under the same political sovereignty? Unless a common purpose binds them together, tribal hostilities will drive them apart. Ethnic and racial conflict, it seems evident, will now replace the conflict of ideologies as the explosive issue of our times.

Bruce Thornton, a research fellow at the Hoover Institution, echoed Schlesinger's concerns 20 years later in an essay on the necessity of assimilation in the American immigration system.

The melting pot, Thornton said, "communicated the historically exceptional notion of American identity as one formed not by the accidents of blood, sect, or race, but by the unifying beliefs and political ideals enshrined in the Declaration of Independence and the Constitution: the notion of individual, inalienable human rights that transcend group identity."[6]

Also noting that, as a country, we have failed numerous times throughout history to respect the inalienable rights of many of our people, Thornton points out that over time the American legislative and judicial systems have worked to correct past wrongs. He also acknowledged that assimilation can be painful for immigrants who necessarily must abandon some old customs to fully join American society. However, Thornton wrote, "No matter the costs, assimilation was the only way to forge an *unum* from so many *pluribus*."

Understanding this shift from melting-pot assimilation to salad bowl multiculturalism helps explain the wide divide in our politics over immigration—and the rising tide of cultural disunity in America today.

POST-MELTING-POT IMMIGRATION

The emergence of multiculturalism and the erosion of the melting pot combined with a rapid uptick in immigration to the

United States over the last several decades (much of it illegal) to make immigration the most explosive political issue in America today.

Millions of Americans came to believe that their government had abandoned them in favor of foreigners who broke the law. Initially people were silenced by the elite's overwhelming condemnation of any effort to discuss immigration, but gradually the growing awareness of American culture being submerged by multiple identities led to a backlash.

This is exactly the feeling candidate Trump identified and gave a voice to during the campaign. It is also the feeling guiding his immigration policies in the White House.

The members of the anti-Trump coalition claim these feelings are simply errant, knee-jerk reactions that have no basis in fact. They are either ignorant, lying, or both.

Consider this: According to the Migration Policy Institute, in 2015, immigrants made up 13.5 percent of the U.S. population. This is not much higher than the statistic in 1930, when immigrants made up 11.6 percent of the population. It is also short of the 1890 high of 14.8 percent. So, in the long view, the relative population of immigrants in the United States has remained flat.[7]

However, the percentage of immigrants in the United States was at an all-time low of 4.7 percent in 1970, and then it nearly tripled in 45 years. The actual number of immigrants in the United States has also more than quadrupled in that time frame, going from 9.6 million to an all-time high of more than 43.2 million.

Critically, because we have moved away from the melting-pot model, many of these new immigrants were not expected to learn our language, customs, or traditions, and therefore never assimilated into American society.

Consider the following:

- In Miami, 60 percent of the population speaks Spanish[8]
  due to large immigrant populations from Cuba,
  Colombia, Guatemala, Honduras, Nicaragua, and
  Venezuela.[9] Native, English-speaking business owners
  there say it has become difficult to conduct business. For
  the entire state of Florida, the foreign-born population
  increased by 60.6 percent from 1990 to 2000, and again
  by 53 percent from 2000 to 2015.[10]
- The radio program *This American Life* aired a show
  in December 2017 telling the story of Albertville,
  Alabama—the hometown of Attorney General Jeff
  Sessions. The population in Albertville shifted from 98
  percent white to one-quarter Latino in a matter of two
  decades starting in 1990. Some of the Latinos interviewed
  had lived in the United States for 20 years and still did
  not speak English well enough to be interviewed in what
  is supposed to be our common language.[11]
- In Minneapolis, the Somali immigrant population exists
  in a neighborhood dubbed "little Mogadishu" that is
  completely isolated by the Mississippi River and two
  highways. I visited there while researching my novel
  Duplicity. The community first started growing in the
  1990s. Importantly, from 2007 to 2013, more than 20
  young Somali men left the community to go fight for
  al-Shabab, a jihadist group in East Africa.[12] Now, the
  community itself has programs to keep young men away
  from street gangs as well as Islamic radicalization. The
  area has always been an immigrant community, however,
  the Germans and Swedes who preceded the Somalis
  decades before assimilated.

These are all examples of immigrant populations coming to
the United States and re-creating small versions of their home

countries rather than becoming American. While this may seem innocuous, it can present real challenges for police and local officials—especially if these mini-nation communities grow large and isolated.

And the problems can go both ways. In some isolated immigrant communities, language barriers prevent victims from reporting crimes to police—or even calling 911 for medical assistance.[13] For police investigating crimes in immigrant communities, it can become almost impossible to gather critical witness testimony—either due to a language barrier or a mistrust of American law enforcement.

When you consider that many Americans voting today have lived in an America that quickly went from having near record-low to near record-high immigrant populations (relative to the total population)—and at the same time watched the American approach to immigration profoundly transform, creating isolated immigrant communities—it is easy to see why people are concerned. It is easy to understand why the Trumpian approach to immigration and assimilation gained support.

Despite media claims, the members of Trump's America are not anti-immigration. We are against illegal immigration. We cannot attract the best and the brightest from across the world if we cease to be a nation of immigrants. However, a key part of the great American comeback involves reestablishing the melting-pot model and getting immigration laws and enforcement under control. This will do wonders for easing tensions and negative perceptions about immigration.

MULTICULTURAL DIVISION

The shift toward multiculturalism over the melting pot has affected more than immigration. The salad bowl model has actually worsened race relations by separating American culture, diminishing our common ground, and ultimately stratifying our citizenry at home by establishing a system in which people self-segregate based on their ethnicity, gender, self-identity, or perceived privilege.

In his 2012 essay, Thornton from the Hoover Institution warned that the salad bowl theory provided the foundation of the identity politics, which drives much of the cultural upheaval in America domestically today. Specifically, he argued that multiculturalism has been used to indict American society as "imperial, colonial, xenophobic," and racist.

According to Thornton, this theory ultimately provides justification for placing the rights of some groups above others— based on the degree to which they had been supposed victims of the newly vilified American history. This, as Thornton wrote, "directly contradicts the core assumption of our liberal democracy: the principle of individual and inalienable rights that each of us possess no matter what group or sect we belong to."

Once again, the purpose behind identity politics seems innocent. Indeed, appreciating and understanding different peoples' perspectives is critical for building strong relationships—particularly across cultural or societal lines. However, today's identity politics seem to have gone awry. Instead of promoting a noble pursuit of equality and understanding, multiculturalism and identity politics have led us into a perverse paradigm of privilege checking.

Instead of judging various points of view on merits, speech and debate are frequently tested and measured based on the ethnicity, gender identity, or sexual orientation of the speaker. Speakers from minority backgrounds, or those with uncommon sexual identities, are uplifted, while those who are deemed to have more privilege are silenced—unless they confess their privilege and preemptively repudiate the validity of their points of view.

Take this way of thinking and consider how it's used in

current politics. Think about how often President Trump has been described as an older white male by elites who were seeking to discredit his positions and goals. Notice, this "criticism" does not address anything about the president's agenda or goals; it simply seeks to imply that he is in the old white male group and therefore couldn't possibly be interested in helping any other group. Not coincidentally, the exact same tactic was used against Bernie Sanders in the Democratic primary.

The privilege theory system does not engender equal and free debate. Nor does it promote the sharing of new ideas. It attempts to divide us into vaguely ranked groups to establish a pseudo hierarchy of entitlement for a minority of Americans. Frankly, it reminds me of George Orwell's novel *Animal Farm*, in which "All animals are equal, but some animals are more equal than others."

In fact, the relevance of Orwell's writing is important in understanding the genuinely radical nature of privilege theory. Orwell was an opponent of communism, a governing system derived from the writings of Karl Marx, and his stories were illustrations of the corruption and moral bankruptcy of that totalitarian philosophy.

As Canadian professor Jordan Peterson has pointed out in a series of YouTube lectures and interviews, privilege theory began to emerge around the time that news of the evil communist Soviet Union became too visible to be ignored by the intellectual class. The reaction from this elite, however, was not to question the underlying philosophy of Marxism, which sought to pit the proletariat against the privileged economic elite, but instead to replace economic dividing lines for racial ones. Privilege theory is, in fact, nothing more than racial Marxism, and left unchecked will lead to the same disastrous, totalitarian end state as the Soviet Union.

Privilege theory in practice is also a complete departure

from what Dr. Martin Luther King Jr. envisioned in his "I Have a Dream" speech. The privilege theory system clearly judges people "by the color of their skin" rather than "the content of their character."

Consider the following examples of privilege-based identity politics in action.

In May 2017, students rioted several times after faculty at Evergreen State College in Olympia, Washington, declined to enforce a student demand that would require white students to stay home from class for a day. This day without white people was reportedly in the name of racial equality. The violence got so bad the college had to hold its graduation ceremony off campus, 30 miles away.[14]

During the 2017 Democratic National Convention candidate forum, candidate Sally Boynton Brown, who is the executive director of the Idaho Democratic Party, said that her purpose at the forum was "to listen and be a voice and shut other white people down" when they deny being prejudiced.

The *Atlantic* published a story in September 2015 that declared, "Color-Blindness Is Counterproductive." The magazine cited sociologists who have decided colorblind theory is just a covert way to ignore racial discrimination.[15]

As a final example, a professor at City University of New York in October 2017 posted a series of tweets in which she claimed that when white families have children, they are promoting systemic white supremacy.[16]

Specifically, the professor, a white woman, wrote: "I mean, if you're a white person who says they're engaged in dismantling white supremacy but…you're forming a white family + reproducing white children that 'you want the best for'—how is that helping + not part of the problem?"

All of these examples fit the Thornton model. The rights of

some people are diminished, and others are uplifted in the name of America's supposedly racist, iniquitous past—for which no people alive today are responsible.

President Trump is working to dismantle this perverse social reconstruction and return our politics and country to a system in which people are treated with equal respect and ideas are judged by their merits rather than the race, gender, ethnicity, or so-called privilege of the people who share them.

Unfortunately, the liberal members of the anti-Trump coalition have latched on to identity politics as a way to isolate and target particular voter groups. It is unclear how this tenuous culture of coalition building will last. As I wrote in my *New York Times* No. 1 best seller *Understanding Trump*, the Left misunderstood the coalition-building success Barack Obama achieved in his 2008 and 2012 elections. While Obama was able to unite many demographic groups on core American principles, today's Left is promoting divisive politics in an effort to hold these groups together.

It clearly did not work for them in 2016. We will see if they continue sowing disunity ahead of the 2018 midterm elections.

SEGREGATING THE MELTING POT

A final side effect of multiculturalism which has arisen in American society is the idea that someone from one culture cannot adopt some aspect of another culture. To do so, the liberal branch of the anti-Trump coalition argues, is "cultural appropriation."

There are plenty of absurd examples, such as the Portland burrito truck that was shamed out of business in May 2017 after its owners were accused of culturally appropriating the burrito. *Cosmopolitan* magazine in October 2017 also decided to inform white parents they should not allow their daughters to dress up as Disney's Moana for Halloween because they would be appropriating Polynesian culture.

Certainly, it is socially unacceptable and morally repugnant for someone to don blackface and denigrate African Americans. Similarly, displaying insulting depictions of people from other cultures or societies falls far short of the shining city on a hill standard.

However, raising pitchforks over white northwestern liberals eating burritos or children admiring and wanting to emulate fictional characters from other (often fictional) countries is ridiculous.

Still, this notion of cultural appropriation is serious because it is an absolute repudiation of the melting pot. If cultures are not socially allowed to blend and adopt new ideas and customs, then the United States will become a collection of isolated, fragmented communities that have little in common. Certainly, had the Founding Fathers believed that it was morally wrong to experience and share new cultures, America would have never been formed.

After all, democracy was culturally a Greek invention—are all democratic countries essentially stealing from Greece? Our representative Republic has roots in Rome. Should we give our Senate back to Italy? Is there a moral imperative that we stop celebrating Cinco de Mayo or St. Patrick's Day—or stop using French, Spanish, or Germanic words that have become English cognates?

The ultimate destination of the multicultural movement in the United States is actually a new era of American segregation. The idea that we can survive as a nation without a unified culture that is grounded in principles rather than heritage is just historically and logically inaccurate. Further, America is a better place (both for immigrants and citizens) when we share common ground and mutual respect rather than picking fights over magnified and often artificial differences.

If we in Trump's America are to complete this great American comeback that the 2016 election started, we must seriously focus as a nation on reestablishing the melting-pot principle that helped us succeed for more than 240 years. It is essential for American culture to continue—and American culture is essential for our country's survival. That is the heart of the Trump appeal.

SECURING THE BORDERS

President Trump has consistently said he supports strong immigration programs that will help America grow and succeed for generations to come. However, the president knows that new immigration laws would be meaningless without safe, secure borders.

The people of Trump's America know it, too.

This is why many Americans have responded positively to President Trump's calls to tighten security at our borders, curtail illegal immigration, and to closely vet refugees coming to the United States from war-torn countries rife with terrorism.

However, throughout 2017, congressional Democrats, federal bureaucrats, leaders in so-called sanctuary cities, and special interest groups have fought tooth and nail to slow construction of the southern border wall, hinder lawful immigration enforcement, and halt temporary travel bans issued by the Trump administration.

In following with the multicultural-privilege theory model, the elites in the anti-Trump coalition have claimed that President Trump's tough positions on immigration are driven by inherent racism—which they insinuate carries over to all members of Trump's America. This assertion is morally bankrupt

and reveals a profound historical (perhaps intentional) ignorance on their part.

This assertion also ignores the facts on the ground. President Trump's immigration plans are succeeding.

Despite the efforts of the elites, illegal crossings (as well as
human trafficking) over the southern border are down,[17] and the
U.S. Supreme Court ruled in December 2017 that a third version of a temporary ban on travel to eight dangerous nations
could proceed over aggressive legal challenges.[18]

The impact President Trump had on illegal immigration
was almost immediate. In May 2017—less than five months into
the president's term—National Public Radio reported on *Morning Edition* that, "The number of people apprehended while trying to cross the Southwest border illegally has plummeted, as
the age-old practice of hopping the border without papers has
changed profoundly in recent months."

This near-immediate drop in illegal crossings was due to
increased security at the U.S.–Mexico border—but also due to
the message President Trump's election sent around the world:
that immigration laws in the United States meant something
again.

The reduction in demand for immigrants to illegally come
to the United States had the added benefit of also drying up
some illegal activity in Mexico. One human smuggler the news
outlet interviewed, who called himself "the Wolf," was quoted
saying, "My business has dropped by more than half.... If it
goes down anymore, I'll have to think about doing something
else. Maybe open a little store or sell cars."

Imagine that. Trump's ability to reduce human trafficking
may lead some criminals to take up honest trades.

Despite this direct connection between increased security and decreased illegal crossings, the Washington elites
are still fighting the president's policy goals. As of the end of

Fiscal Year 2017, total apprehensions of unattended immigrant children were down from 2016 by 30 percent—from 59,757 to 41,456. Apprehensions of accompanied children, parents, and or guardians was down 2.6 percent—from 77,857 to 75,802.

I'm confident President Trump will build the wall—and reestablish law and order at the border. Once security is achieved, he will further work to reestablish policies to promote assimilation and reassert that the United States is one, indivisible nation including those who come here legally and want to become Americans.

CHAPTER THREE

THE COMEBACK OF "UNDER GOD"

In addition to reaffirming that the United States is one, indivisible nation, the Trump comeback is also about reestablishing America as a nation under God.

President Trump gave his most illustrative speech on the importance of religious freedom in the first days of his presidency, when he spoke at the annual National Prayer Breakfast on February 2, 2017.

In his remarks, the president said, "America is a nation of believers. In towns all across our land, it's plain to see what we easily forget—so easily we forget this—that the quality of our lives is not defined by our material success, but by our spiritual success."[1]

Shortly after this speech, President Trump signed an executive order to protect the rights of America's believers, which instructed executive branch employees to promote free speech and religious liberty in their duties.[2]

This order was necessary because the Obama administration had consistently used the power of the government to diminish religious freedom. Obama aggressively struck down regulations that would have protected religious groups from paying for health care coverage for procedures which they opposed on moral grounds. His Department of Homeland Security also produced a report on "right-wing extremism" identifying pro-life advocates and other traditional conservatives as "extremists."

Reversing the Obama anti-religious pattern, President Trump in May 2017 signed an order instructing government personnel that, "It shall be the policy of the executive branch to vigorously enforce Federal law's robust protections for religious freedom."

Trump moved quickly to defend religious liberty in America to quell the immediate threats from the Obama administration, but faith in America has been under attack for decades.

Since the 1960s, secular elites in government, media, and academia—who are now part of the anti-Trump coalition—have been carrying out a campaign to erode the public practice of faith and religious liberty in America. They have fought to replace the traditional American pattern of religious freedom with a system of strict secularism. Essentially, the anti-Trump coalition has twisted freedom *of* religion into freedom *from* religion by casting faith as a source of oppression that should be removed from public life.

This inversion of the traditional American understanding of freedom is in direct service of the coalition's goals and in perfect keeping with their rejection of other key components of American exceptionalism.

Part of what has made America unique in this world is our belief, set forth in our founding document, that our rights come from our Creator, not from the government. Thus, our nation's belief in God checks the growth of government and helps keep us free.

For the anti-Trump coalition to succeed in creating bigger,

more powerful government that submerges the sovereignty of U.S. citizens, it needs to remove the essential bulwark for freedom that strong religious faith provides.

In addition, because religious faith is a primary source for Americans to learn the precepts of traditional morality, some in the coalition seek to undermine religion as part of their campaign in support of unrestricted abortion rights and the supposed rights of increasingly fringe sexual identity groups.

THE JUDICIAL ASSAULT

A favorite tool of the secular elite wing of the anti-Trump coalition in attacking religious liberty is the courts.

In 1962, the U.S. Supreme Court ruled it was unconstitutional for teachers, principals, or other educators to lead prayers in public schools. In 1980, the court barred schools from displaying the Ten Commandments on campus. Since these cases, courts have gone further. The high court said in 1985 that even a moment of silence could potentially be unconstitutional, and in 1989, it ruled that nativity scenes celebrating Christmas in government buildings were unlawful.

In 2002, a federal court even ruled that the phrase "under God" in the Pledge of Allegiance ran afoul of the First Amendment's Establishment Clause—which prohibits the federal government from establishing an official religion. The Supreme Court overturned the lower court's ruling, but the justices stopped short of clarifying that this phrase is in fact constitutional. This is profoundly troubling, after all, the official motto of the nation is still In God We Trust.

In addition to the courts, some in the anti-Trump coalition have also waged a wide-ranging cultural campaign that impacts every aspect of American society. The First Liberty Institute documented 1,400 attacks on religion in America in 2017. The Institute's "Undeniable: The Survey of Hostility to Religion in

America" looks at instances of religious hostility across four categories: the public arena, which includes government, workplaces, markets, and other public spaces; the schoolhouse, which includes K–12 and collegiate institutions; attacks against places of worship by local communities, and local, state, and federal governments; and religious attacks within the military. The Institute reports that instances of religious intolerance increased by 15 percent since 2016—and 133 percent over the last five years.[3]

Some of these attacks include companies that have been threatened with consequences by government for refusing to provide insurance coverage for contraception or abortion drugs and procedures. In one example cited by the Institute, elderly Americans at a senior citizens' center were told they could not pray, listen to religious messages, or sing religious songs because the facility was a government building. In other instances of religious persecution, a high school football coach was fired for praying alone on the field after a football game, and a Navy chaplain was investigated for counseling his fellow seamen according to his religious beliefs.

More and more often, we are seeing the First Amendment, which was written to protect our freedom to practice religion, misused as a tool to strip religion out of our public lives. Not only is this push for a religion of public secularism a departure from the historic American approach to faith, it is a threat to our liberty and the principles on which our country was founded.

The Founding Fathers regularly—and intentionally—engaged in public religious observances, and they knew that faith was vital to our country's survival. They understood that religious freedom underpinned all our other liberties and provided an important limit to the federal government's reach into our lives.

Critics of Donald Trump question his piety. After all, they point out that he is a divorced, wealthy real estate tycoon, and casino owner. However, he does have a very personal faith. At the National Prayer Breakfast in February, he shared some of his personal beliefs, saying, "I was blessed to be raised in a churched home. My mother and father taught me that to whom much is given much is expected. I was sworn in on the very Bible from which my mother would teach us as young children. And that faith lives on in my heart every single day."

This personal faith helped President Trump recognize how religious rights in our country have been diminished over the years—particularly during the previous administration—and he has worked to restore these rights. President Trump knows that America is strongest and most successful when its people are free to live and worship as they wish.

This is why the freedom of religion is an essential pillar of America—and a key to the American comeback.

FAITH AS THE FOUNDATIONAL BASIS FOR FREEDOM

Make no mistake, the Founding Fathers viewed religious liberty and faith as the basis for all our individual freedoms.

In the Declaration of Independence, Thomas Jefferson cited "the Laws of Nature and of Nature's God" as the authority under which Americans had the right to claim autonomy from England. He went on to write "that all men are created equal, that they are endowed by their Creator with certain unalienable Rights."

This statement serves as the cornerstone of our individual liberties because it recognizes that our Creator is the ultimate authority over any government of human beings, and that we receive our rights from our Creator—not our government.

As Founder Alexander Hamilton wrote in February 1775, more than a year before the Declaration of Independence was ratified, "The sacred rights of mankind are not to be rummaged for, among old parchments, or musty records. They are written, as with a sun beam, in the whole volume of human nature, by the hand of the divinity itself; and can never be erased or obscured by mortal power."[4]

These words from one of our Founders show that religious freedom was not some vague notion meant to simply ensure people had the ability to attend the church of their choice—or to choose not to attend religious services. The idea—the dictum—that government lacked the authority to infringe on fundamental rights was unique and vital to America's founding.

The Founders believed this so thoroughly that according to Founder Samuel Adams, people didn't even have the ability to surrender their own rights. In a paper Adams wrote concerning the rights of colonists in November 1772, he said, "If men through fear, fraud or mistake, should in terms renounce and give up any essential natural right, the eternal law of reason and the great end of society, would absolutely vacate such renunciation; the right to freedom being the gift of God Almighty, it is not in the power of Man to alienate this gift, and voluntarily become a slave."[5]

President Trump understands this principle with perfect clarity. Once again, we saw this in his words at the second National Prayer Breakfast that he attended, in February 2018:[6]

> Our founders invoked our Creator four times in the Declaration of Independence. Our currency declares, "In God We Trust." And we place our hands on our hearts as we recite the Pledge of Allegiance and proclaim we are "One Nation Under God." Our rights are not given to us by man; our rights come from our Creator. No matter what, no Earthly force can take those rights away. That is why the words "Praise be to God" are etched atop the Washington Monument, and those same words are etched into the hearts of our people.

The belief that rights come from a divine source (and the acknowledgment that human beings were fallible) also led the first leaders of our country to ensure our government was accountable to the people. In "Federalist Paper No. 51," the author (who is believed to be James Madison) wrote, "If men were angels, no government would be necessary. If angels were to govern men, neither external nor internal controls on government would be necessary."[7]

Now, the secular elite who make up part of the anti-Trump coalition like to claim the Founding Fathers were agnostic deists (or complete atheists who professed religious beliefs only for social and political reasons). Further, the elites claim the founding principles of America were products of the Enlightenment rather than religious belief. However, many of the Founders would have seen this as a false dichotomy. To them, the principles of the Enlightenment reinforced the belief that our rights came from our Creator. The principles of the Enlightenment and religion were not mutually exclusive.

This is simply left-wing fiction.

In an October 25, 2006, piece for the *National Review*, authors Michael and Jana Novak pointed out that "Among the 89 signers of the Declaration and/or the Constitution, nearly a dozen had studied theology, were ordained ministers, were preachers though not ordained, were chaplains to a militia unit, or were officers of national Bible societies and the like."[8]

Within their analysis, the Novaks highlighted:

- George Washington's insistence that chaplains accompany the men he was leading to defend the western frontier and his coining of the phrase "under God" in his General Orders to the Continental Army on July 2, 1776;
- Hamilton's repeated pleas to receive the Holy Eucharist while on his deathbed;

- and Ben Franklin's letter to the president of Yale, wherein he said plainly: "I believe in one God, creator of the universe. That he governs it by his Providence. That he ought to be worshiped. That the most acceptable service we render to him is doing good to his other children. That the soul of man is immortal and will be treated with justice in another life respecting its conduct in this."

In the letter, Franklin doubted the divinity of Christ, however, expressing doubt is very different from being faithless.

The Novaks chalk up the current academic mischaracterization of faith in early American leaders to the largely secular world of academia failing to understand the nuances and differences between religion today and religion from the eighteenth century.

That is a gracious, diplomatic view of the situation.

A more critical view would be that those secular academics are intentionally proselytizing their own atheist worldview and imposing it upon their students.

In either case, the consequences for removing foundational faith from American society would be dire.

Stripping religious freedom—and the notion that rights are endowed upon us by our Creator rather than government—from the American system would undermine the entire concept of American liberty. The Founding Fathers knew this, and so does President Trump.

ESSENTIAL MORALITY

Many in the anti-Trump coalition have completely misunderstood—or misrepresented—the Establishment Clause in order to drive religion out of the American system. They say that the Founders intent in prohibiting the establishment of a national religion was to shield American politics entirely from theological or religious ideals. This is the argument they have made for removing religion from our public institutions.

Chiefly, the secular elites point to Thomas Jefferson's 1802 letter to the Danbury Baptists Association in which he wrote, "I contemplate with sovereign reverence that act of the whole American people which declared that their legislature should 'make no law respecting an establishment of religion, or prohibiting the free exercise thereof,' thus building a wall of separation between Church & State."[9]

However, the separation Jefferson referenced stressed government's inability to regulate religion. It was not intended to be a blanket prohibition against public religious activities. In fact, two days after writing the "Church & State" letter, Jefferson attended religious services at the United States Capitol. The service was led by Baptist Minister John Leland, who was himself a key helper to James Madison with the inclusion of the Establishment Clause in the First Amendment.

Further, as governor of Virginia, Jefferson regularly called on the commonwealth to pray and fast—and worked to institute laws for punishing those who disrupted worship services or broke the Sabbath.

In fact, Jefferson and the other Founders believed religion was the principle source of morality—and morality was essential for a free society. They included the Establishment Clause in the First Amendment because there was a healthy and diverse religious community guiding America—and they wanted it to continue to grow unhindered by government.

President Trump cited this desire for diverse religious practice as the basis for his executive order, saying, "The Founders envisioned a Nation in which religious voices and views were integral to a vibrant public square, and in which religious people and institutions were free to practice their faith without fear of discrimination or retaliation by the Federal Government."

Consider the words of John Adams, our second president, in a letter he wrote to Founder Benjamin Rush in 1811. Among other things, Rush had asked Adams to advocate for the establishment of "national social, domestic, and religious virtues."

Adams's response totally rejects the current assumption that the Founders did not want an established religion because they were irreligious. Adams wrote:

> I agree with you in sentiment that religion and virtue are the only foundations; not only of Republicanism and of all free government: but of social felicity under all governments and in all the combinations of human society. But if I should inculcate this doctrine in my will, I should be charged with hypocrisy and a desire to conciliate the good will of the clergy towards my family as I was charged by Dr. Priestly and his friend Cooper and by Quakers, Baptists and I know not how many other sects, for instituting a national fast for even common civility to the clergy, and for being a church going [animal].
>
> If I should inculcate those "national social, domestic, and religious virtues" you recommend; I should be suspected and charged with an hypocritical, [Machiavellian], Jesuitical, [Pharisaical] attempt to promote a national establishment of Presbyterianism in America. Whereas I would as soon establish the Episcopal Church; and almost as soon the Catholic Church.[10]

This passage perfectly illustrates the Founders' belief that religion was essential to maintaining morality—and that the Establishment Clause was largely about not having the government favor one of the many faiths active in early America over the others.

The French diplomat and historian Alexis de Tocqueville noted the societal importance of religion in early America in his

1830 book *Democracy in America*. In the work, he said religion, "takes no direct part in the government of society, but it must be regarded as the foremost of the political institutions of that country; for if it does not impart a taste for freedom, it facilitates the use of it."[11]

AMERICA'S GUIDING LIGHT

More pressing than any historical discussion about religious liberty and practice in America, the foundation of faith has guided and delivered our country through its most perilous challenges.

As mentioned, faith was largely what drove the Founders to declare independence from England, which immediately put them in a war with the most powerful empire in the world at the time. Religious convictions also helped them overcome this seemingly insurmountable foe and successfully complete the American Revolution.

While American soldiers stormed the beaches of Normandy, France—executing the largest amphibian invasion in history—on the evening of June 6, 1944, President Franklin D. Roosevelt addressed the American people by radio. He did not dictate a report about the progress of the D-Day mission or explain the military strategy, he asked Americans to join him in prayer, saying:

> Almighty God: Our sons, pride of our Nation, this day have set upon a mighty endeavor, a struggle to preserve our Republic, our religion, and our civilization, and to set free a suffering humanity.
>
> Lead them straight and true; give strength to their arms, stoutness to their hearts, steadfastness in their faith.
>
> They will need Thy blessings. Their road will be long and hard. For the enemy is strong. He may hurl back

our forces. Success may not come with rushing speed, but we shall return again and again; and we know that by Thy grace, and by the righteousness of our cause, our sons will triumph.

This historically and spiritually important prayer rallied Americans to prepare for the brutal fight ahead. It was an animating force for American patriotism leading into World War II.

As an important side note, despite this prayer's significance, the Obama administration's Bureau of Land Management objected to a congressional proposal to include Roosevelt's words on a plaque at the National World War II Memorial, saying it would "dilute this elegant memorial's central message and its ability to clearly convey that message to move, educate, and inspire its many visitors."[12]

This barring of Roosevelt's prayer was Obama's secular-socialist agenda at its sickest. To diminish and ignore the deep, spiritual, moral underpinnings beneath America's efforts in World War II is irresponsible and contemptuous to every American who prayed along with Roosevelt as their loved ones faced great peril to destroy the evils that had come out of Germany and Japan. If nothing else, World War II was a battle between good, peace-loving children of God across the world and the worst agents of evil we had seen in modern history.

In fact, President Roosevelt described the war as a contest between "pagan brutality" and the "Christian ideal" and said, "We choose human freedom—which is the Christian ideal." Later, Presidents John F. Kennedy and Ronald Reagan struck similar tones during the Cold War. Both presidents described the contest with the Soviet Union as a struggle between atheist, communist ideals, and Judeo-Christian values of the West.

In Kennedy's words, the Cold War—and particularly the nuclear arms race—was "a struggle for supremacy between two conflicting ideologies: Freedom under God versus ruthless, godless tyranny."

Reagan echoed Kennedy and contrasted the Soviet legacy with our own, saying, "Two visions of the world remain locked in dispute. The first believes all men are created equal by a loving God who has blessed us with freedom. Abraham Lincoln spoke for us.... The second vision believes that religion is opium for the masses. It believes that eternal principles like truth, liberty, and democracy have no meaning beyond the whim of the state. And Lenin spoke for them."

Finally, religious faith and liberty were also crucial to the success of the civil rights movement. Dr. King repeatedly—and correctly—cast segregation and the iniquitous treatment of African Americans in our country at the time as moral and spiritual failures.

Specifically, King cited religious liberty enshrined in our founding documents as the absolute justification that segregation was counter to American ideals. He made this point clearly in his "Letter from a Birmingham Jail":

> One day the South will know that when these disinherited children of God sat down at lunch counters, they were in reality standing up for what is best in the American dream and for the most sacred values in our Judeo-Christian heritage, thereby bringing our nation back to those great wells of democracy which were dug deep by the founding fathers in their formulation of the Constitution and the Declaration of Independence.

THE TRUMP REVIVAL

President Trump's executive order to protect religious liberty was an important first step toward bringing our nation back in line with its founding principle of freedom of religion.

He followed up this action in January 2018 by announcing a new Conscience and Religious Freedom Division at the Department of Health and Human Services. The new division, which is a part of the HHS Office for Civil Rights, will restore the enforcement of federal laws which protect health care workers from being forced to violate their conscience in order to practice medicine and healing.

However, there is more work that needs to be done.

President Trump and Republicans must strive to completely restore rights to our nation's religious institutions. This means they must repeal the Johnson Amendment—a provision in the U.S. tax code which prohibits 501(c)(3) organizations from endorsing or opposing political candidates. Most churches and faith-based charitable organizations are designated as 501(c)(3) organizations, which exempts them from paying federal taxes.

President Trump raised the issue of getting rid of the Johnson Amendment at the Republican National Convention, then he continued that charge at the 2017 National Prayer Breakfast. Quoting Thomas Jefferson, Trump said, "'The God who gave us life, gave us liberty.... Can the liberties of a nation be secure when we have removed a conviction that these liberties are the gift of God?'

"Among those freedoms is the right to worship according to our own beliefs. That is why I will get rid of, and totally destroy, the Johnson Amendment and allow our representatives of faith to speak freely and without fear of retribution."

The law, which was named for former president Lyndon B. Johnson, who proposed it when he was a senator, is billed as a way to prevent people from making tax-deductible campaign contributions by giving money to churches that support particular candidates. This seems like a reasonable goal. However, the provision completely violates the First Amendment rights of clergy and other faith leaders by threatening to revoke their organizations' tax exemptions if they express political opinions about candidates.

This essentially divides the First Amendment for religious leaders and makes their freedom of speech and freedom of religion mutually exclusive if they want to keep their tax-exempt status. Thus, the federal government is regulating churches—a notion the Founders would have wholeheartedly rejected.

Furthermore, churches have been traditionally tax-exempt since the founding of our country. There was no rampant tax abuse by American congregants from 1776 to 1954. The Johnson Amendment was an act of revenge against conservative pastors who had opposed Johnson's reelection. Despite Johnson's petty attack, liberty for pastors matters. Historically active clergy members—such as Leland, who I mentioned previously—were critical to the founding of our country. It seems foolish to decide that the opinions and ideas of today's John Lelands are not worth protecting.

Even those who support the Johnson Amendment, such as the *Washington Post* Editorial Board, acknowledge that the provision "puts government in the business of evaluating speech's content and is bound to have some chilling effect on someone."[13]

President Trump has blunted enforcement of this bad law by ordering the Department of the Treasury not to take "any adverse action against" clergy members, churches, or other faith-based organizations "on the basis that such individual or organization speaks or has spoken about moral or political issues from a religious perspective." However, it is up to Congress to finish this work with legislation repealing the Johnson Amendment.

House Republicans have put forward a repeal that would protect the ability of religious leaders to speak on politics during regular activities, but it would limit extra political activity or spending by the organizations. This bill was introduced by Representative Jody Hice (R-GA) and House Majority Whip

Steve Scalise (R-LA). It has a Senate sponsor in Senator James Lankford (R-OK).

This plan mirrors a proposal supported by the Alliance Defending Freedom, a group which opposes the Johnson Amendment and provides legal help for people whose religious freedom has been infringed.

The Alliance suggests taking the advice of a commission formed by the Evangelical Council for Financial Accountability, which suggested changing the rule to allow:

1. Speech that would be no added cost or a very minimal cost to the organization (such as a sermon, not an expensive advertising campaign)

2. If the speech of the organization would cost more than that minimal amount, then the Johnson Amendment would only prohibit speech that clearly identifies candidates and directly calls for those candidates' election or defeat.[14]

These proposals may be the right answer, and it will be up to Congress to pass a bill that the president can sign.

President Trump and Republicans must ensure that religious faith and its practice remain protected as essential parts of Trump's America.

Individual religious liberty is absolutely vital to the continued strength of our country.

As President Trump said in February 2017:

America will thrive as long as we continue to have faith in each other and faith in God.... Because that's what we are and that is what we will always be, and that is what our people want: one beautiful nation, under God.

CHAPTER FOUR

THE COMEBACK OF SOVEREIGNTY, ENDING THE NEW WORLD ORDER

Imagine a world wherein you could freely escort your loved ones up to an airport departure gate to bid them farewell.

Imagine that, in this world, the idea of holding a handheld computer that allowed you to connect with millions of human beings across the globe seemed as far-fetched as flying cars.

Imagine that, in this world, you could walk into almost any clothing store in America and still find items with "Made in the U.S.A." on the tags.

Now, stop imagining. I'm describing America in 1990, when President George H.W. Bush outlined his administration's commitment to creating a "new world order."

At the end of the Cold War, the United States remained at center stage as the world's sole superpower. Cast as the world's leading protagonist, President Bush seized the opportunity to rewrite the narrative of U.S. foreign policy and international relations by borrowing a page from President Woodrow Wilson's playbook and embarking on a heroic global quest toward a new world.[1]

Bush imagined a new world order where many nations would equally share financial, diplomatic, and military responsibility to enact collective security measures against aggressive forces.[2] He envisioned a world whereby nations would hold one another accountable for acts of injustice and would be made to answer to the international community for crimes against humanity or the global order. He spoke of a new world that would follow in the American example, based upon the ideas and values of westernized democracy, that would actively pursue securing freedoms and liberties for all.

This was the absolute dream of the people who now make up the orderly institutionalist wing of the anti-Trump coalition. This new world order was supposed to be their crowning achievement—the height of their political accomplishments.

But after four presidents and 26 years, the new world order failed to materialize.

Instead of a global order, wherein all of the member countries are benevolent and look out for one another, we developed a system wherein the United States was benevolent, and many in the global community took full advantage of that benevolence.

This is the common denominator spanning throughout many of our foreign policy and national security decisions over the past two and a half decades. The Obama administration especially operated in a way which was completely out of touch with reality, leading to critical and continuous failures to stand up for American interests.

Instead of an international utopia, the new world order established an international bureaucracy, a global swamp that makes the one in Washington look like a mud puddle.

This elite global bureaucracy set up organizations, international relationships, and deals that forced America's interests to take a back seat. Our diplomats worked to appease this global bureaucracy rather than prioritize the values and concerns of American citizens.

The 2016 election made clear that millions of Americans were sick of being sold out by bureaucrats to bureaucrats. The men and women of Trump's America had reached their breaking point.

These Americans had witnessed (or lived through) devastating attacks in New York City and DC and subsequent attacks in Boston, Paris, Orlando, Brussels, and more. While Americans mourned for the loss of these victims and were resolute in their belief that such evil had to be defeated, they grew frustrated by seemingly endless wars as Islamic terrorism continued to spread throughout the globe.

At the same time, Americans experienced a technological revolution creating a range of new inventions spanning from the smartphone to battle-ready drones. These advancements connected millions through the Internet and social media networks, and simultaneously opened the door to security vulnerabilities from global competitors who wish to steal data and ideas or influence national opinions.

Meanwhile, American companies stockpiled $2.5 trillion overseas because it made more sense than bringing it home and losing a third of it to taxes.[3] We also saw a dramatic increase of the United States' deficit in the trade of goods with other world nations—up from a $185.5 billion deficit in 1990[4] to $736.8 billion at the end of 2016.[5]

In constructing his foreign policy and national security initiatives, President Trump has chosen to end the failed, outdated pursuit of a new world order and instead has chosen to recognize the new world reality. In order to protect American interests and keep America safe, we must start by putting America first.

This replacement of the idealistic fantasy of a new world order with the principled realism of President Trump's America first strategy is a critical component of America's great comeback.

A NATIONAL SECURITY STRATEGY FOCUSED ON WINNING AGAIN

Standing on the steps of the United States Capitol building, Donald J. Trump addressed the American people for the first time as the 45th president of America.[6] He said:

> The oath of office I take today is an oath of allegiance to all Americans. For many decades, we've enriched foreign industry at the expense of American industry; Subsidized the armies of other countries while allowing for the very sad depletion of our military; We've defended other nation's borders while refusing to defend our own; And spent trillions of dollars overseas while America's infrastructure has fallen into disrepair and decay.
>
> We've made other countries rich while the wealth, strength, and confidence of our country has disappeared over the horizon. One by one, the factories shuttered and left our shores, with not even a thought about the millions upon millions of American workers left behind. The wealth of our middle class has been ripped from their homes and then redistributed across the entire world. But that is the past. And now we are looking only to the future. We assembled here today are issuing a new decree to be heard in every city, in every foreign capital, and in every hall of power.
>
> From this day forward, a new vision will govern our land. From this moment on, it's going to be America First. Every decision on trade, on taxes, on

immigration, on foreign affairs, will be made to benefit American workers and American families.

We must protect our borders from the ravages of other countries making our products, stealing our companies, and destroying our jobs. Protection will lead to great prosperity and strength. I will fight for you with every breath in my body—and I will never, ever let you down.

America will start winning again, winning like never before.

On this inauguration day, President Trump emphasized one core promise to the American people—that they will never be forgotten and will always be put first. Every decision he has made thus far as president, particularly in the realm of trade, national security, and foreign policy, has always been made with this promise in mind.

The president enshrined his America first approach into official policy in December 2017, when he issued his National Security Strategy report.

The report starts by declaring:

An America that is safe, prosperous, and free at home is an America with the strength, confidence, and will to lead abroad. It is an America that can preserve peace, uphold liberty, and create enduring advantages for the American people. Putting America first is the duty of our government and the foundation for U.S. leadership in the world.

A strong America is in the vital interests of not only the American people, but also those around the world who want to partner with the United States in pursuit of shared interests, values, and aspirations.

This National Security Strategy puts America first.[7]

Importantly, one of the four pillars outlined in the National Security Strategy report is to "Promote American Prosperity." The central idea of this pillar is that, "rebuilding economic strength at home and preserving a fair and reciprocal international economic system will enhance our security and advance prosperity and peace in the world."[8]

Simply put, the United States must be economically competitive, particularly in the areas of manufacturing and technology, to protect and advance our national interests.

This is a significant departure from the beliefs of many in the orderly institutionalist wing of the anti-Trump coalition, who argue that trade deficits don't matter, and that the United States can be competitive in the world so long as it maintains a strong service economy and benefits from cheap foreign goods to keep prices low.

But this argument falls apart upon scrutiny.

Without a strong manufacturing base, the United States cannot domestically manufacture and produce the defensive technologies and weapons that are required to protect ourselves and our allies from enemies. The same is true for many critical energy and infrastructure needs for which relying on foreign production would present national security vulnerabilities.

Furthermore, without a strong technological base, the United States would be incapable of maintaining the strongest and most technologically innovative military in the world.

This rational thinking was incomprehensible to the bureaucratic policymakers who spent years pursuing the new world order through complex multilateral agreements, bad deals, and unreciprocated relationships that resulted in a hemorrhaging of manufacturing jobs from America, while failing to protect critical industries from intellectual property theft and other acts of economic aggression.

The men and women of Trump's America elected Donald

Trump to put an end to the fantasies and failures of the globalists and international bureaucrats. And boy, has President Trump delivered.

THE TRANS-PACIFIC PARTNERSHIP

Three days after taking office, Donald Trump fulfilled one of his core campaign promises and withdrew from the Trans-Pacific Partnership (TPP).

Backers of this agreement, negotiated under President Obama and signed in 2016, promised it would boost trade, contribute to economic growth, and strengthen economic ties between the 12 involved countries. Together, these countries represented about 40 percent of the world's global economy.[9] Though the deal had yet to take effect, as Congress still had to approve the participation of the United States, the historic significance of President Trump backing out of this bad deal cannot be overstated.

Instead of buying the rhetoric espoused by President Obama and the orderly institutionalist wing of the anti-Trump coalition, President Trump understood the reality of the TPP— that ultimately, it would hurt Americans.

A 2016 brief published by the Roosevelt Institute noted that while 18,000 tariffs would be cut for American exporters under TPP, it would have little positive impact on our domestic industry and would not likely increase our economic competitive advantage.[10]

With such a significant slash of tariffs, how could this be possible?

First, the author, Joseph Stiglitz, Senior Fellow and Chief Economist states, "tropical, impoverished Vietnam will eliminate tariffs on skis, snowplows, and caviar," while Brunei and Malaysia, countries that consist mostly of a Muslim population, would do away with tariffs on pork.[11]

Moreover, Stiglitz found that the United States did not

provide any exports to TPP countries in 2015 in over half of the categories covered under the 18,000 tariff cuts. As for the other 7,500 categories, the United States only sent small amounts of products to other TPP countries during 2015.

This analysis shows how useless the deal was to America. In fact, citing a study conducted by the Economic Research Service, Stiglitz writes the "TPP would have zero effect on U.S. GDP."[12] He points to a different study by Tufts University that utilized a different model to conduct its research, which found the United States would actually suffer a net gross domestic product (GDP) loss.

Much of the pushback that resulted from President Trump's decision was centered around the idea that U.S. withdrawal from this deal would ultimately result in the United States losing influence in the Indo-Pacific region. The anti-Trump coalition argued this would then in effect lead to China stepping up to fill the great economic power void in the region—a consequence counter to U.S. interests.

But take a look at the root of this argument. By arguing that TPP is required to contain and balance Chinese influence, no matter what the impact is on the American economy, it puts American workers second to geopolitical theory.

Or as Derek Scissors, a China policy specialist from the American Enterprise Institute, said in an article published by NBC, "This is all diplomacy. There is no benefit," adding that "the idea was diplomatic rather than economic."[13]

This is exactly the type of process before results thinking which defines the orderly institutionalists that Donald Trump's America first foreign policy seeks to end.

Promoting a trade deal that had no economic benefit for America, all in a flimsy diplomatic attempt to contain China and at the cost of American prosperity is indisputably irrational and shortsighted. The United States instead should work to remain the largest market in the world and encourage foreign investors and businesses to come do business on our home field. A dominant American economy will check China better than the TPP ever could.

President Trump's aim is to encourage foreign countries to want to come negotiate with us and to have the incentive to want to become a part of the American market—which won't happen if we have a weak economy, no jobs, and a country filled with workers who are struggling to make ends meet.

Trump's executive order withdrawing from the TPP, issued within the first 72 hours of his presidency, set a definitive precedent for the future of his administration. As president, Donald Trump has attached action to rhetoric, while unfailingly and unapologetically delivering on his promise to put the interests of the American people first, both at home and abroad.

He saw withdrawing from the TPP agreement as one of his first acts as commander in chief to be an easy way to communicate just how different a leader he was going to be for our country. He defiantly broke out of the old globalist mold by refusing to continue with the TPP and, in effect, shook up the status quo on a global scale.

This decision was a great shock to members of the orderly institutionalist wing of the anti-Trump coalition, who were comfortable continuing on in the new world order global establishment at the expense of American success.

This clear shift away from the global bureaucracy affirmed that the America first policy was not simply empty campaign jargon and it effectively assured the American people that this would be a core philosophy for President Trump's administration going forward.

THE PARIS AGREEMENT

The Paris Agreement—a bad deal which would provide framework for and implement measures to eliminate problems with climate change while providing financial assistance to under-developed countries—was heavily supported by the Obama administration and was a perfect example of the orderly institutionalist wing of the anti-Trump coalition's pattern of structuring foreign policy around fantasies.

A perfect example can be found in former secretary of state John Kerry's hyperbolic 2014 declaration that "climate change can now be considered the world's largest weapon of mass destruction, perhaps even the world's most fearsome weapon of mass destruction."[14]

How can the American people trust leaders such as these to correctly manage global threats and ensure our national security if they are this out of touch with reality? How can leaders justify indulging in these distant fantasies when there are real, present dangers right in front of them that put the lives of Americans and our foreign allies at risk?

Let's be clear: A rogue nation or terrorist organization's possession of a nuclear weapon is an immediate weapon of mass destruction and, in the short run, vastly more dangerous than global warming. The Left hides from real, immediate weapons of mass destruction by focusing on distant potential problems, which suddenly become today's focus of energy and excitement.

When President Trump took office, as a principled realist, he immediately recognized that the Paris Agreement was an ineffective initiative and a bad deal for Americans.

A study conducted by NERA Consulting found that in order to meet the requirements of the Paris Agreement as outlined under the Obama administration, over the next several decades, the U.S. economy would incur costs amounting to $3 trillion dollars.[15]

As negotiated under President Obama, the Paris Agreement would destroy our coal industry[16] and would force the United States to meet unrealistic carbon emission reduction goals.[17]

And while the international community has incredibly high expectations for the United States, the Paris Agreement would give what President Trump accurately called a "free pass" to other countries for years.[18]

Furthermore, if implemented, the Paris Agreement would have cost the United States 6.5 million industrial sector jobs—including 3.1 million manufacturing jobs—by 2040.[19]

As if all the terrible economic figures were not enough, the Paris Agreement wouldn't have even stopped climate change.

A statement from the Trump administration, citing researchers at the Massachusetts Institute of Technology (MIT), stated that even with all member nations fulfilling their obligations under the Paris Agreement, "By the year 2100, the impact on the climate would be negligible."[20]

In fact, these MIT researchers found that the "impacts have been estimated to be likely to reduce global temperature rise by 0.2 degrees Celsius in 2100."[21] That is a lot of lost jobs for a tiny change.

This is far short of the Paris Agreement's goal and requirement that the average global temperature must be kept to "well below 2°C above pre-industrial levels."

Amazingly, the crafters of the agreement even acknowledge that the multinational accord wouldn't make a dent in climate change.[22]

The United Nation's proposal notes that even with all member countries contributing and meeting the requirements outlined in the agreement "much greater emission reduction efforts will be required than those associated with the intended nationally determined contributions in order to hold the increase in the global average temperature to below 2°C above pre-industrial levels."

So, the Paris Agreement would cost America $3 trillion and not solve the problem. Yet, when President Trump withdrew the

THE COMEBACK OF SOVEREIGNTY   69

United States from this inarguably harmful and feckless deal, the anti-Trump coalition reacted with apoplectic rage.

Here are some of the most over-the-top reactions, as compiled by the *Federalist*:

- Tom Steyer, a left-wing billionaire who funds radical environmentalist causes, called the withdrawal "a traitorous act of war."
- The Huffington Post ran the headline "Trump to Planet: Drop Dead."
- The American Civil Liberties Union somehow managed to bring race into the issue, calling the withdrawal "a massive step back for racial justice, and an assault on communities of color across the United States."[23]

It is important to note that in issuing the U.S. withdrawal from the Paris Agreement, President Trump is not in any way opposed to continue working toward initiatives that aim to preserve our planet's environment.

In a statement made on June 1, 2017, President Trump said, "I'm willing to immediately work with Democratic leaders to either negotiate our way back into Paris, under the terms that are fair to the United States and its workers, or to negotiate a new deal that protects our country and its taxpayers."[24]

Trump's decision therefore sent a message to the global community that this particular agreement wasn't good enough, and member nations must return to the negotiating table. He wasn't going to put the global bureaucracy before the American people.

THE NORTH AMERICAN FREE TRADE AGREEMENT

The North American Free Trade Agreement (NAFTA), negotiated under President George H.W. Bush in 1992 and implemented under President Bill Clinton, was a free trade agreement designed to ease trade barriers that would, in effect, lead to increased trade and spur economic growth between the United States, Canada, and Mexico.

When President Clinton presented the agreement to Congress in 1993, many Republicans—myself included—supported the NAFTA proposal. As the Republican whip at the time of the Congressional NAFTA vote, I helped deliver more Republican votes in favor of the agreement than the Democrats.

Unfortunately, we were trapped in a new world order mentality and failed to see how lopsided the deal was in favor of Mexico.

NAFTA was implemented in 1994, and according to the World Bank, for that year, the United States had a per capita GDP of $27,777[25] and, comparatively, Canada's per capita GDP was $19,859.[26] However, in 1994, Mexico's per capita GDP was much lower, at $5,710.

This disparity resulted in Mexico benefiting from the NAFTA agreement in a much greater capacity than the United States. The removal of tariffs under the implementation of this agreement had a heavy impact on multiple U.S. industries, particularly in the fields of auto manufacturing, textiles, agriculture, apparel, and others.[27]

Manufacturing jobs in the United States dropped from 16.8 million in 1993[28] to 12.5 in 2017.[29] Moreover, U.S. jobs in the automotive manufacturing industry are down from 1.1 million to approximately 940,000 in 2017.[30] Some of this job loss can be attributed to automation and technological advancements, however, NAFTA undoubtedly exacerbated the job loss.

A study published in 2016 by two economists from the University of Virginia (UVA) that compared census data from 1990 and 2000 described the profile of the workers and industries where the negative impacts of NAFTA were most likely to be experienced.[31]

One of the co-authors, UVA economics professor John McLaren, when asked during an interview to describe how NAFTA affected U.S. wages, said, "For the average worker, there is not much of an impact, but for certain important pockets of workers, the lowered import barriers resulting from NAFTA do seem to have lowered wage growth well below what it would have been. This is particularly true for blue-collar workers."[32]

The study found that workers who were most negatively affected by NAFTA were high school dropouts who were employed in particular industries that could no longer rely on various tariff protections as a consequence of the agreement. Comparing the wages of these affected workers with workers in unaffected industries, the former saw a wage growth drop of up to 17 percent compared to the wage growth of the latter.

"If you are a blue-collar worker at the end of the '90s and your wages are 17 percent lower than they could have been, that could be a disaster for your family," McLaren said.

The study also showed that NAFTA had indirect negative impacts on American workers who weren't involved in the industries that were covered by the agreement. This is where geography comes into play.

For example, he suggested that a waitress working "in a town that depends heavily on apparel manufacturing might miss out on wage growth even though she does not work in an industry directly affected by trade."

McLaren asserted in the interview that this geographic component was in fact, "one of our most striking findings."

So, President Trump is not opposed to trade agreements, but such agreements must be beneficial to U.S. workers overall. NAFTA fails that test.

As such, at the time of this writing, the Trump administration continues to engage in negotiations with Mexico and Canada to try to reach a new trade agreement that is fair to

American workers and their families. Because President Trump has already shown the global swamp that he will not agree to a deal that jeopardizes the national security and prosperity of the United States, the American people can remain steadfastly confident that their interests will be prioritized throughout the negotiating process.

A DANGEROUS DEAL FOR AMERICA: THE IRAN DEAL

Multilateral trade agreements are not the only deals President Trump has scrutinized.

He is also reassessing President Obama's Iran deal—or the Joint Comprehensive Plan of Action (JCPOA) as it is officially known. This deal was billed as a way to keep Iran from building or obtaining nuclear weapons.

In practice, however, it has done little to achieve this goal—and provided the dangerous Iranian regime with an enormous infusion of cash.

The Iran deal is a perfect example of how naive and weak the Obama administration was in handling the unpredictable Iranian dictatorship—which has consistently threatened American security, interests, and lives for decades. It also illustrates how eager President Obama was to appease the global bureaucracy and leave some type of global legacy—even if it meant putting the interests and security of Americans at risk. The Obama legacy was clearly more important to him than the American legacy or the safety of the American people.

In the terms laid out by the current agreement, Iran can keep its military installations secret. International inspectors are not permitted to search for violations on military facilities. This nullifies our ability to effectively verify Iran's compliance with the agreement's terms.

To add to this, the same day this catastrophic deal was

implemented, the Obama administration secretly flew in $400 million of Swiss francs, euros, and other currencies on wooden pallets to Iran.[33] Four U.S. hostages were released on this day as well. Over the course of just a few weeks in early 2016, two more airline shipments containing $1.3 billion in cash were sent by the Obama administration to Iran—totaling $1.7 billion.[34]

This cash exchange not only violated the United States' policy to not pay ransom for hostages—or appear to do so—and negotiate with terrorists (Iran is the leading state sponsor of terrorism), but it jeopardized the safety and security of American lives.

And instead of this cash being used by the Tehran regime to build up its own country, the Iranian dictatorship allocated these funds toward supporting violent campaigns and increasing the power of the regime, while simultaneously keeping the Iranian people in a state of continued repression.

Under the nuclear deal, according to a *Wall Street Journal* editorial released in early 2018, $100 billion in Iranian assets became unfrozen through the lifting of international sanctions.[35]

The editorial reflected on the "illusions about Iran" the Obama administration held to be true when the deal was made. The article quoted Vice President Joe Biden's national security advisor, Colin Kahl, who absurdly said the Iranians "are not going to spend the vast majority of the money on guns, most of it will go to butter."

However, the piece points out that, "instead of using the money to improve the lives of Iranians, Tehran has used its windfall to back clients making trouble throughout the region. The mullahs have spent billions propping up Syria's Bashar Assad with troops, weapons and energy shipments. Iran funds Shiite militias in Iraq, Hezbollah terrorists in Syria and Lebanon, and Houthi fighters in Yemen."

A February 2018 *Washington Times* article further reported that "The U.S. government has traced some of the $1.7 billion released to Iran by the Obama administration to Iranian-backed terrorists in the two years since the cash was transferred." This list also included Hezbollah.[36]

Evidently, not a lot of these funds were allocated toward "butter" as predicted.

President Obama clearly did not understand his opponent in Tehran. He did not recognize how dangerous Iran's dictatorial regime was (and still is). He also didn't understand that rogue dictatorships don't often play by the rules.

It is also worth noting that President Obama was not only naive about the nature of the Iranian regime, he was also remarkably dishonest with Congress and the American people.

In a May 2016 article in *New York Times Magazine*, Obama National Security Advisor Ben Rhodes was remarkably frank about the lengths to which they went to sell a false bill of goods about the Iran deal. In the article, Rhodes bragged about controlling the "narrative" of the Iran deal story, since most reporters "literally know nothing" and creating an "echo chamber" in the press by lining up a steady stream of arms control experts to parrot their talking points.[37] The article also makes clear that many of the Obama administration talking points about the deal were false. For instance, the Rhodes-constructed narrative said that negotiations began when the (relatively) moderate Hassan Rouhani was elected president. In reality, they began when the ultraradical Mahmoud Ahmadinejad was still in office.

In addition, *Politico* reported in December 2017 that the Obama administration was so desperate for a deal with Iran that they derailed an eight-year effort to map Hezbollah's billion-dollar criminal enterprise in the United States, which includes the smuggling of cocaine.[38] The problem was that the investigation had traced the criminal terrorist network's activities back to its state sponsors in Iran. As the Obama administration feverishly worked toward a deal, *Politico* reports, they erected bigger and more cumbersome roadblocks in front of the investigative team, such as denying requests for prosecutions and arrests of high profile Iranian and Hezbollah leaders.

Here, we had President Obama using the power of the White House to obstruct the FBI from doing its job—largely for imaginary political gain and Iran's benefit. This is another real example of the deep-seated bias in the media and Washington. Had President Trump even thought about slowing down or impeding FBI investigations the way Obama did, the entire elite class would be screaming for impeachment hearings—or criminal charges.

During President Trump's first year in office, he immediately worked to undo the damage done by Obama's naive and dishonest pursuit of this truly dangerous deal.

Under the Corker-Cardin "Iran Nuclear Agreement Review Act" (INARA/PL 114-17), the president is required every 90 days to ensure that Iran is abiding by the terms of the JCPOA through a certification process.[39]

As I described in an op-ed for Fox News back in October 2017, "full compliance under this law requires the United States to certify that: (1) Iran is fully implementing the JCPOA and all related agreements; (2) Iran has not committed (or if committed, has cured) a material breach; (3) Iran has taken no action to significantly advance its nuclear weapons program; and (4) that continued suspension of nuclear-related sanctions is both appropriate and vital to our national security interests."[40]

While making the decision to certify and deciding if all four points had been met, President Trump took a look back at all of the events that had occurred throughout the first year of his presidency.

He could see that the Tehran regime had become even more

dangerous. Trump recognized that the Iran deal was doing nothing to curtail the rising threat. In fact, since the agreement lifted many sanctions on Iran, the regime had new access to billions of dollars that were being used for violence. All the while, the United States was not able to guarantee that Iran wasn't working to obtain a nuclear weapon.

In fact, UN Ambassador Nikki Haley observed that since the nuclear agreement was signed, "the undeniable fact is that that the Iranian behavior is growing worse."[41]

The failed launch of a missile by Iran in January 2017; a faked missile launch in September; and the enthusiastic chanting of "death to America" by the Iranian parliament after a unanimous vote was passed, according to the AP, "to increase spending on its ballistic missile program and the foreign operations of its paramilitary Revolutionary Guard" made it impossible to reasonably assert that the aforementioned criterion No. 4 of the Iran Nuclear Agreement Review Act (that continued suspension of nuclear-related sanctions is both appropriate and vital to our national security interests) had been followed.[42]

Considering all of this, President Trump decertified the Iran deal in October 2017. Keeping in line with the America first policy, the president rejected the desires of global bureaucrats and prioritized the safety of Americans.

Decertification, however, does not kill the nuclear agreement with Iran. Rather, it provides President Trump with more flexibility and options by increasing America's leverage to fix the broken parts of the deal, which *is* in the vital interest of American national security.

In January 2018, President Trump made the decision to extend the waivers on Iran nuclear sanctions, which he said is the final effort he will put toward fixing this failed agreement.[43]

Fox News reported, "In a stern statement, Trump said he's waiving the sanctions to secure European allies' agreement to address the 'terrible flaws' in the 2015 deal negotiated by his predecessor.

"'Despite my strong inclination, I have not yet withdrawn the United States from the Iran nuclear deal. Instead, I have outlined two possible paths forward: either fix the deal's disastrous flaws, or the United States will withdraw,' Trump said.

"He added, 'No one should doubt my word.'"

HOLDING INTERNATIONAL ORGANIZATIONS ACCOUNTABLE

President Trump's dedication to putting America and its interests first in foreign affairs even extends to our largest international relation—the United Nations.

On former governor Nikki Haley's first day as the U.S. ambassador to the United Nations she clearly articulated President Trump's position to the international body. At UN headquarters in New York, Haley told members, "For those who don't have our backs, we're taking names."[44]

In December 2017, the list of names grew.

During the campaign, President Trump pledged to move the U.S. embassy in Israel to Jerusalem and declare it the capital of Israel. Presidents Bill Clinton and George W. Bush also made this promise but realized once they were in office that it would upset the international bureaucracy and shake up the global order. They backed off.

President Trump did not. He is fulfilling the promise that he made to the American people—and supporting a key ally in the Middle East. The new embassy, according to Vice President Mike Pence, is set to open in 2019. The global bureaucrats in the United Nations did not like this decision.[45]

The United Nations voted in December on a resolution that demanded that the United States reverse its decision. An overwhelming 128 nations voted in favor of this resolution, in direct defiance *against* America and its interests.[46] Some of these nations were (traditionally) major allies of the United States, such as Britain, France, Germany, and Japan.[47]

According to the *New York Times,* this vote is "nonbinding and therefore largely symbolic" but it provided an opportunity for the United States to clearly see "who has our back."[48]

This massive level of global condemnation by the international bureaucracy was shocking. Haley reiterated her "taking names" warning in a tweet:

> At the UN we're always asked to do more and give more. So when we make a decision, at the will of the American people, about where to locate OUR embassy, we don't expect those we've helped to target us.[49]

In a statement to the *New York Times*, she further said, "We will remember it when we are called upon once again to make the world's largest contribution to the United Nations....And we will remember when so many countries come calling on us, as they so often do, to pay even more and to use our influence for their benefit."[50]

In response to the UN's vote, the Trump administration plans to significantly scale back funding contributed to the United Nations.

According to the *Guardian*, the United States contributes 22 percent of the UN's operating budget annually,[51] amounting to approximately $1.2 billion for the 2017–2018 year.[52] The United States is additionally responsible for 28.5 percent of peacekeeping operation funding, totaling an estimated $6.8 billion for the 2017–2018 year. Keep in mind, there are 193 member nations.

In response to the pushback from the members and in recognizing the inefficient monetary and management expenditures of the UN, the Trump administration announced it negotiated a cut to the UN budget of more than $285 million for the 2018–2019 fiscal year.

Regarding the budget slash, Ambassador Haley said in a press release issued at the end of December, "The inefficiency and overspending of the United Nations are well known. We will no longer let the generosity of the American people be taken advantage of or remain unchecked. This historic reduction in spending—in addition to many other moves toward a more efficient and accountable UN—is a big step in the right direction."[53]

As such, President Trump agreed, and said, "People that live here, our great citizens that love this country—they're tired of this country being taken advantage of and we're not going to be taken advantage of any longer."[54]

COMPETITION WITH CHINA

President Trump's actions with China are perfectly in line with the National Security Strategy report's goal to "respond to the growing political, economic, and military competitions we face around the world."[55]

The report further states:

> We welcome all economic relationships rooted in fairness, reciprocity, and faithful adherence to the rules. Those who join this pursuit will be our closest economic partners. But the United States will no longer turn a blind eye to violations, cheating, or economic aggression. We must work with like-minded allies and partners to ensure our principles prevail and the rules are enforced so that our economies prosper.

Simply put, President Trump is finally holding nations accountable that violate trade agreements and engage in unfair economic practices that target American industry.

President Trump's actions with China are a perfect example.

In January 2018, President Trump decided to place tariffs on solar panel imports.

Over the past five years, approximately 30 U.S.-based businesses that manufacture solar cells and modules have either gone bankrupt or closed[56] due in large part to the devastating effects stemming from foreign corporations dumping their products into the U.S. market.[57]

Dumping is a technical term for what happens when a foreign entity (in this case, China) floods a market with goods that are priced substantially lower than the price in the country where they are made. The goal of dumping is to drive other manufacturers out of business by dramatically underbidding them on prices.

At the request of President Trump, an investigation into the solar panel dumping issue was conducted by the U.S. International Trade Commission.

The Commission responded with a 4–0 ruling recommending action to protect the U.S. solar industry and, in a follow-up document, confirmed that most of these cheap imports were coming from China, even though they may have been manufactured elsewhere.[58] The report shows that in response to previous tariffs placed specifically on Chinese solar products, Chinese companies simply moved their manufacturing to other countries. Furthermore, the Commission found that these Chinese manufacturers were able to offer such low prices because the Chinese government had been subsidizing them—an action that violated China's obligations outlined under the World Trade Organization.

In other words, China was cheating, and President Trump caught them.

It is also worth noting that in 2014, five members of the Chinese military were charged with stealing the intellectual property of a U.S. solar cell manufacturer, as well as other companies.[59]

Alarmingly, Chairman Rhonda K. Schmidtlein wrote that the solar cell manufacturing industry "would likely cease to exist in the short term" if relief was not provided for these struggling U.S. corporations. She further explained that this would in effect create "significant long-term consequences for US economic and national security interests."

Chinese and foreign control of our solar cell manufacturing industry has serious economic and national security implications. Not only does it pose a threat to the U.S. power grid, but just as critically, the U.S. military uses solar power as a backup energy source. Allowing China, which is already a very competitive global economic force, to control the prices and supply of a component so integral to our society is unacceptable.

It is a national security imperative that the United States does not relinquish control of this industry to foreign competitors. It's equally important domestically that our solar cell manufacturers are competing on a level playing field.

In response to China's attempts to cheat the system, President Trump issued a tax of up to 30 percent on imported solar cells and panels.[60]

The orderly institutionalists in the anti-Trump coalition responded by fretting that the tariffs would start a trade war with China and lectured about the benefits of free trade. Very few, however, acknowledged the foundation upon which President Trump reached his decision: The Chinese government was illegally subsidizing its industries and dumping its products to harm U.S. industry.

An editorial in the *National Review* titled "Against the Tariffs," for instance, was long on economic theory but totally avoids providing an answer to the question "What do you do when your trading partners are determined to flout the rules?"[61] They are so stuck in the new world order mind-set that they can't comprehend that their huge, complicated, multilateral trade agreements are powerless to stop some countries from taking advantage of the United States.

President Trump understands that we have to be tough with China. It's the only language its leaders respect.

As China has shown, it is capable of economically expanding at an incredibly rapid pace and is determined to do so—even if it means capitalizing on unfair practices. Moreover, China has expressed goals to dominate more than the solar power industry.[62] It is hoping to gain market share in the next-generation information technology sector, the aerospace and aviation equipment industry, biomedicine, the agricultural machinery industry, and robotics.

Since we know the types of actions they will take to try and dominate the solar power sector, failure to respond would guarantee that China would pursue the same sort of economic aggression in those industries.

The United States cannot allow China to control future industries, and we cannot let the Chinese take advantage of our domestic markets for their own economic gain. President Trump has recognized this and, through imposing this tariff on the solar industry, has shown that we must make both rational and smart decisions in order to maintain our competitive advantage with growing economic powers, such as China.

The only way to beat competitors as strong as China is to refuse to allow our domestic industries to be taken advantage of in any way, at any point.

GOING FORWARD

Presidents Trump's National Security Strategy Report lays out an important strategy that embraces the idea that the binary terms "at war" or "at peace" are largely irrelevant in today's world. Instead, it asserts the United States is in "an arena of continuous competition."

Further, the report declares, "We will raise our competitive game to meet that challenge, to protect American interests, and to advance our values."

Though remarkably impressive strides have been made toward reasserting American dominance on the global stage, there is still much more work to be done to suppress and eliminate the threats facing our country.

After all, while ISIS has been largely destroyed, radical Islamic terrorism still thrives in the Middle East. The outcome of the proposed denuclearization talks with North Korea remains uncertain. Competition with China—both in economic and world influence—will likely be a centerpiece of U.S. foreign policy for decades to come. To top things off, Russia's use of hybrid warfare—the utilization of a broad spectrum of methods to attack numerous aspects of an enemy, particularly through aggressive cyber, information, and economic tactics—poses challenges that will evolve and change at the breakneck pace of technology.

Facing these prominent global challenges, President Trump has recognized that clinging to the outdated, failed "new world order" would ultimately lead to America's downfall and inevitable destruction.

President Trump's acute sense of the reality of our world, his principled, optimistic, yet realistic, approach to foreign and national security policy, and his recognition that economic prosperity is a critical component to keeping America safe has led him to make bold, influential, and beneficial decisions during the first year of his administration.

Most importantly, the American people can already clearly see that President Trump's America first policy is working.

The president helped create a counterterrorism alliance with more than 50 Arab and Muslim nation leaders at the Arab Islamic Summit in Riyadh, Saudi Arabia. This coalition helped dismantle and destroy ISIS's territorial dominance.

He has also stared down the global bureaucracy and elicited more defense funding from members of NATO who had not been paying their fair share in the defense of alliance countries or the war on radical Islamic terrorism.

Thanks to the efforts of the Trump administration, America has been placed in a position to boldly and successfully "meet the challenge."

There is no doubt, many in the anti-Trump coalition—in particular the globalists and news media—have been alarmed by the president's efforts. However, Trump's America is pleased. The Americans who elected President Trump see him doing exactly what he said he would do on the campaign trail to protect American jobs and keep people safe. As the president's efforts continue, America will only become more secure and prosperous.

The Trump administration's decisions to withdraw from or renegotiate bad agreements, hold other nations accountable for their actions, not engage in unreciprocated relationships, and address economic cheating head on have initiated America's comeback on the global stage.

CHAPTER FIVE

THE COMEBACK OF FREE SPEECH

Thanks to President Trump, free speech is making a comeback in America today.

Even as a candidate, President Trump recognized that, in addition to reshaping our nation's unifying principles and limiting our religious liberties, the left-wing members of the anti-Trump coalition have been chipping away at our fundamental right to speak our minds and express ourselves freely.

They do this while waving a banner of inclusion and diversity, but their ultimate goal is a profound, unhealthy change to America's fabric.

Through the dogged enforcement of political correctness, the elites in Washington, the media, and academia have been working diligently to convince Americans that freedom of speech is limited to "acceptable" speech. They say some speech is offensive, hateful, or otherwise distasteful and does not warrant protection. They have been persuading people that free speech needs to be confined to "free speech zones." They seek to create "safe spaces," where dissenting views cannot be expressed. Some "safe spaces" include entire university campuses. They have even begun a campaign to convince Americans that inappropriate speech is a form of violence. In fact, these efforts are not so thinly veiled attempts to silence views which the elites oppose.

According to the Foundation for Individual Rights in Education, 16 speakers were disinvited from speaking at U.S. college campuses in 2017 alone.[1] In 13 of these cases, student groups on the Left petitioned to have right-leaning speakers barred from speaking—or simply overwhelmed the events with violence forcing administrations to cancel speaking engagements for public safety.

Other colleges have used these violent outbursts as excuses to head off conservative speakers. In August 2017, the University of California, Berkeley, levied a $15,000 "security fee" on Young America's Foundation, the group that invited *Daily Wire* editor in chief Ben Shapiro to speak on campus.[2] This is ironic, as Berkeley is the supposed home of the free speech movement.

These are limitations that the Founding Fathers never intended—and would have wholeheartedly rejected. While some people hold views which are indeed abhorrent, it is critical to our liberty that all Americans are able to speak their minds without fear of punishment by the state or censorship by academic institutions.

The men and women of Trump's America understand this, which is why they rallied to Trump as a candidate and continue to support him today. President Trump rejects these limitations as well and is working to ensure that our core freedoms and values are not simply limited to those with whom the elites agree.

REJECTING POLITICAL CORRECTNESS

If President Trump has a single defining characteristic, it is his willingness to say what he believes, regardless of who might be offended.

This was the first jarring reality of the Trump candidacy. He was willing to say things that no typical leader could have imagined saying. The bluntness and, at times, crassness of Trump's language has proven to be a force in its own right. People are stunned and forced to pay attention to Trump just because they have never heard a modern political leader speak like him.

As a candidate, Trump defeated more than a dozen Republicans and the Clinton political machine by branding opponents as "low-energy," "little," "lying," and "crooked." He unabashedly called out past Republicans for failures in the Middle East in dealing with radical Islamic terrorism. As president, he has answered nearly every criticism from hostile leaders with defiance. He calls North Korean leader Kim Jong-un "Rocket man" in response to missile tests. Even when British Prime Minister Theresa May, who is an ally, criticized him for retweeting a video about Islamic terrorism posted by a controversial group, he tweeted, "Don't focus on me, focus on the destructive Radical Islamic Terrorism that is taking place within the United Kingdom." His whole attitude toward opinion leaders, other political figures, and the news media has been "if you want to go after me, I will go after you ten times harder."

When the news media began to attack him relentlessly, he brilliantly co-opted the term *fake news* and began branding his critics as liars and propagandists. His 50 million Twitter followers enabled him to fight the anti-Trump media to a standstill.

Consistently, the president insists that the southern border must be secured and that so-called sanctuary cities must cooperate with federal law enforcement in deporting criminals who are in our country illegally. He also says we must halt immigration from countries wracked by terrorism until we can assure security measures are in place to protect Americans. For these comments, the political correctness thought police maliciously claim that he is a xenophobic isolationist who is offending all people of Latin American, Hispanic, or Islamic descent.

However, Trump has not backed away. Instead, he has reinforced his political incorrectness as defined by the elites by picking fights that are virtually indefensible on the other side. Instead of talking about illegal immigration, in general, he talks about the vicious brutality of the MS-13 gang. Similarly, instead of talking about immigration at large, he focuses on sanctuary cities and emphasizes the cases where the cities released someone who then harmed an American. His opponents then grow frustrated because they can't really defend the murderers and rapists who are at the heart of MS-13, or other criminals who are in the country illegally and hurting and killing Americans.

President Trump also represents the 83 percent of Americans who identify as Christians[3] and the 67 percent who routinely say Merry Christmas (25 percent say happy holidays and 4 percent refuse to say anything).[4] While the secular multiculturalists in the anti-Trump coalition insist on toning down all religious references, many Americans are deeply pleased that President Trump breaks the mold and emphasizes Christmas.

When faced with this overwhelming acceptance and support of Christmas by most Americans, the elites disingenuously claim they never waged a war on Christmas—despite spending decades filing lawsuits seeking to ban nativity displays, tree lighting ceremonies, and other religious iconography from public areas.

FACT VERSUS IDEOLOGY

Political correctness is enforced in part by having a commitment to mindlessly repeat what is ideologically necessary.

It is ironic that America, the birthplace of pragmatism, is now home to elites who believe in a philosophy that facts should be reshaped to fit ideology. One of the reasons it has become so hard to reform government has been this rise of the ideologically defined reality. Nowhere has this preference for ideology over facts been more obvious than in trying to analyze the threat from Islamic supremacists.

The elites in Germany refused to recognize mass harassment, assaults, and in some cases, rape of German women during the 2015–2016 New Year's Eve celebration in Cologne and other parts of Germany. Only when social media blew up with indignation and outrage did the authorities admit that there had been more than 1,200 assaults.

Similarly, the news media has had a long tradition of trying to avoid religious motivation as a key to understanding terrorist violence.

In 2016, New York City Mayor Bill de Blasio's first reaction to a bomb that injured 29 people in the Chelsea neighborhood of Manhattan was to avoid using the word *terrorism* until police fully investigated the matter.[5]

Again and again, authorities are cautious to the point of absurdity in reporting on and analyzing terrorist attacks. Whenever possible, the elite media shades the facts to fit its ideological preconceptions. Thus, the truck driver who instantly killed 84 people and injured hundreds more during the July 2016 Bastille Day celebration in Nice, France, was reported to be a French resident. Initially, there was no mention that he was originally from Tunisia. Similarly, attackers can yell "Allahu Akbar" before committing or attempting mass murder, and the elite's first reaction is to say motivation is not known.

President Trump's willingness to be blunt about the threat of Islamic supremacists is a major break with the elites. For two decades the elites did everything they could to downplay the religious motivation of international terrorists. It was considered xenophobic and racist to even raise questions about the people who were trying to kill us. Trump blew all that away and insisted on telling the truth even if it conflicted with the elite ideology.

Another example of ideology dominating facts is the absolute refusal of American elites to hold large, bureaucratic schools accountable for their failure to educate. No matter how bad the schools are, or how much they cheat their poorest children, the elites insist that these failing schools are paragons of citizenship and progress—and they just need more money.

However, facts, if confronted, can be devastating.

At schools in the city of Baltimore, only 15 percent of elementary and middle school students who took the Partnership for Assessments of Career and College Readiness assessment passed the English portion and 11.9 percent passed the math section.[6]

Some schools in the District of Columbia have half or more students absent for more than half the year, but these students still somehow graduate. The school faculty is still paid with our tax dollars for "teaching" empty seats. Furthermore, the students still receive passing grades, despite not going to class. In a fact-based society, this would be considered fraud, and these teachers would be at least fired and at most prosecuted. However, in the ideologically defined world of big city, left-wing, union-dominated politics, it is just bureaucracy as usual.

President Trump is redefining the very structure of American political and governmental dialogue by insisting on fact-based conversations—even if they are politically incorrect and even if they offend Republicans and Democrats alike.

However, President Trump's commitment to fight political correctness has its own downside. There are times when President Trump gets himself in trouble that traditional leaders might have avoided. His lack of timidity sometimes leads to overreach and, at times, indefensible statements. The Trump technique is to learn from the mistakes and keep moving forward, without apology. His philosophy is that the next fight will drown the last fight.

Trump's ferocity in counterattacking is also a part of his strategy. As someone who spent his career with blue-collar workers, Trump understands that someone punching you becomes an existential moment. You either fight back or you back down. Trump always chooses to fight. In some ways, President Trump is the first president since Andrew Jackson to understand barroom brawling at a practical level. He applies this brawl model to politics. You have to counterpunch or you will lose.

Clearly, President Trump has been fighting a nonstop battle with political correctness, and I expect he will continue that fight.

This has been a total shock to the political establishment—and a breath of fresh air to many Americans. Trump's rejection of political correctness and promotion of the free expression of ideas tapped a feeling many Americans share. It has been a key to his success as a candidate and as president.

In fact, the CATO Institute found in its 2017 Free Speech and Tolerance Survey that 71 percent of Americans polled in August 2017 thought political correctness has prevented important conversations about a range of societal issues. As a result, the poll shows 58 percent of Americans have opted not to share their political opinions in public.[7]

For these Americans, and millions like them, President Trump has heralded a return to the traditional idea that America is inherently diverse, people are going to disagree about many things, and for our country to grow, we must freely speak about our differences.

The results of the CATO survey clearly show why this return to traditional freedom of speech has been welcomed. Across the political spectrum, Americans are self-censoring. Even on the Left, 45 percent of those who identified themselves as liberal said they agreed with the statement: "The political climate

92THE GREAT COMEBACK

these days prevents me from saying things I believe because others might find them offensive." Thirty percent of self-identified strong liberals agreed as well. As the graph tracks to the right, more and more people say they silence themselves to avoid social consequences. Fifty-seven percent of moderates, 70 percent of conservatives, and 76 percent of strong conservatives all reported keeping their political views to themselves to avoid ridicule by the political correctness thought police.

The fact that this many people—of all political persuasions—have been afraid to publicly share their beliefs in America tells you that the cudgel of political correctness has done serious damage to our right of free speech.

The CATO poll also found that Americans are getting tired of biting their tongues. Overall, 59 percent of those surveyed said people should be able to express their opinions publicly even if others are offended. The importance of this nationwide frustration over political correctness can't be overstated. People are starting to reject it.

In fact, a predictive computer model made by clearthinking .org found that opposition to political correctness was the second-highest motivator for Trump voters in the 2016 election—behind party affiliation.[8] The nonpartisan organization developed a machine learning program, which analyzed survey results from 800 people who had already decided how they would vote one month before the election.

On a seven-point scale (with –3 representing total disagreement and +3 meaning total agreement), 90 percent of Trump voters agreed with the statement: "There is too much political correctness in this country." In fact, 54 percent reported the strongest possible agreement rating. Interestingly, even 49 percent of Clinton voters expressed some level of agreement with the statement.

It's not surprising so many people are rejecting political correctness. The very idea that one must not air ideas which some may find offensive is totally counter to the American system of freedom.

Consider the words of Founder Ben Franklin, who wrote an article on freedom of speech for the *Pennsylvania Gazette* in November 1737:

> Freedom of speech is a principal pillar of a free government; When this support is taken away, the constitution of a free society is dissolved, and tyranny is erected on its ruins. Republics and limited monarchies derive their strength and vigor from a popular examination into the action of the magistrates.

Our country is based, thrives, and depends on the free flow of opinions and robust public debate. The process of hearing and weighing ideas, and ultimately uplifting some over others, is the key to maintaining a vibrant civil discourse in our society. Frankly, constantly grappling with new opposing viewpoints—especially in politics—keeps our civilization honest and helps to stave off tyranny.

In the words of George Washington, "the freedom of Speech may be taken away, and, dumb and silent we may be led, like sheep, to the Slaughter."

This is one of the main reasons some in the anti-Trump coalition are trying to limit the exchange of ideas. They are trying to promote a system in which ideas they don't like can be deemed unacceptable and summarily dismissed. Currently, they are issuing these dismissals in the name of tolerance, inclusion, and diversity. However, as Franklin warned in the *New-England Courant* in 1722, "in those wretched countries where a man cannot call his tongue his own, he can scarce call anything else his own. Whoever would overthrow the liberty of a nation, must begin by subduing the freeness of speech."[9]

ACADEMIC ATTACKS ON FREE SPEECH

Since its beginning in the 1980s, the political correctness movement has waged the brunt of its war on America's college campuses. The reason is simple, the elites want to train young minds
to accept restrictions on speech and opinions as soon as they
begin forming solid political opinions.

Some of the results of these efforts are completely ridiculous. For example, in a January 2, 2018, op-ed for the *Wall Street
Journal*, Steve Salerno criticized an article written by a pair of
University of Northern Iowa professors which aimed at putting
an end to what they called "white-informed civility."[10]

According to Salerno, "their core contention is twofold:
One, that civility, as currently practiced in America, is a white
construct. Two, that in a campus setting, the 'woke' white student's endeavor to avoid microaggressions against black peers
is itself a microaggression—a form of noblesse oblige whereby
white students are in fact patronizing students of color. Not
only that, but by treating black students with common courtesy
and expecting the same in return, white students [ignore] black
grievances, bypassing the 'race talk' that is supposed to occur
in preamble to all other conversations."

The takeaway here is: According to political correctness
doctrine, all white people are racist, and their ideas are illegitimate unless they sufficiently atone for their inherent racism—
which only reinforces their inherent racism and delegitimizes
their opinions. It is a negative feedback loop.

The article Salerno references is outlandish; however, it represents a real, constant movement in the academic wing of the
anti-Trump coalition to fundamentally alter our freedom of
expression.

If you have any doubt that the academic elite view freedom of speech as malleable and think it should be applied to
some speakers differently than others, simply read the April 24,

2017, *New York Times* op-ed by New York University professor Ulrich Baer.[11]

In the op-ed titled "What 'Snowflakes' Get Right About Free Speech," Baer quite clearly argues that instead of following the founding principle of free expression promoted by the Founders of our country, we should instead adopt the definition developed by contemporary French philosopher Jean-François Lyotard.

Baer argues that some opinions are simply too wrong or hurtful to be allowed. Specifically, he said:

> Lyotard shifted attention away from the content of free speech to the way certain topics restrict speech as a public good. Some things are unmentionable and undebatable, but not because they offend the sensibilities of the sheltered young. Some topics, such as claims that some human beings are by definition inferior to others, or illegal or unworthy of legal standing, are not open to debate because such people cannot debate them on the same terms.[12]

Baer said speakers with bigoted, maligned, overtly controversial opinions rob others of their humanity and voice. Baer applied this faulty idea as a justification for recent violent efforts by college students to bar people he called controversial from speaking on campus. Specifically, he named Richard Spencer, Milo Yiannopoulous, and Charles Murray. According to Baer, these efforts to silence speakers "should be understood as an attempt to ensure the conditions of free speech for a greater group of people, rather than censorship."

Sure, Spencer and Yiannopoulous may be racist and outlandish, respectively. However, Murray is a serious academic and an emeritus scholar at the American Enterprise Institute.

Regardless of the character of the speaker, condoning—or rather failing to condemn—violence aimed at silencing speech is dangerous and un-American.

Ultimately, Baer's position is that free speech doesn't count for some people—and it just depends on what they have to say.

> We would do better to focus on a more sophisticated understanding, such as the one provided by Lyotard, of the necessary conditions for speech to be a common, public good. This requires the realization that in politics, the parameters of public speech must be continually redrawn to accommodate those who previously had no standing....
>
> The idea of freedom of speech does not mean a blanket permission to say anything anybody thinks. It means balancing the inherent value of a given view with the obligation to ensure that other members of a given community can participate in discourse as fully recognized members of that community.

To be clear: Racial epithets; slurs based on gender, sexuality, or ethnicity; and other personal attacks and denigrations have no place in civil society or discourse. However, Baer is suggesting that we should put in place what the U.S. Supreme Court has repeatedly called prior restraints on free speech.

Baer's pseudosophisticated model applied at our nation's colleges and universities would result in regular censorship. This is dangerous because students are supposed to learn to debate and overcome bad ideas with words, facts, and reason rather than violence, censorship, or government suppression.

In fact, this is exactly what happened when Charles Murray tried to speak at Middlebury College in Vermont in March 2017.[13] Rather than listen to his arguments and debate him, students attacked Murray and another professor. After successfully disrupting a planned speech by Murray, the students tracked Murray and a professor down to where they had fled and assaulted them. The professor, Allison Stranger, was ultimately hospitalized.

Applying Baer's model to society at-large would bring about a system of government-led speech oppression that would place the United States in the company of China, Russia, and North Korea.

Who, after all, should be the one to decide whether a speaker's opinion meets Baer's "conditions for speech to be a common, public good?" What authority should Americans trust to be "balancing the inherent value of a given view."

The answers are: no one, and no authority. What Baer is suggesting is an absurd counter to the ideals of free society that would empower elites (such as Baer) to dictate which opinions are valuable and which should be silenced.

Baer is remarkably close to the governing party in Orwell's novel *1984*. That frightening description of a Britain turned totalitarian has a dictatorship based on three slogans: war is peace, freedom is slavery, ignorance is strength.

As the modern left explains its thinking, it is remarkably close to the Orwell description of a totalitarian elimination of free thought.

STICKS AND STONES

The latest alarming, reckless attack on the First Amendment by the politically correct elites is the effort to equate words with actual violence. Some have even used this line of illogic to justify violence as an appropriate response to speech they find offensive.

Indeed, Natasha Lennard wrote in the liberal magazine *The Nation* on January 19, 2017, that President Trump was a fascist, represented "violent racist forces," and that "counter-violence" was necessary to oppose his agenda.[14]

Keep in mind, Trump had not yet been inaugurated nor taken any actions as president when Lennard wrote this piece. He was sworn in the day after it was published.

Nevertheless, Lennard espoused the virtues of violent anti-fascist movements throughout history and made clear that while some liberals "cling to institutions" such as freedom of speech or "investigations and justice," the brand of liberalism she supported "does not tolerate fascism; it would give it no platform for debate."

This was a clear call to arms for the actually violent, dangerous so-called Antifa members who harassed Trump supporters and vandalized cities across the country on Inauguration Day.

Their actions, which led to injured police, destroyed property, and endangered Americans, had zero impact on President Trump's presidency—except to highlight how truly crazy the Left was.

Yet this is exactly the kind of activity Lennard would seem to support in her piece:

> Those of us who long before Trump have defended counter-violence against oppression—as in Ferguson, as in Baltimore, as in Watts, as in counter-riots against the Klu Klux Klan, as in slave revolts—know where we stand.
>
> …disruption, confrontation, doxxing and altercation remain tactics anyone taking seriously a refusal to normalize Trump-era fascism should consider. Liberals who reject such a strategy in defense of the right to [freedom] of speech and assembly engage in an historical NIMBYism, in which only in the past, or in other countries, has militancy against white supremacy been a legitimate resistance.

Lennard is clearly an extremist, but this is an example of what happens when politically correct ideology replaces freedom of speech: "Incorrect" speech is viewed as violence; therefore, actual violence is justified to combat it. Lennard's labeling of Trump supporters as fascists is simply a verbal way to justify the illegal, violent activity she is promoting.

Now, to practice what I'm preaching and civilly consider an opposing viewpoint, I'll point out that Northeastern University psychology professor Lisa Feldman Barrett addressed this concept of speech as violence much more eloquently.

In a July 14, 2017, op-ed for the *New York Times* titled "When Is Speech Violence?" Barrett rightly pointed out that prolonged, pervasive stress—such as the stress caused by being in a verbally or emotionally abusive home or relationship—is medically harmful.[15] Certainly, prolonged stress can cause depression, weaken the immune system, and cause measurable harm to many bodily systems.

This is a reasonable position, and it led her to her thesis: "If words can cause stress, and if prolonged stress can cause physical harm, then it seems that speech—at least certain types of speech—can be a form of violence."

Barrett also makes clear that human beings are perfectly equipped to deal with short-term stress caused by "fleeing from a tiger, taking a punch, or encountering an odious idea in a university lecture." She even gave an anecdote about a time her students refused to engage in a mock debate defending eugenics for the sake of understanding how science has been misused in the past. She actually brought in an African American colleague to argue for the merits of eugenics, while she debated him. (They switched sides halfway through to show the students how civil discourse is supposed to work.)

This is all well and good. However, Barrett lost me when she argued that the opinions of speakers such as Yiannopoulos offer no public benefit and therefore don't qualify for free speech protections—while Murray's opinions were "only offensive" and therefore worthy of debating.

The issue with this position is twofold: First, like Baer, Barrett is suggesting someone (presumably some elite group of highly educated persons) should weigh the content of speech, decide whether or not it has merit, then decide whether there is anything "to be gained from debating" it. This is the same prior restraint that has been continuously ruled unconstitutional by the U.S. Supreme Court.

Second, she's equating the stress someone might feel by listening to a speech by Yiannopoulos with the kind of stress caused by being in a prolonged abusive relationship or imprisonment. This completely ignores the fact that Yiannopoulos's speech is a voluntary event. Students who do not agree with or do not wish to debate him are welcome to do something else with their time.

Along those lines, as Dr. Pamela Paresky pointed out in a rebuttal of Barrett's piece on the website psychologytoday.com, Barrett is ignoring the fact that stress isn't felt universally, and it's largely in the eye of the beholder. Paresky argues that Barrett's position can actually lead to more harm because some people may feel more stress simply by being told they might. According to Paresky:

> If one person tells herself that listening to a speaker is going to be intolerable and harmful, it stands to reason that the experience will be more stressful for her than it will be for the person who tells herself it will be illuminating, or an opportunity to defeat a bad idea. (Or a chance to take a nap...)[16]

Make no mistake, the argument that words are violence is a poor attempt by the elites to grant themselves authority over speech. Violence is violence, speech is speech. It would do all Americans well to remember that sticks and stones may break our bones, but words can never hurt us.

THE THOUGHT POLICE, KILLING INNOVATION

College campuses have always been a battleground for freedom of speech. However, the effort to silence ideas is expanding to America's private sector—particularly in our growing tech industry. Since President Trump took office, American businesses have experienced incredible growth. Now is not the time to stifle that growth in the name of political correctness.

Consider the firing of former Google engineer James Damore, who was relieved of his post after circulating an internal memo in July 2017 expressing grievances about Google's hiring practices, diversity programs, and how "Google's left bias has created a politically correct monoculture that maintains its hold by shaming dissenters into silence."[17]

Central to Damore's essay is the assertion that some of Google's attempts to close the gender and racial gaps in its company's employment were discriminatory and actually served to worsen relations among employees.

Certainly, Damore expressed some views in the memo about the biological and behavioral differences between men and women as they related to the workplace that were of questionable veracity—and this is the theme on which the elite media latched. However, he prefaced the entire document by saying:

> I value diversity and inclusion, am not denying that sexism exists, and don't endorse using stereotypes. When addressing the gap in representation in the population, we need to look at population level differences in distributions. If we can't have an honest discussion about this, then we can never truly solve the problem.

These don't seem to be the words of a disgruntled, mean-spirited, bigoted misogynist. They seem like the words of someone who wanted to start—and participate in—a real discussion. In fact, virtually every section of Damore's more than 3,000-word essay included statements that acknowledged the harmful societal impact of bias, supported equality, and suggested ways to improve the company.

The elites skipped right over these comments. They also ignored Damore's other main point: that Google alienated conservative employees and caused them to "feel like they need to stay in the closet to avoid open hostility."

Google caved under the elite media pressure (and maybe also the internal culture of conformity Damore had challenged) and fired Damore for writing and sharing the memo, saying it was offensive. He lost his job, not because he had failed as an engineer, but because he had expressed opinions which the media and Bay Area elite found offensive.

Another employee at tech-giant Apple, Denise Young Smith, was spared a public firing—but she did have to apologize after she suggested that people of the same ethnicity and gender could still have diversity of opinion. Specifically, she was criticized for suggesting that white people could have diverse ideas. Ironically, Smith, who is black, was the vice president of inclusion and diversity for Apple.

She was pilloried by the elite thought police for suggesting that "there can be 12 white blue-eyed blonde men in a room and they are going to be diverse too because they're going to bring a different life experience and life perspective to the conversation."

Despite spending 20 years at the company, Smith resigned from Apple in November 2017, roughly a month after sending her apology.

It's not a huge surprise that the left-leaning American tech industry is a bastion of PC culture; however, some in its ranks are warning that the deep ideological undercurrents in Silicon Valley are chasing away talent.

Sam Altman, the president of the tech startup accelerator Y Combinator, wrote on his blog in December 2017 that he "felt more comfortable discussing controversial ideas in Beijing than in San Francisco"[18] because political correctness had run amok on the West Coast.

The thrust of his short essay—for which he was widely criticized—was that "restricting speech leads to restricting ideas and therefore restricted innovation—the most successful societies have generally been the most open ones."

This seems like a fairly reasonable position to take in America—except, apparently, in San Francisco.

Altman said he knew people in "pharmaceuticals for intelligence augmentation, genetic engineering, and radical life extension" who were leaving the Bay Area because the intolerant political climate had become "toxic." Critics of his departing colleagues had argued that human beings harm the environment; therefore, those who wanted to try to extend human life were unethical.

Political correctness, he said, "ends up being used as a club for something orthogonal to protecting actual victims." He posited that if the space transport company SpaceX had been founded in San Francisco it "would have been attacked for focusing on problems of the 1 percent."

Altman got into trouble with the elites because he "inelegantly" suggested in a footnote to the post that homophobic comments online aren't likely to convince reasonable people to hate homosexuals, but banning speech which is deemed controversial could prevent or hinder societal progress.

In a clarification he posted the next day, he stressed that "the biggest new scientific ideas, and the most important changes to society, both start as extremely unpopular ideas," and we must be able to tolerate them.

Altman is exactly right. If we do not return to the foundational principle of freedom of speech and expression in America, which welcomes new ideas (even bad or zany ones) for debate, we will pay dearly for it. At this moment in our history, we are facing numerous watershed moments in computing, medicine, space exploration, and all manner of technological achievement.

If our innovators are walking on eggshells and unable to pursue new ideas for fear of consequences by the thought police, we will decline as a society and be eclipsed by our global competitors who are less concerned about hurt feelings.

NO LEGISLATIVE ANSWER

The trickiest part about preserving and restoring freedom of speech is there is no obvious legislative fix. The law (the First Amendment) is already on the side of freedom of expression, so there is not much Congress can meaningfully do to protect it further. The proponents of silence know they are unlikely to get rid of the First Amendment—but they have been diligently working to culturally change the way Americans think about it.

The Trump administration, on the other hand, is in the perfect position to ensure that the law of the land is properly executed and not being infringed.

To this end, Attorney General Jeff Sessions announced in September 2017 that the Department of Justice (DOJ) would start filing legal briefs in court cases across the country involving students whose rights to free speech had been infringed. Such briefs will allow the DOJ to speak in support of such claimants without technically being part of the case.

The first such case, according to *U.S. News and World Report*, involved a student at a Georgia College who was barred from handing out Christian-themed fliers on campus. He has sued, rightly claiming his First Amendment rights had been trampled.[19]

Sessions announced that the DOJ would seek to support the Georgia student during a speech at Georgetown Law. During his speech, he noted, "freedom of thought and speech on the American campus are under attack."

He went on to say:

> The American university was once the center of academic freedom—a place of robust debate, a forum for the competition of ideas. But it is transforming into an echo chamber of political correctness and homogenous thought, a shelter for fragile egos.

Hopefully, the DOJ's decision to come to the defense of silenced students will cause colleges and institutions of higher learning across the country to think twice before imposing restrictive speech policies.

Even if some of the more ardently PC colleges hold out, the administration could find more direct ways to defend the rights of speakers on campus.

In February of 2017, after "150 agitators...threw commercial-grade fireworks and rocks at law enforcement, started fires with Molotov cocktails and broke windows of the building where Yiannopoulos was set to speak at UC Berkeley,"[20] President Trump suggested that he might seek to withhold federal funding from schools that do not protect speakers from such violence.

In many ways, President Trump is the best person to combat the efforts of the elites because he has been relentlessly fighting his own culture war since he entered public life. He is totally unafraid to speak his mind—and he will quickly defend the rights of those the elites are trampling.

Trump supporters can follow the lead of the president and the attorney general. They can help fund conservative student activist groups. They can help finance student lawsuits. They can demand that their alma maters have conservative faculty and host conservative speakers. They can join together to endow conservative professorial chairs and student internships (the Bill Buckley program at Yale is a model of this kind of pro-conservative engagement on a liberal campus).

Freedom of speech is the foundation of all our freedoms and it must be protected and cherished as such.

THE COMEBACK OF THE AMERICAN ECONOMY, PART 1—CUTTING RED TAPE

The bureaucracy is the anti-Trump coalition's favorite weapon.

For the Left, it is the primary vehicle through which to subvert the will of the people by using regulations to control almost every aspect of our lives.

For members of the economic and political establishment, the regulations which the bureaucracy creates and enforces are an important tool for gaining market share and amassing power. Corporate interests use their lobbying muscle to create regulations that shut out their competitors—usually smaller, start-up companies that cannot afford the lobbyists. Likewise, for members of the political establishment, the ability to manipulate regulations on behalf of their donors keeps a steady stream of campaign cash flowing in.

Trump's America, on the other hand, resents an omnipresent government in their lives, micromanaging small business owners with job-killing regulations and trying to impose weird liberal values on ordinary Americans. Plus, many members of Trump's America are hurting economically. They are victims of jobs going overseas and the slow economic growth of the Obama administration following the 2008 recession. They cheer any steps which will create jobs and spur economic growth.

Fortunately for Trump's America, when it comes to repealing regulations and reducing the power of the bureaucracy, the president has delivered "big league," as he would say. The deregulatory effort led by President Trump is jaw-dropping and historic, and a key reason why the economy boomed in his first year, even before the tax cut was passed.

If you want to understand the truth about America's comeback in job creation and economic growth, you need to understand how bad the regulatory state had become and the scale of the president's effort to review and roll back job killing, expensive federal regulations.

A DAUNTING TASK

As soon as President Trump took office, he began his aggressive campaign to cut red tape in Washington.

This is no easy feat. At the end of 2016—just before President Trump was inaugurated—the Code of Federal Regulations (CFR), which includes all final rules published by the government, contained 185,053 pages in 242 bound volumes, including a 1,170-page appendix.[1] This figure is up from only 22,877 pages in 1960—a more than 700 percent increase over 56 years.

To put a finer point on it: The Mercatus Center at George Mason University regularly gathers data from the CFR and logs the frequency of phrases and words, including "may not," "must," "prohibited," "required," and "shall," in an effort to track the number of restrictive regulations in the code. According to the

Center's research,[2] such restrictions increased by 107 percent from 1975 to 2016.

This increase in regulations—and specifically restrictive ones—matters because this huge spike in government controls and rulemaking across American industry is choking out innovation and making it harder for businesses to grow, create jobs, and provide opportunities for Americans. Indeed, there is a place in our society for reasonable regulations. No one wants toxic, lead-laden drinking water. No company in America should be able to exploit child workers. However, when regulations go too far, or are poorly written, they add tremendous costs to U.S. businesses.

For example, the Environmental Protection Agency (EPA) determined in 2015 that dust—what comes off gravel roads or recently tilled fields—was dangerous particulate matter. That is the same pollutant classification it gives coal ash or soot. This meant farmers had to start spending their time and money not on growing crops but mitigating the dust that could potentially come off the natural land.

As another example, on January 19, 2017—days before President Trump was inaugurated—the Department of Energy under President Obama published a rule that required ceiling fans to be more energy efficient. This 62-page rule will do little more than make new ceiling fans more expensive. Republicans have been fighting the Obama administration's ceiling fan rule since 2013.

Another last-minute Obama rule was an Occupational Safety and Health Administration (OSHA) regulation that put limits on workers' exposure and handling of beryllium—a lightweight, strong metal used in construction, electronics, and maritime and aeronautical vehicles. If handled improperly over a long period of time, beryllium can cause lung disease and other health issues.

However, it can be safely handled with proper protection. Originally, the rule was meant to only cover manufacturers, but OSHA expanded its reach to include construction and maritime industries. Alabama Congressman Bradley Byrne cautioned the added costs of complying with this expansion could endanger the livelihoods of more than 400,000 American workers.[3]

The cost of these ridiculous regulations adds up. The Competitive Enterprise Institute's Ten Thousand Commandments 2017[4] report estimated the economic impact of compliance with federal regulations to be $1.9 trillion a year. That equals half of our federal spending for 2016 and accounts for 10 percent of our gross domestic product (GDP). The cost in taxpayer dollars for the agencies to administer regulations was estimated at $63 billion for 2016.

To express these large numbers in a more relatable way: If the regulatory machine in America were a country, it would be the seventh largest economy in the world—ranking just ahead of Italy but behind India.

Much of this cost increase has built up from regulatory actions taken over the last few decades. Another report by the Mercatus Center found that if the level of U.S. regulation had remained static from 1980 forward, "the economy would have been nearly 25 percent larger by 2012 (i.e., regulatory growth since 1980 cost GDP $4 trillion in 2012, or about $13,000 per [person])."

Imagine for a moment what it would mean for our country if GDP had been $4 trillion larger in 2012. How quickly would we have climbed out of the 2008 recession—would there have been a recession at all? My bet is had we stayed on the path which President Reagan put us on, we would have avoided many of the economic struggles we've faced in the last several decades.

According to the White House Council of Economic Advisors,[5] small businesses pay a disproportionate share of the cost of regulations. The White House report estimated the per-employee regulatory compliance costs for small businesses was $11,724 in 2016. Meanwhile, firms with more than 100 employees paid $9,083 per employee. Ninety-nine percent of the employers in our country are small businesses, and small businesses employ almost half of our private-sector workforce. On top of this, small firms create 75 percent of the new jobs in America. When you raise the cost of hiring employees, fewer Americans get jobs. It's that simple.

Finally, U.S. regulations have a real impact on American taxpayers as well. The Ten Thousand Commandments 2017 report found that regulatory costs added to food, health care, petroleum, and transportation create what is essentially a hidden tax. On average, this costs U.S. households $14,809 a year. The White House Council noted that this hidden regulatory tax on necessities, which are the most heavily regulated products in our economy, hits lower-income Americans hardest. While higher-income earners may not be harmed when regulations drive up the price of eggs, milk, or gasoline, those who struggle to make ends meet are forced to make tough decisions.

So, the Trump administration's drive to cut red tape in America is not simply anti-Washington rhetoric. The unchecked growth of federal regulation has kept jobs, prosperity, and the American dream out of reach for many Americans. President Trump understands this perfectly, and this is why he started fighting the regulatory machine as soon as he took office.

His success in this effort has been one of the most important—and underreported—achievements of President Trump's first year in office.

ONE-IN, TWO-OUT

President Trump's deregulation effort started in earnest with Executive Order No. 13771[6]—the directive that said for every cost-bearing regulatory action federal agencies proposed, they had to identify two existing ones for removal. The order also instructed agencies that the net cost of their final regulatory actions for Fiscal Year 2017 could not exceed $0—unless the law required otherwise, or the actions had clearance from the White House Office of Management and Budget (OMB) director.

According to the White House Office of Information and Regulatory Affairs (OIRA),[7] by July 2017, the Trump administration had withdrawn 469 proposed regulatory actions requested by agencies in Obama's final months in office. Another 391 Obama-era actions had been reclassified as either long-term or inactive, so the new administration could more carefully review them. At the time, OMB Director Mick Mulvaney said the administration was more than meeting the one-in, two-out directive by eliminating 16 regulatory actions for each one it created. To be clear: Mulvaney was talking broadly about regulatory actions—not final rules. By February 2018, OIRA Director Neomi Rao said at a meeting of the National Space Council that the deregulation ratio was actually 22-to-1.

Deregulation may not seem exciting, but cutting these regulations has a tremendous potential to boost the American economy. The OIRA reported that the number of "economically significant" proposed regulations in the pipeline had dropped to 58—a 50 percent reduction since the fall of 2016. The office defines such regulations as "likely to have an annual effect on the economy of $100 million or more, or adversely affect in a material way" any aspect of the economy. The administration requires agencies to perform more thorough cost benefit analyses for economically significant regulations as well as analyses for other feasible alternatives.

As the White House was working with agencies to cut regulations, the Republican Congress made excellent use of the Congressional Review Act (CRA), which became law as a part of the

Contract with America when I was Speaker of the House. We included the CRA in the Contract because we believed a powerful administrative state posed a serious threat to the Republic.

It is Congress's duty to make law; it is the executive branch's duty to implement it, both through enforcement and by creating specific regulations that carry out the law's intent. However, we realized in 1994 that the administrative state had grown so large and left-leaning it could use the regulation issuing process to subvert the will of the people as expressed through elections and the laws passed by Congress. This represented a serious imbalance to the checks and balances set forth by the Constitution of the United States.

The CRA was our solution to this problem. It provides Congress with a 60-day window to expeditiously revoke regulations made by federal agencies. Since these bills require the president's signature to be enacted, they are most useful for getting rid of regulations made during the final months of a presidency after a new president takes office. In addition to revoking regulations, the CRA makes it impossible for cagey agencies to write similar regulations without an act of Congress.

Today's Republican Congress, with President Trump's aid, negated 15 Obama-era regulations with CRA resolutions in the first 60 legislative days of Trump's term. This was a record. Previously, the CRA had only successfully been used once before, during the George W. Bush administration, to negate an expensive rule requiring companies to revamp their workplaces to make them more ergonomic. This 600-page rule had been made by Bill Clinton's Labor Department and would have greatly hampered U.S. businesses. Back in 2000, the Heritage Foundation said the rule was "the broadest and most costly workplace regulation ever published." The foundation estimated it would have cost businesses $4.7 billion a year.[8]

Similarly, the CRA actions taken by Republicans and the Trump administration during year one will provide immediate economic benefits. Sam Batkins at the American Action Forum (AAF), which has closely tracked the Trump deregulation effort, wrote on May 10, 2017,[9] that impact analyses created by federal agencies indicate the repeal of these regulations under the CRA "will save $3.7 billion in total regulatory costs ($1.1 billion annually) and eliminate 4.2 million hours of paperwork." Batkins wrote that nongovernment estimates were much higher. According to AAF, industry analysis showed repealing the rules would save more than $34.8 billion in costs.

No wonder the economy took off so fast under President Trump and a Republican Congress.

Now, in addition to cutting regulatory actions and revoking rules from previous administrations, federal agencies under Trump are also producing fewer regulations.

The *Wall Street Journal*[10] reported on July 26, 2017, that the Trump administration at the time had proposed the fewest number of rules in 17 years. Furthermore, many of those proposed rules actually overturned previous rules. For example, citing Sofie Miller of George Washington University's Regulatory Studies Center, the newspaper reported one-third of the EPA's 66 regulatory actions at the time were rule withdrawals.

When you combine Congress's CRA efforts with final regulatory actions made by the Trump administration, AAF[11] found in another analysis from October 3, 2017, that by the end of Fiscal Year 2017 there had been 26 final rules repealed and only five enacted since President Trump took office.

That is remarkable. By comparison, the *Weekly Standard*[12] noted on October 30, 2017, that over the last two decades, the federal government has added 13,000 new regulations annually.

Under President Trump, "the increase in regulatory restrictions...has been near to zero."

Federal regulations are expensive. Rand Paul points out a number of burdensome, expensive, and overreaching regulations in his book *Government Bullies*, in which he describes how federal regulations have invaded virtually every aspect of our lives from determining the size, shape, and efficiency of our toilets to dictating the type of light bulb Americans can purchase.

EPA regulations cost us about 5 percent of our more than $15 trillion GDP in 2012, according to Paul.

These are just a few examples. The regulatory regime in the United States has grown at an astonishing rate for decades. Even with President Trump's significant deregulatory efforts, the American regulatory system is still gigantic. I suspect cutting red tape will be a constant effort throughout his presidency.

Despite this huge challenge, President Trump and his cabinet members have been diligent in their effort to shrink the federal government and to shield Americans from damaging, costly regulations. The White House has seen success in virtually every sector.

ENERGY AND ENVIRONMENT

Some of the most controversial, expensive regulations the government has imposed in recent years have been environmental rules—many of which target the energy sector. Some of these rules have proved tough to dismantle; however, President Trump and Republicans are making progress.

Obama's so-called Clean Power Plan is perhaps the best example of overreaching environmental regulation. In the plan, the Obama White House attempted to regulate coal-fired power plants out of existence by setting new standards for the emission of greenhouse gases, such as carbon dioxide.

While Obama was in office, the massive regulatory effort faced numerous legal challenges with mixed results. Federal courts ruled that the EPA did have authority to regulate greenhouse gases. However, in June 2014, the U.S. Supreme Court said the Obama EPA had overstepped its bounds by attempting to rewrite part of the Clean Air Act. Only Congress has the authority to change law. On February 9, 2016, the high court ruled 5–4 to stay the Clean Power Plan until all the current legal challenges for and against the plan were settled.

Once President Trump took office, he directed the EPA to perform a comprehensive review of the Clean Power Plan, and on October 16, 2017, EPA Administrator Scott Pruitt announced a proposal to rescind the rule.

Trump is also seeking to do away with another controversial rule known as the Waters of the United States rule. Through this rule, the Obama administration sought to redefine what waters the EPA and the U.S. Army Corps of Engineers had the authority to regulate under the Clean Water Act. Specifically, Obama's White House sought to expand the definition of "navigable waterways" to an absurd degree in an effort to increase its regulatory power.

U.S. Senator Lamar Alexander, the Republican who leads the Senate Energy and Water Development Appropriations Subcommittee, has vehemently opposed this rule since its proposal, saying it gives federal authorities the ability to regulate mud puddles that form on a farmer's pasture.

Imagine for a second that Hillary Clinton had won and her administration had the power to regulate mud puddles.

Fortunately, American farmers were spared this nightmare. After one month in office, President Trump, on February 28, 2017,[13] ordered the EPA and the U.S. Army Corps of Engineers to reevaluate the rule. In July 2017, the administration proposed to rescind the rule and replace it with regulations which had applied earlier.

While working to cut red tape at the EPA, the Trump administration has also ended a destructive practice known as "sue and settle," which has cost taxpayers billions and allowed special interest groups and past EPA regulators to conspire to skirt the normal process by which Americans can offer feedback on how proposed regulations would affect them.

Under a normal procedure, an environmental group or concerned citizen makes a complaint. The EPA then takes time to investigate the alleged violation, seek public comment, and transparently form a regulation or enforcement action to correct the issue—if one existed at all.

Under "sue and settle," however, an environmental group would sue the EPA for allegedly failing to do its job. The case might be over a potentially polluted waterway, a city's air quality, or a construction project that allegedly harmed the environment.

Since Obama's EPA was in league with the far-left environmental activists, it wouldn't fight the charge in court or dispute whether it was responsible for the underlying violation. Instead, it would agree to a settlement with the group and craft what is called a consent decree. These decrees would allow the court to dictate regulatory action—permitting the EPA to bypass the normal regulatory process, including public comment, as a backdoor way of imposing environmental regulations on businesses and states. In the end, the group bringing the case would get what it wanted, leaving the American people out of the process entirely, except for being stuck with the legal cost of the litigation.

The AAF studied a database of economically significant EPA rules[14] from 2005 to 2016, which included judicial deadlines, the hallmark of a sue-and-settle rule. The Forum found 23 regulations that fit the sue-and-settle profile. In total, these litigated regulations cost taxpayers $67.9 billion.

On October 16, 2017, Administrator Pruitt wrote a directive aimed at ending the sue-and-settle practice. Going forward, lawsuits against the EPA will be posted online within 15 days of being received by the EPA. Pruitt also ordered EPA staff to notify states and industries that would be affected by the suit and to get input from the public through hearings or comments before settling lawsuits or entering consent decrees.

This added transparency will help the EPA do its important work in the light of day—and make the agency more accountable to the taxpayers for whom it works.

Republicans in the House of Representatives have been working on a bill that would bring similar transparency measures to every federal agency. The Sunshine for Regulations and Regulatory Decrees and Settlements Act of 2017 closely mirrors Pruitt's directive and could help tear down barriers between the people and the onerous regulatory process. As of this writing, the bill has passed the House and has been sent to the Senate for consideration.

ECONOMY AND BUSINESS

President Trump and Republicans have made considerable progress in getting rid of economically harmful regulations governing the financial and labor sectors.

For example: Congress used the CRA to nullify what was known as the arbitration rule, a costly regulation created by the totally unaccountable Consumer Financial Protection Bureau, which benefited trial lawyers rather than ordinary Americans and cost taxpayers $76 million annually.

After Trump appointed, and the Senate confirmed, two new members of the National Labor Relations Board (NLRB) in 2017, the board moved to revoke a destructive Obama-era standard that drastically expanded the definition of "joint employer" under federal rules.[15]

Obama's labor board in 2015 set a new standard that said any company that had even the vaguest control over working conditions or terms for employees at another company was a "joint employer." This rule greatly complicated business for franchise companies—of which there are 780,000 locations in the country—as well as contractors.

The Obama standard meant that any company that had even "indirect control" over an employee could potentially be held liable for violations at the employee's workplace—even if the company had no way of directly overseeing or preventing the bad behavior. So, as an example, the Subway corporation could be held liable for virtually any violation that occurred at any of its 26,291 franchise[16] stores across the country—along with the person who owned the franchise.

This huge expansion of risk and liability made it more beneficial for large restaurant chains or other franchise businesses to own all of their stores outright rather than provide opportunities for franchisee-owned small businesses.

Under Trump and Republican leadership, the labor board returned the joint employer standard to include only employers with direct control over employees' workplaces and employment. This was the standard that had been constant from 1984 until Obama's labor board changed it. However, in March, the labor board's inspector general decided one of the NLRB's Trump-appointed members should have recused himself from the case that overturned Obama's horrible rule because a law firm he previously worked for represented a company involved in the NLRB case that set Obama's standard. In response, the board vacated that ruling, effectively readopting Obama's broad joint employer definition. This decision by the labor board's inspector general showed a blatant double standard at the NLRB. The same inspector general found no issues when one of Obama's former board members, who was previously a lawyer for the Service Employees International Union, oversaw cases for that body. As I am writing this, Obama's horrible rule is in place, however, the House has already passed a bill to fix this regulatory overreach and define joint employers as direct employers in law.

The bureaucracy also fought Trump's first effort to get rid of the fiduciary rule—a controversial regulation passed by the Department of Labor under Obama that would make sound investment advice harder to get for many in America's middle class.

The fiduciary rule drastically redefines the role of financial advisors who manage retirement investments. Instead of being advisors who give people "suitable" advice on their investments, the fiduciary rule would force financial planners to have the same legal and ethical accountability to their clients as doctors and lawyers. The rule is estimated to cost the industry more than $4.7 billion per year to cover compliance of the rule. Any sane person who understands business recognizes this cost will be shifted to consumers. Do we really want to make retirement planning services comparable in cost to legal and medical services? I think not.

Shortly after taking office, President Trump ordered the Labor Department to review the fiduciary rule in order to delay its implementation. While Senate Democrats slow-walked Trump's appointment for secretary of labor, the bureaucrats at the department ignored the president's order and actually sped up implementation of the fiduciary rule. They claimed it was "uncontroversial" despite it being called a "terrible, horrible, no good, very bad rule" by then acting Securities and Exchange Commission Chairman Michael Piwowar. Ultimately, two pieces of the regulation went into effect, however, once the Senate confirmed Alex Acosta as secretary of labor in April, he was able to delay the remainder of the rule.

The administration is aggressively working to strip away other burdensome, backward regulations that are keeping small community banks from being able to lend money and giving labor unions outsized power.

However, the most important effort the administration is taking to spur our economy through deregulation is its effort to reign in the Consumer Financial Protection Bureau (CFPB).

The CFPB is an entirely partisan, unaccountable, anti-capitalist institution created by the 2010 Dodd-Frank Act and shaped by hyper-liberal Senator Elizabeth Warren. Its original mandate was to provide transparency to consumers who were borrowing money from banks, credit unions, and other financial institutions to prevent shady lenders from taking advantage of people. Since its creation, however, the bureau has abused its power and become a liberal weapon to carry out an anti-capitalist agenda by placing burdensome regulations on banks, which have made it harder for them to lend money. Specifically, the bureau has used its bureaucratic power to prevent banks from lending money to industries that the Left opposes. For years, I have warned that the CFPB is a dangerous, unconstitutional, economically damaging, out-of-control federal bureaucracy. Time and time again, the bureau has validated my concerns.

In July 2013, the *Washington Times*[17] reported that some CFPB officials were being paid more than U.S. Supreme Court justices, congressmen, state governors, and White House officials. At the time, the newspaper reported that 741 of the bureau's 1,204 employees were bringing home six-figure salaries, with 56 being paid more than $199,700 a year. Also, 111 CFPB employees were being paid the same salary as Federal Reserve governors, who make $179,700 annually. The highest-paid worker was getting $251,288. Overall, the average pay for a CFPB bureaucrat was $118,000, and the median salary was $113,000, according to the paper. On its face, this is absurd.

CFPB employees regulate banks and other financial institutions. Supreme Court justices, members of Congress, governors, and executive appointees are essential members of our government and shape the future of America.

Prior to the 2016 elections, Republicans have repeatedly introduced legislation that would bring CFPB salaries in line with other federal employees. All attempts were blocked by Democrats.

Pay is far from the only problem at this agency.

In April 2014, CFPB senior attorney Angela Martin testified before a congressional committee that there was a "pervasive culture of retaliation and intimidation that silences employees and chills the workforce from exposing wrongdoing" at the bureau's office of enforcement, according to the Cleveland .com[18] news website.

An outside investigator looking into Martin's claim found the agency rife with "exclusion, retaliation, discrimination, nepotism, demoralization, devaluation and other offensive working conditions."

These instances illustrate the complete disregard the CFPB has for any other federal authority.

The CFPB has been able to get away with this defiant activity because it isn't accountable to the American people or any branch of government. The bureau gets its funding from part of the Federal Reserve's operating budget, so it doesn't need Congress for anything. Its director is also one of the only federal bureaucratic leaders that the president of the United States cannot fire at will. According to the Dodd-Frank Act, the CFPB director can only be fired with cause.

This point leads to one of President Trump's first victories over the CFPB—which the media first distorted and then promptly ignored.

On November 24, 2017, former CFPB Director Richard Cordray, who was appointed by President Obama, abruptly announced he was resigning. He had eight months left in his term. Before Cordray left, however, he tried to prevent President Trump from steering the future of the rogue consumer bureau by appointing his chief of staff, Leandra English, to be deputy director, which effectively made her acting director in his stead. According to a provision in the Dodd-Frank Act, the deputy director assumes the role of acting director if the director leaves.

President Trump quickly appointed OMB Director Mick Mulvaney as acting director, in accordance with existing law that gives the president authority to fill executive vacancies. An extremely brief legal battle ensued.

Citing Dodd-Frank, English and her attorney asked a federal judge to bar Mulvaney from becoming acting director. They failed.

Cordray and English apparently thought their absurd scheme would allow the entrenched bureaucracy to continue hindering President Trump's agenda until he could get a permanent director confirmed by the Senate. It was a ludicrous plot, especially since the CFPB's own general counsel acknowledged Mulvaney was the rightful acting director.

Through it all, the media treated English's claim that she somehow had more authority over the agency than the president of the United States as legitimate. After English's restraining order was denied, the mainstream media simply stopped following the story.

Another big win for the Trump deregulation effort came in December, when Trump's Federal Communications Commission (FCC) voted to repeal the 2015 Obama overreach known as "net neutrality."

The rule put a number of new restrictions on Internet service providers such as Comcast and Verizon. The aspect of the law that the Obama administration touted was a restriction that disallowed these Internet service providers from speeding up or slowing down upload and download speeds on certain apps or websites. So, for instance, it prohibited Comcast from slowing down Internet speeds when its customers went to Verizon's website.

The bureaucrats' pitch was that this would make the Internet a free, unspoiled, information landscape that was unhindered by corporate motives. This seemed like an OK idea. However, it was a perfect example of a federal bureaucracy overreaching to solve a problem that never existed. The Internet has been widely accessible to Americans since the mid-1990s.

The net neutrality rule has roots in similar "open Internet" rules passed by the FCC in 2010, which have been continuously challenged in court by communications companies. In earlier cases, federal courts ruled the FCC lacked authority to regulate the Internet. By 2015, when the current net neutrality rule was enacted, there had never been any significant evidence that the large telecommunications companies had been engaging in the behavior the FCC was trying to halt.

Despite this, the U.S. Court of Appeals for the District of Columbia Circuit ruled in a 2–1 decision in 2016 that broadband Internet was a utility that could be regulated, therefore allowing the FCC's rules to stand. This is ridiculous. Water is a utility. People could die if they don't have access to clean water. The Internet is important but does not fall into the same life-and-death category. Now that the net neutrality rule is vacated, communications companies can focus on their customers instead of their lawyers.

The truth is, as the nation has moved away from wide reliance on the electromagnetic spectrum (in which radio and broadcast TV operate) the FCC as an agency has become more and more obsolete. It was originally founded to essentially be a federal real estate manager for the electromagnetic spectrum by renting specific parts of the spectrum to various broadcasters. This is how radio and broadcast TV stations secured their claim to their call frequencies (or channels).

There is still a role for the FCC in managing cellular phone communications, satellite signals, and other uses of the spectrum. However, over the last decades, the radio and television industries have been gradually moving to Internet-based, cable, or fiber-optic formats that don't need to use the electromagnetic spectrum. Instead of shrinking the bureaucracies within the FCC that managed those industries' use of the spectrum, the agency has simply determined they have the authority to regulate these other formats—which aren't scarce, are created by private companies, and don't really need regulating.

Net neutrality was the bureaucratic establishment's effort to declare the Internet a utility that government has purview to micromanage. It was a naked attempt by government bureaucrats to justify their increasingly unnecessary jobs.

As FCC Chairman Ajit Pai said when the rule was repealed:

Following today's vote, Americans will still be able to access the websites they want to visit. They will still be able to enjoy the services they want to enjoy.... There will still be cops on the beat guarding a free and open internet. This is the way things were prior to 2015, and this is the way they will be once again.

President Trump's effort to free American businesses from arduous federal regulations has been a key driver in restoring and energizing our economy. As more red tape gets cut, America will become more prosperous.

EDUCATION

President Trump also took action to make sure students continue to have access to the type of certificate and associate degree training programs which are a key requirement for many well-paying jobs.

Under the guise of protecting students, the Obama administration created a rule which measured the success of a program not by whether the student learned the material, but by whether they earned an arbitrary amount of money relative to their student loans after they graduated. Programs whose graduates did not earn enough money two out of three consecutive years were barred from receiving student loans.

The so-called Gainful Employment Rule was devastating to trade schools. Many of these schools are small businesses and the reporting requirements alone are daunting. Furthermore, measuring the earnings of a graduate immediately upon entering the workforce is absurd. Most first jobs out of college are not high paying. The rule didn't consider expected wage increases in the industry students enter.

For instance, many electricians attend trade schools to learn the basics. They then move on to apprenticeships to hone their crafts and many remain apprentices for several years. These apprenticeships do not pay much, but they prepare electricians for very high-paying jobs down the road. The Gainful Employment Rule doesn't take this into account when measuring the success of the programs.

In truth, the Gainful Employment Rule was a thinly veiled attack on the for-profit school sector. For one, the rule applied to all programs offered by proprietary schools while only applying to nondegree programs (certificates) at public and nonprofit ones. So left-wing schools that offer basket weaving and unemployable humanities degrees, whose graduates end up working in coffee shops, unable to repay their student loans, are left untouched.

This attack was a continuation of the failed national education policy that has spent years funneling all students into college—whether it made sense for their futures or not. This effort has only contributed to a massive skills gap in the American workforce.

More fundamentally, since these private schools are not subsidized by state and local taxes, as community and state colleges are, they have higher tuitions—making it harder for their students to meet the rule's arbitrary debt-to-earnings ratio. However, students choose for-profit schools despite the higher tuitions for a variety of reasons—including class flexibility and condensed schedules. It should be up to the student to decide. All the Gainful Employment Rule did was reduce student choice.

The Trump administration recognized all the problems this rule presented, halted enforcement of the rule, and went back to the drawing board in an attempt to create a fairer set of rules. The new rules are still being revised, but the proposed framework suggests that it will apply to all schools and all programs, instead of just targeting one sector, and promote transparency across all forms of higher education so students can make the best choice that fits their needs.

ONLY THE BEGINNING

Remember, the Trump presidency has only existed for a little more than one year. President Trump and Republicans are going to continue to aggressively reduce the U.S. regulatory state.

The Office of Management and Budget is collecting destructive federal regulations via a public website it set up.[19] Republican governors across the nation should follow suit and identify regulations at the state level that can be modified or revoked to make living and working in America easier and more prosperous.

President Trump and Republicans nationwide have a tremendous amount of work cut out for them, and eliminating the decades of red tape which have accumulated in our country is vital to freeing up America to be great again. Many Americans elected President Trump because he pledged to get America back to work. His deregulation effort is central to that mandate.

CHAPTER SEVEN

THE COMEBACK OF THE AMERICAN ECONOMY, PART 2—THE TAX CUTS AND JOBS ACT OF 2017

The most memorable, immediately impactful accomplishment President Trump and Republicans made in the first year of his term, without question, was passage of the Tax Cuts and Jobs Act of 2017. It is a key part of America's great comeback, and along with the repeal of regulations is the major reason the economy has boomed under President Trump.

The left-wing of the anti-Trump coalition hates tax cuts because their working assumption is that all money should belong to the government so that more enlightened people (non-deplorables) can decide how to spend it. Every time taxes are raised, the power of the Left is increased. Every time taxes are lowered, the power of the Left is reduced.

The men and women of Trump's America, on the other hand, believe that they should decide how to spend their own money, and the idea of a tax cut appeals to them. They're not

ideologically anti-government, but they do believe that government is full of waste and should be forced to run on a budget the
same way families have to live within a budget. Furthermore,
many of the "forgotten men and women" of Trump's America
who have been left behind by the globalist economic vision of
the orderly institutionalist wing of the anti-Trump coalition have
gone years without real pay raises, if they were lucky enough to
keep their jobs at all. Despite months of concerted effort by the
Democrats and other left-wing members of the anti-Trump coalition to stop the tax cuts, Republicans were able to deliver this
monumental achievement by Christmas 2017—a tight, meaningful deadline brilliantly imposed by President Trump. Meeting the
end-of-year goal was important politically, and the Left knew it.

The Tax Cuts and Jobs Act was the largest reform to the
nation's tax code in 31 years. The last time Congress and a president were able to give the American people tax relief of this mag-
nitude was passage of the 1986 tax cuts under President Ronald
Reagan. The left-wing members of the anti-Trump coalition feared
that Americans would be pleased with Republicans due to the
results of the tax cuts, and even some of the institutionalists who
oppose him just wanted to keep Trump from any sort of victory in
his first year. Instead, the anti-Trump coalition wanted to keep the
focus on the first half of 2017, when Republicans were completely
consumed in the endless Obamacare repeal and replace effort.

Wisely, Speaker Paul Ryan decided in July to move to tax
cuts. This was critical because Ryan recognized that the health
care problem was too big and would take too long to solve in
2017. He also saw that, for six months, the media and the Left
were happily watching Republicans fight one another over the
best ways to replace the Democrats' deeply flawed health care
law without producing an enormous disruption to the insurance markets that would ultimately inflict pain on Americans.

Ryan needed to unify the party, and he did. Working with President Trump and Senate Majority Leader Mitch McConnell, Ryan and House Republicans were able to immediately change the narrative by banding together to announce the new Republican tax reform framework.[1] This served as the foundation of common principles which ultimately guided the Tax Cuts and Jobs Act.

Some in the party—and especially those in the media—wanted to keep hashing out the Obamacare fight, but Republican leadership stood strong and insisted on moving forward to a new focus. This proved vital to the GOP's success. The newly minted GOP unity drove the Democrats and the elite media nuts. They desperately wanted to keep Republicans divided because they knew it helped the Left's chances to make gains in the House and Senate in the 2018 elections.

But the elites were out of luck. Republicans across Congress quickly realized that working together earned them much more praise from the people they serve at home. This goodwill empowered them to ignore media and political attacks in Washington and keep grinding forward toward their goal.

Only five months after President Trump, Speaker Ryan, and Leader McConnell unveiled the tax framework, the House of Representatives and the Senate passed the bill, and the president signed it into law. This pace was incredible for writing, negotiating, and passing legislation of this complexity. Similarly, it took President Reagan and Republicans six months to propose, write, and pass tax cuts in 1981.

So, the short takeaway is: After the tumultuous 2016 elections, it took Republicans a little time to come together, but they did. The Tax Cuts and Jobs Act was the result of this effort. Going forward, Republicans must keep this successful, unified model in mind and apply it to everything they do.

HISTORIC TAX RELIEF

As mentioned, the Tax Cuts and Jobs Act of 2017 was the most thorough overhaul of the tax code in three decades. This was not a collection of small tweaks. The tax cuts represent significant tax relief for American families and businesses of all sizes—and a vast improvement in America's ability to compete on the world stage.

The results of the tax cuts and reforms will mean more jobs, higher wages, more investment in American companies, and more companies bringing foreign earnings back to the United States.

American families receive tremendous tax relief under the new law. According to the House Ways and Means Committee,[2] most four-member families who earn the median household income of $73,000 a year get a $2,059 tax cut in 2018. Instead of paying $3,557 in taxes, these families pay $1,499. This is a 58 percent tax cut, according to the committee.

Most single parents who have one child and who earn $41,000 a year receive a $1,300 tax cut. For most, this is a roughly 73 percent reduction in their federal taxes, with their final bills dropping from $1,792 to $488.

Married small business owners who make $100,000 a year ($85,000 in personal income from the business, and $15,000 of small business income) get a 24 percent tax reduction, according to the committee. A typical final tax bill for this type of family will drop from $10,982 in 2017 to $8,379 under the new law. Importantly, people began to see the benefits of this as soon as they started receiving paychecks for 2018 work in February. This significant tax savings for families is due to several provisions in the new law.

First, the overall tax rates were reduced across the board. The lowest individual tax rate is 0 percent for individuals who report less than $9,525 taxable income, and the highest individual rate is 37 percent for those who make more than $500,000.

For joint filers, the 0 percent rate applies to those who make less than $19,050, while the top rate is for couples who make more than $600,000. The intermediate tax rates are 10 percent, 12 percent, 22 percent, 24 percent, 32 percent, and 35 percent.

For perspective, households that make the median national income of $73,000 fall squarely into the 12 percent bracket.

However, the most significant benefit for individuals and families comes from the law almost doubling the standard deduction. The Tax Cuts and Jobs Act raised the standard deduction for single taxpayers from $6,500 to $12,000. Similarly, the deduction for joint filers raised from $13,000 to $24,000.

This change drives tax reduction for our nation's low- and middle-income earners more than any other provision in the law by greatly expanding the 0 percent tax bracket—and dropping everyone's taxable income. It means individuals will pay no taxes on the first $12,000 they earn, and families pay no taxes on the first $24,000 they earn.

This huge jump in take-home pay will have a profound effect on Americans across the country. The House Ways and Means Committee studied the impact the increased standard deduction will have by looking at the median income levels in every congressional district in the nation for both families of four and single taxpayers with no children. After crunching the numbers, they found tax cuts in every congressional district for both groups. This fact will be difficult to reconcile for Democrats, who universally voted against the tax cut in both the House and Senate. It will be especially difficult for Democrats in states Trump carried in the 2016 election.[3]

These reductions take into account another tremendous tax benefit for Americans with children. The Trump tax reform law doubles the Child Tax Credit from $1,000 to up to $2,000. This means most Americans with children will see a $2,000 reduction of their final tax bill for each of their dependent children. Even if the reduction exceeds their final tax bill, they can get up to $1,400 as a refund. This credit is available to all lower- and middle-income American families with children; however, it begins to phase out for families who make $400,000 a year or more.

The added benefit of having a larger standard deduction is that more families will be able to file their taxes on a simple form. Currently, 68.5 percent of tax filers use the standard deduction. Speaker Ryan estimated that with the larger standard deduction, 90 percent of taxpayers will choose this option and be able to file their taxes on a form that is slightly larger than a postcard.

Here's my prediction: If only 85 percent of American taxpayers choose to take the standard deduction in 2018, the media will fall over itself to say that Speaker Ryan was wrong—and they will completely miss the point that 85 percent of Americans saved money on tax preparation by doing their taxes at their kitchen tables.

However, for families and individuals that do not take the doubled standard deduction, the Trump-Republican tax law retains many important tax deductions, such as those for mortgage interest, extraordinary medical costs, charitable giving, educational costs, and state and local taxes up to $10,000.

The tax law also stripped away the Obama-era mandate that every American is obligated to purchase health insurance. This was an important first step to solving many of the problems created by Obamacare. It also spared more Americans from the individual Alternative Minimum Tax (AMT). The income threshold that determines who has to pay the AMT increased from $54,300 to $70,300 for individuals and from $84,500 to $109,400 for joint filers.

The Republican tax law was also an enormous win for small businesses in America.

Small business owners, who report their business income on their individual income tax as pass-through income, get to apply a 20 percent deduction on the first $315,000 their businesses make. This applies to S corporations, limited liability corporations, partnerships, and sole proprietorships. Such businesses that make higher incomes will have their effective tax rate capped at 29.6 percent.

Tax relief for America's small business owners is essential to spurring our economy because small businesses make up 99.7 percent of our nation's employers, according to the U.S. Small Business Administration.[4] These firms employ nearly half of the U.S. private-sector workforce and are responsible for creating three-fourths of all new jobs in this country.

The Left and the elite media have desperately tried to convince Americans that these small business owners are ultrarich one percenters in disguise. However, data[5] from the U.S. Treasury and a National Federation of Independent Business report[6] tell a different story. In fact, only 2.4 percent of small businesses make more than $250,000 a year. The vast majority (88 percent) of small business owners report less than $200,000 of adjusted gross income on their tax returns. Additionally, 71 percent of these business owners reported less than $100,000 in adjusted income.

The relief provided by the Tax Cuts and Jobs Act will be a huge boon for these small businesses. In addition to having a lower overall tax burden, small business owners will be able to write off the costs of capital investments in the year they are made. So, if the owner of a small manufacturing business, like a tool and die shop with 25 employees, buys equipment to help increase production, that owner will be able to deduct that entire expenditure in his or her 2018 taxes rather than having to spread the deduction across multiple years. This will allow business owners to make calculated decisions about growing business and relieve some of their risk.

These tax cuts for small businesses will lead to very quick growth, hiring, and wage increases in communities across America.

Finally, the Trump-Republican tax cuts will help America successfully compete for the world's business.

The tax law cuts the corporate tax rate from 35 to 21 percent. This is the deepest cut to the corporate income tax rate in our nation's history, and it could not have come at a better time. Prior to passage of the Tax Cuts and Jobs Act of 2017, the United States had the third highest business tax in the developed world.

Aside from the tax cuts, the Republican law also updated and reformed the way we collect taxes on profits American companies earn overseas. Under the old tax scheme, U.S. businesses that operated in foreign countries paid U.S. taxes on money they made there—unless they invested their earnings in foreign countries. This provided a perverse incentive for companies to build facilities and create jobs and products outside of America.

As Kyle Pomerleu wrote for the Tax Foundation[7] on August 1, 2017:

> The U.S. worldwide tax system discourages companies from repatriating foreign earnings, causing what some call the "lock-out effect." Companies make inefficient financial arrangements and investments to avoid repatriating this income and facing additional U.S. tax. In some cases, the system incentivizes companies to avoid the domestic tax on their foreign profits by moving their corporate headquarters out of the United States. As a result, the U.S. worldwide system has been one of the major drivers of corporate inversions in the last few decades.

Under the worldwide system, CNBC reported in April 2017[8] that U.S. multinational companies had more than $2.6 trillion tied up overseas to avoid paying the exorbitant corporate tax rate. Meanwhile, many of the countries with whom we compete maintain territorial tax systems that do not domestically tax profits made in other countries when those profits are brought home.

The new tax law finally brought the United States in line with the modern global marketplace, joining the ranks of 35 other Organization of Economic Cooperation and Development countries, which have designed territorial systems. Under the new law, companies will be able to bring the more than $2.6 trillion in foreign earnings back to the United States for a one-time, low rate of 15.5 percent for liquid assets and 8 percent for real estate and other investments. After that, foreign profits will not be subject to corporate income taxes—however, there are provisions that will prevent companies from hiding U.S.-earned profits in foreign subsidiaries.

These changes to the corporate tax rate—and the international tax system—will attract more foreign businesses to the United States and make it easier for American multinational companies to bring money they make in other countries back to the United States.

LEFT-WING LIES

As soon as it became clear that Republicans were galvanizing and making progress on the tax bill, Senate Minority Leader Chuck Schumer and House Minority Leader Nancy Pelosi started an aggressive campaign of lies and propaganda to poison Americans against the Republican bill.

Despite the doubled standard deduction, the greatly increased Child Tax Credit, and all the other provisions that lowered the tax burden on the vast majority of hardworking Americans, Democrats tried to convince people that the law was only going to benefit corporations and incredibly wealthy individuals. They also pitched an entirely false narrative that most Americans' tax bills would actually increase.

Note the following tweets from Senate Democrats:

- Senator Kamala Harris (D-CA), October 27, 2017, "On average, middle class families earning less than $86,000 would see a tax increase under the Republican 'tax reform' plan."
- Senator Robert P. Casey Jr. (D-PA), October 24, 2017, "The average tax increase on families nationwide earning up to $86,100 would be $794.00."
- Senator Jeff Merkley (D-OR), October 24, 2017, "Under GOP plan, U.S. families making ~$86k see avg tax increase of $794."

This lie was so egregious even the *Washington Post*[9] had to call the Democrats out on it. The claim received four Pinocchios from the *Post*'s fact-checkers. According to the newspaper, the senators had misrepresented a finding by Democrats on the Joint Economic Committee, which claimed *8 million households* making less than $86,100 would see an average tax increase of $794. The Dems happily decided to say this applied to all middle-class households.

In a stunning moment of honesty, the *Post* acknowledged that while 8 million families *might* see an increase, "more than 97 million (80 percent) will receive a tax cut. Doing the math the same way the [Joint Economic Committee] staff did, we come up with an average tax cut of about $450 for those 97 million households."

So, 8 million could pay an extra $794 on average, while 97 million could save an extra $450 on average. This is the level of dishonesty to which Democrats are committed.

This honesty from the *Washington Post* was a small drop in a bucket of media lies about the tax cuts.

In October, before the bill had even been introduced by Republicans, the *New York Times* dutifully parroted its

Democrat allies' charge that the Tax Cuts and Jobs Act was a "middle-class con job"—even acknowledging in the article that "crucial details" of the plan had not yet been finalized. In a later *Times* op-ed, Paul Krugman referred to policies within the plan as "leprechaun economics."

In *Newsweek*, Doug Wirth wrote, "Trump's tax reform will make America poorer and sicker." In the piece, Wirth dutifully carried on the Left's lie that middle- and lower-income Americans would receive a tax hike under the plan. He further harped on the claim that eliminating the individual mandate, which the tax bill effectively did, will cause 13 million people to lose health insurance—ignoring the fact that many of those people will *choose* not to buy it.

On the other end, *Business Insider* wrote wildly out-of-touch articles bemoaning the claim that elite colleges with billion-dollar endowments were going to be taxed under the plan and that the Tax Cuts and Jobs Act would make it "a lot harder to buy a $1 million home." I have to wonder what the editors were thinking. According to the Federal Reserve Bank of St. Louis, the median sales price of homes in the United States in the third quarter of 2017 was $315,200.[10] Why on earth should regular, hardworking Americans feel sympathy for those who have trouble paying $1 million for a house?

Finally, the *Atlantic* wrote that the provisions in the bill, which opened up part of Alaska for oil exploration, could "forever alter" the lives of Alaskan natives. Dramatically, the piece focused on only two possible outcomes for these Alaskan natives: The bill would either destroy their lives or make them rich. And, of course, the Alaskans themselves overwhelmingly favor more oil leading to more jobs and creating more income.

After erroneously persuading many Americans their taxes would increase, the media then polled support of the bill—based on the Democratic lies the media had cheerfully repeated. Then, for weeks, the media inundated Americans with the reports of those skewed surveys to show how unpopular the bill supposedly was and how it was going to sink Republican chances to make gains in the 2018 elections. However, despite the staunch Democrat-media opposition, the bill passed, and the Left has been completely proven wrong. One of the best examples of the media realizing and acknowledging the depths of its own dishonesty was a report made by CBS News, which I have mentioned before on Fox News.[11]

CBS interviewed three families and asked for their expectations about how their personal tax burden would be impacted by passage of the GOP tax bill. Next, a CPA the network brought on analyzed the families' taxes and told them on camera what they could actually expect to pay.

Since these three families had been completely misled by Democrats and the media for months, all expected to have to pay more or see no change in their taxes.

In fact, all three save money under the Republican plan.

The first interviewee, a single mother in North Carolina who makes under $40,000 a year, didn't think her taxes would change. However, she will save roughly $1,300 more per year thanks to the tax cuts.

Two college professors in Rhode Island interviewed by the network, who make a combined salary of $150,000 a year, expected a higher bill, yet they will save about $650.

Finally, a California couple with three children, a small business, and approximately $300,000 in annual income believed their taxes would go up—because California is a high-tax state and state and local tax deductions are capped at $10,000 under the GOP bill. Much to their surprise, they will save $13,000 annually under the Tax Cuts and Jobs Act.

It was amazing to watch the utter surprise on the faces of these people—who had been told for months by the media that the Republican plan was going to cost them money.

As the CBS analyst put it, "every one of the families will have more money in their pocket next year."

After watching the CBS report, a colleague sent me an email saying, "This segment drove me crazy. As if CBS was incapable of doing math before the tax cuts passed."

Another huge lie that the media ceaselessly repeated throughout the debate of the tax bill was that workers wouldn't benefit from the massive reduction in the corporate income tax rate or the change to the way foreign earnings were taxed.

Again and again, the Left and its media allies insisted that businesses would simply give shareholders big payouts and refrain from investing in U.S. facilities, boosting wages, hiring, or otherwise improving the economy.

Boy, were they wrong.

In January 2018 alone, more than 100 companies announced they were giving up to $2,000 bonuses for employees, increasing matching contributions to 401(k) plans, increasing wages of workers, or ramping up capital investments in the United States—specifically because President Trump signed the Republican tax cuts into law.

Americans for Tax Reform has been keeping an up-to-date list of companies that have announced benefits for employees as a result of tax cuts. As of February 23, 2018, the list included 401 companies that had announced bonuses, raises, or increases to 401(k) contributions because of the tax cuts.[12] Consider the massive effect this has had on the hundreds of thousands, indeed millions, of American workers and families who have seen a direct benefit from the tax cuts. In addition to seeing larger paychecks from reduced tax rates, they are seeing more take-home pay because the private sector responded to this tremendous Republican law.

Along with bonuses and expansions, the *Baltimore Sun*[13] reported on January 5, 2018, that Baltimore Gas & Electric Co. (BGE) planned to pass on about $82 million in tax savings to customers through rate cuts. The company attributed the action directly to passage of the Republican tax cuts.

The newspaper quoted BGE CEO Calvin G. Butler Jr. as saying, "For us it was real simple.... We wanted to share those benefits with consumers."

Faced with the facts of just how wrong they were, Nancy Pelosi and the hard-left leaders of the Democratic Party didn't acknowledge their error. Instead, they doubled down, saying the raises and bonuses weren't anything to celebrate, that they were "pathetic" and "crumbs," in the words of Nancy Pelosi.

According to the Center for Responsive Politics, Nancy Pelosi's net worth was $100.64 million in 2015.[14] Maybe $2,000 is crumbs to her, but to most Americans living paycheck to paycheck, that money is a huge increase in their disposable income. It's the difference that can mean paying a bill on time or taking the family on vacation for the first time in years. Plus, the salary increases, even if they are just by $2 per hour, add up significantly over time. Assuming a 40-hour workweek, that additional $2 per hour is an additional $4,000 per year.

To the forgotten working men and women of America who form the core of Trump's America, that extra financial security is a godsend.

THE POLITICAL IMPACT

The success of the Tax Cuts and Jobs Act will become the cornerstone of Republican campaigns in 2018.

As the benefits of the tax cuts set in, the American people will see how completely dishonest and wrong Democrats and the media were about this tremendous accomplishment by President Trump. As Americans see their paychecks, 401(k)s, and savings increase, they will remember the huge bias of the liberal media. This will only further weaken the media's already declining influence on American policy.

A *New York Times* SurveyMonkey poll in late February found that 50 percent of people approved of the tax cuts. This was a huge increase from a December poll they had done, which found only 37 percent of people surveyed approved of the tax cuts.[15] This was a common trend. According to BusinessInsider.com, Gallup and Monmouth University polls saw similar increases in the first two months of 2018.

Passage of this historic overhaul to our tax system will also show Americans that the GOP can lead and achieve tremendously important goals that help improve the lives of Americans. This squarely delineates Republicans as the party for lower taxes, higher wages, more jobs, better economic growth, and a stronger America.

Meanwhile, the Democrats who opposed this bill—especially the 10 Senate Democrats who are running in states that President Trump won in 2016—will have to explain themselves to their constituents. They will have to explain why they were for higher taxes, lower wages, fewer jobs, slower economic growth, and a weaker country.

Americans received their first post–tax cuts paychecks in February, and we immediately saw this shift start to happen. On the day the tax cuts passed, Real Clear Politics generic ballot congressional polling showed Democrats up by 15 points in a nationwide average. By February 23, 2018, that gap had closed to an eight-point lead.[16]

I suspect once the American people hear these two arguments—and see the reality of the GOP tax cuts—they will overwhelmingly choose Republicans to represent them in the House and Senate in 2018.

CHAPTER EIGHT

THE COMEBACK OF THE CONSTITUTIONAL JUDICIARY

President Trump made a bold prediction early in his presidency.

At one of his first cabinet meetings, Trump said, "a big percentage of the court will be changed by this administration over a very short period of time."

President Trump was right.

When Trump took office, there were more than 100 judicial vacancies. Although Democrats have tried to block his progress at every chance, President Trump has managed to get federal judges confirmed at a faster pace than any of his predecessors. As of January 2018, 23 Trump-appointed judges have been confirmed by the Senate. By comparison, only 10 judges had been confirmed by January 2010 under Obama.[1]

Trump's unprecedented success with getting federal judges appointed to the court is one thing that the elite media cannot deny. As Trump continues to appoint federal judges, he solidifies a legacy that will last much longer than his tenure in office.

President Trump understands that federal judges are appointed for life and that they are instrumental in making sure that our judicial system rules according to the Constitution and not according to a judge's political agenda.

Instead of acknowledging Trump's unparalleled success in filling federal judge seats, the mainstream media and the anti-Trump coalition have only sought to discredit his accomplishments. The media has latched on to the narrative of a disgruntled group of lawyers who are upset about losing influence—the American Bar Association (ABA).

Since the Eisenhower administration, the ABA has played a role in judicial selection, mostly by screening judicial nominees before presidents officially nominate them. Typically, the group rates judicial candidates as well-qualified, qualified, or unqualified. This gave the group a tremendous amount of influence.

Since this activity began, the ABA has built a record of clear preference for liberal nominees. The group also continues to promote liberal agendas under a paper-thin veil of nonpartisanship. It has a long history of fighting for abortion rights and other staunchly liberal stances, for which the group's president, Hilarie Bass, frequently advocates.

Bass has openly expressed her liberal views on Twitter and advocated for tight gun restrictions. She has also praised Democrats for pushing radical environmental rules. Bass has also shown her bias against Attorney General Jeff Sessions. Bass questioned Sessions's independence while criticizing his strong stance on separation of powers within our government. This is ironic considering the heat Sessions took from President Trump when Sessions recused himself from the Russia investigation simply because he was part of the Trump campaign. Whether or not it was wise to recuse himself, Sessions clearly proved he would act based on his own conscience and not on orders from above.

Consistently, liberal nominees do better in the ABA process

than conservative ones. One study found that 65 percent of nominees under Clinton received the ABA's highest rating compared to just 17 percent of the Bush nominees. Also, conservative judges without prior judicial experience do significantly worse than liberal judges without experience.[2]

This history of bias led President George W. Bush to reject the group's influence. Bush informed the ABA that he would not use them to screen judicial nominees before they were reported to the Senate, but he would welcome their ratings, along with ratings from other groups, after the judges had already been publicly nominated. The Bush administration's argument was no one group should have "a unique, quasi-official role and thereby have its voice heard before and above all others."

Obama, on the other hand, fully reversed Bush's action and relied heavily on the ABA for judicial recommendations. President Trump has returned to the Bush policy, denying the elite ABA its coveted insider position in judicial nominations. Naturally, the group is upset about its loss of prestige (and elite status), so it is attacking Trump's nominees. The group is declaring many of Trump's nominations as "unqualified" and conveniently keeping its criteria to itself.

As Republican U.S. Senator James Lankford of Oklahoma said, "they're very secretive about the process and why they make the decisions they do." Naturally, the elite media, lobbyists, and liberals in the anti-Trump coalition are repeating these claims with glee and treating the ABA's word as infallible.

Ultimately, Senator Lankford is being generous. The fact is, President Trump has promised since the beginning of his campaign to drain the swamp. This includes ditching bad 50-year-old traditions that undermine the power of the president and elevate the power of left-wing DC interest groups. The great American comeback requires putting great people in great positions, which will invariably upset swampy Washingtonians.

THE CONSTITUTIONAL JUDICIARY

As White House press secretary Sarah Huckabee Sanders said:

> This is a president who is focused on making sure we have judges in place that understand what their role is. That's not to create law, that's not to change laws. But it's to be actually focused on the Constitution.

In an effort to preserve the original intent of the Constitution, President Trump has instead relied on the advice of the Federalist Society and the Heritage Foundation to seek out and find federal judges who will be constitutional originalists.

In particular, Leonard Leo, the executive vice president of the Federalist Society, has been vital to the Trump administration. Leo clearly expressed the impact President Trump's nominations will have in an op-ed he wrote for *Newsweek* in January 2018:[3]

> Since the 2016 election, President Donald Trump has nominated judges who have a demonstrated commitment to, as the president puts it, interpreting the Constitution "the way it was meant to be." In so doing, Trump is ensuring that his legacy will last far beyond his term in office. Tax and health care reform can quickly evaporate with future changes in congressional majorities, but federal judges serve for life, often making decisions about our Constitution and laws that affect one or two generations.

JUSTICE NEIL GORSUCH

The crowning achievement of President Trump's judicial agenda up to now is the appointment of Supreme Court Justice Neil Gorsuch. Justice Gorsuch is exactly the type of judge that our country needs—one who will uphold the Constitution over political agendas and seek to ensure consistency and fairness under the law.

During Gorsuch's confirmation hearings, many Democratic senators tried their best to make Gorsuch seem as if he had a political agenda or that he would rule according to President Trump's agenda. Many pointed to Gorsuch's judicial history when he served on the U.S. Tenth Circuit Court of Appeals. One of the main rulings Gorsuch made that the Left has tried to demonize was his ruling in *Hobby Lobby v. Sebelius.*

Hobby Lobby is a store with a strong commitment to religious values that sells arts and crafts. Anyone who visits a Hobby Lobby store can immediately recognize the Christian values expressed in their business protocol. They are closed on Sundays to respect the Sabbath, even though it costs them a lot of money to do so, and they play Christian music in their stores.

Under the Affordable Care Act, or Obamacare, Hobby Lobby was required to provide health insurance that covers contraceptives, even though some of the required covered contraceptives violate Christian values. The owners of Hobby Lobby argued that the mandate forced them to do something that was against their deeply held religious convictions. Gorsuch agreed. In his concurring argument, he wrote that the mandate in fact would force them to assist in activity "their religion teaches to be gravely wrong."

When Democrats interrogated Judge Gorsuch about his ruling during his confirmation hearings, Gorsuch explained that he was influenced by a law sponsored by none other than Democratic Senate Minority Leader Chuck Schumer, when he was serving in the House of Representatives. The law, the Religious Freedom Restoration Act (RFRA), was an attempt to further strengthen freedom to practice religion guaranteed under the First Amendment.

The law stated that the government cannot abridge sincerely held religious belief without a compelling reason under "strict scrutiny." As Gorsuch explained in his hearing, requiring strict scrutiny puts a heavy burden on the government because the strict scrutiny standard is the highest legal standard to meet. Given the facts of the case, the government had neither a compelling reason nor a narrowly enough tailored law for abridging the religious rights of Hobby Lobby, according to Gorsuch. His ruling was based completely off the Schumer law, which was sponsored in the Senate by the late Senator Ted Kennedy. Gorsuch suggested if Congress had a problem with the RFRA's application, then it could change the law.

Gorsuch's Hobby Lobby ruling was later upheld by the U.S. Supreme Court and has remained one of the most important court cases to successfully challenge the merits of the Affordable Care Act.

Gorsuch also demonstrated his respect for the First Amendment's protection of religious freedom by dissenting in a case in which two other federal judges ruled that memorial crosses on the side of public roads in Utah amounted to the government's endorsement of Christianity. In his dissenting opinion, Gorsuch wrote, "we can't be sure he [a driver] will even bother to stop and look at a monument before having us declare the state policy permitting it unconstitutional." He further elaborated that a reasonable observer might not even be able to see the names on the memorial as they sped past them and this was clearly an instance of trying to find a problem where there wasn't one.

As I discussed earlier in this book, the Establishment Clause is meant to protect our right to practice religion—not ban its practice in public spaces. These cases give us insight into Gorsuch's commitment to the law—not his political beliefs, as Democrats allege.

In his relatively brief time on the Supreme Court, Justice Gorsuch has further demonstrated his commitment to the Constitution. In June 2017, Gorsuch wrote a strong dissent, along with Justice Clarence Thomas, after the Court opted not to hear the case *Peruta v. California*. In the case, Edward Peruta was denied permits in his county to carry concealed weapons. Gorsuch and Thomas argued the Court should take up the case.

The central question in *Peruta v. California* is whether the Second Amendment to the Constitution allows citizens to bear arms outside of their homes or whether those rights can be infringed by the state by requiring carry permits. Peruta fought the case through the federal system because he felt his right to bear arms had been violated.

The elite anti-Trump media has tried to frame the Gorsuch-Thomas dissent as being politically motivated. However, this completely ignores that hearing the case would provide very clear answers about basic constitutional protections, which many states have questioned, challenged, or blatantly undermined. This is a foundational function of the U.S. Supreme Court.

In their dissent, Gorsuch and Thomas wrote, "The most natural reading of this definition [of the right to bear arms] encompasses public carry. I find it extremely improbable that the Framers understood the Second Amendment to protect little more than carrying a gun from the bedroom to the kitchen."

Throughout his career, Justice Gorsuch has shown his commitment to interpreting the Constitution as written. This is totally counter to what the left-wing faction of the anti-Trump coalition wants. Instead, the Left wants to consider the Constitution a "living document." In fact, there is a proper way to change the Constitution—the amendment process. This is a multitiered process that involves several big hurdles—not the least of which are two-thirds majority votes in both houses of Congress and ratification by the states. The Left would rather the Constitution be made malleable, based on the whims of left-wing judges, so it can be interpreted to meet current political goals. This is counter to the intent of the Founding Fathers.

Justice Gorsuch is a good indication that President Trump is committed to nominating originalist, Constitution-following justices to the U.S. Supreme Court. If the president has the chance, I expect he will continue to follow this pattern.

LOWER-APPELLATE COURT JUDGES

The media's gross mischaracterization of Trump-appointed judges has not been limited to Gorsuch.

One of the first attacks launched by the anti-Trump coalition was directed toward judicial nominee Amy Coney Barrett. Despite Judge Barrett being an extremely accomplished judge and esteemed law professor at Notre Dame, Democrat Senators Dianne Feinstein of California and Dick Durbin of Illinois tried to say that she could not be a fair judge because of her religious beliefs.

Feinstein and Durbin questioned how Barrett could rule fairly on cases concerning abortion when she is a devout Catholic. This line of questioning truly exposed the depths to which the anti-Trump coalition will go to oppose the president. Senators Feinstein and Durbin were essentially suggesting a religious test for federal judges. Not only was it a blatant, insulting attack on Judge Barrett, and a blatant, insulting attack on all Catholics, it was a blatant, insulting attack on the First Amendment.

In their effort to discriminate against Catholics and uphold the Left's pro-abortion agenda, Senators Feinstein and Durbin also discriminated against common sense.

The Left also waged an attack on the confirmation of Judge John K. Bush. Their focus was a personal Internet post Judge Bush had made in which he commented that abortion and slavery were "the two greatest tragedies in our country." This, of course, enraged the Left. To the Left, equating ignoring the rights and lives of the unborn with ignoring the rights and lives of African Americans in early America is anathema. It perfectly illustrates the selective morality of the Left. However, what likely

infuriated them more were Judge Bush's answers to their inter-
rogations. Judge Bush rightly pointed out that his political views
were irrelevant to the judgeship because "it is not appropriate
to bring politics to the bench." This, of course, is the opposite of
the Left's worldview when it comes to the role of a judge.

The most vicious attacks on a Trump nomination to the
court came against Matthew Spencer Petersen. Petersen's
résumé includes serving as counsel to the U.S. House of Representatives Committee on House Administration; as chief counsel to Republicans on the U.S. Senate Committee on Rules and
Administration; and as chairman of the Federal Election Commission. He has indisputable knowledge of the law.

However, at his confirmation hearing, he could not answer
procedural questions, which could be considered common knowledge to most trial attorneys. The anti-Trump media went into a
complete uproar, writing headlines such as: "Trump Judicial Nominee Struggles to Answer Basic Legal Questions at Hearing" and
"Trump Nominee for Federal Judgeship Has Never Tried a Case."

The worst part about this attack is that the media completely
overlooked Petersen's own acknowledgment that he did not follow the same legal path that many federal judges take. Some lawyers rarely try cases. Instead, they handle disputes and matters of
law through the transactional exchange of contracts and paperwork. These lawyers don't argue cases like those seen on TV, but
they still have to have a profound knowledge of the law to be successful. By all accounts, Petersen was a very successful attorney
with a wide knowledge of transactional, procedural law.

Rather than tell the truth, the anti-Trump media presented
Petersen as just some guy who went to law school who had
no legal experience. Unfortunately, the media's blatant mischaracterization led Petersen to withdraw his name from consideration. He said he didn't want to distract from the Trump
administration's goals. He went on to say, "I had hoped that my

nearly two decades of public service would carry more weight than my worst two minutes on television."

The greatest irony here is none of those reporters or anchors who criticized Petersen have an ounce of his legal expertise, yet they feel entitled and qualified to question his credentials. This perfectly illustrates the arrogance of the media.

THE POTENTIAL TRUMP IMPACT

Federal courts play an enormous role in shaping the future of our country. As I have already discussed, court decisions on gun rights, abortion, religious liberties, and freedom of speech can fundamentally change America.

This is why the success President Trump has had in getting originalist judges appointed to the federal courts is so important. These judges serve for life, so the more Constitution-focused judges the president can name to our court system, the more protected our founding principles will be.

In fact, while the appointment of Justice Gorsuch is tremendously important, Trump's circuit court judge appointments will have a more enduring effect on the way our laws are interpreted. On average, the Supreme Court only hears 100 to 150 cases a year. It selects those cases from more than 7,000 appeals cases that request rulings annually.

The circuit and appellate courts across the nation serve as the testing grounds that funnel cases up to the Supreme Court. However, because the Supreme Court hears a relatively small number of cases, the appellate courts have the final word on most federal cases. These courts handle judicial questions and matters of law in every town, city, and state in the union on a daily basis. While the Supreme Court is unquestionably important, Americans are far more likely to encounter circuit or appellate courts in their daily lives.

President Trump surpassed both Presidents Richard Nixon

and John F. Kennedy in appointing appellate court judges. Both Nixon and Kennedy had 11 appellate judges confirmed in their first year in office. President Trump appointed and had confirmed 12. By contrast, Obama had only three appellate judges confirmed in his first year.

As the *Wall Street Journal*'s Kimberley Strassel said, "every new president cares about the judiciary, but no administration in memory has approached appointments with more purpose than this team."

Strassel rightly pointed out that much of the media has missed the biggest story of the early Trump presidency:

> The media remains so caught up with the president's tweets that it has missed Mr. Trump's project to transform the rest of the federal judiciary. The president is stocking the courts with a class of brilliant young textualists bearing little relation to even their Reagan or Bush predecessors. Mr. Trump's nastygrams to Bob Corker will be a distant memory next week. Notre Dame law professor Amy Coney Barrett's influence on the Seventh U.S. Circuit Court of Appeals could still be going strong 40 years from now.

By filling the federal courts with judges who read and interpret the Constitution as it is written, President Trump is protecting the constitutional rights of Americans for generations to come. Regardless of any of his other successes as president, this single achievement will remain the longest-lasting impactful aspect of his legacy.

Trump is reestablishing and protecting the principles on which our country was formed. Despite staunch opposition from the anti-Trump coalition every step of the way, President Trump continues to blaze a trail of unassailable success.

CHAPTER NINE

THE COMEBACK OF AMERICAN HEALTH CARE

Under President Trump, America is beginning its comeback toward affordable health care.

Of course, you wouldn't know this from watching the news. The anti-Trump pundits and analysts view the legislative failure to repeal and replace Obamacare in one big bill as proof that health care has been a zone of failure for President Trump.

But as we have covered in previous chapters, President Trump doesn't accept failure. He just doubles his resolve and tries something new.

So instead of trying to solve health care in one giant, unwieldy bill, the Trump administration has taken an incremental, 1,000-step approach to health care.

Across the administration, different departments are exercising their authority over various aspects of the health care sector to not only fulfill the campaign promise to repeal Obamacare, but to also migrate us toward a twenty-first-century system. This system will deliver lower costs, increased access to care, and improved health outcomes. Congress has played a key role as well, passing some significant reforms as part of other bills.

I have been arguing for such an approach for over a decade, going back to a book *Saving Lives and Saving Money*, which I wrote in 2003.

Our current crisis of health care cost inflation, as well as the challenge of uneven access and quality of care, is caused by thousands of different factors. Each of these factors has evolved over decades. It is an act of hubris to try and solve something this complicated and important in one giant bill. No one is that smart.

In my previous book, *Understanding Trump*, which went to print before the American Health Care Act (AHCA) failed to pass the Senate, I warned against this all-at-once approach on health care. Given the disastrous results of Obamacare (the last attempt to solve health care all at once) and the inability to pass the AHCA, I am encouraged to see the Trump administration adopt a 1,000-step strategy of incremental change.

Here are some of the many successful steps the administration has already taken.

REPEALING OBAMACARE ONE STEP AT A TIME

Bit by bit, Obamacare is being repealed.

The individual mandate, which required all Americans to purchase insurance or face a tax penalty, was always broadly unpopular. A July 2013 poll from HealthPocket showed that only 12 percent of Americans wanted the individual mandate to go into effect the next year as scheduled by Obamacare. Even after three years of implementation, most Americans still opposed it. A February 2017 poll by YouGov found that the mandate was opposed by 65 percent of Americans.

The entire idea of the federal government forcing you to purchase something you don't want is a violation of the American tradition of limited government and free choice in the marketplace. If the government can force you to purchase health insurance for the greater good of lowering the cost of health insurance for all by getting more healthy people into the marketplace, who is to say it could not enforce other changes in purchasing and behavior? A healthier population is less expensive. If an individual mandate to purchase health insurance is acceptable, why not an individual mandate to exercise? Or an individual mandate to eat your vegetables?

With this in mind, it is no surprise that the left-wing portion of the anti-Trump coalition supports the individual mandate. It is a foot in the door for an ever more expansive and invasive government. Similarly, it is no surprise that a majority of Americans, most of whom would be considered part of Trump's America, are dead set against an individual mandate.

Evidence also shows it didn't even achieve what it was intended to accomplish. The mandate was actually a poor incentive for people to sign up for insurance. For one, premiums in Obamacare grew so expensive that for many people, paying the penalty was more affordable. Also, as Chris Pope from the Manhattan Institute pointed out, if the mandate was effective, you would have expected enrollment to increase as the penalty increased from 2014 through 2016. Instead, it remained relatively flat.

So, the individual mandate in health insurance posed a serious threat to the American tradition of freedom, and it was ineffective. This is why one of Donald Trump's most significant accomplishments in health care has been repealing it through the Tax Cuts and Jobs Act, which passed in December 2017. Ditching Obamacare's individual mandate was a key part of America's comeback.

Remember, when the Supreme Court upheld the individual mandate as constitutional, it did so under the rationale that Congress had the power to tax Americans. This makes repealing it as part of a tax bill totally appropriate.

Other key parts of Obamacare have been repealed or neutered.

Many people did not notice that the January 2018 Continuing Resolution (CR), which reopened the federal government after its brief, Chuck Schumer-led shutdown, suspended the health insurance tax for one year. The CR also put off the medical device tax for two years and delayed the Cadillac tax until 2022. Each of these taxes were simply passed on to consumers in the form of higher premiums. These tax delays will put more downward pressure on premiums in 2019.

The Trump administration also took steps to make it more affordable and practical to purchase health insurance on websites other than healthcare.gov, such as insurance company websites and purchasing aggregators like e-healthinsurance .com. Finally, the Trump administration closed loopholes in Obamacare, which some people were using to game the system to avoid paying their premiums and wait until they got sick to get coverage by falsely claiming a "Special Enrollment Period." This cheating drove up costs for everyone.

EXPANDING ASSOCIATION HEALTH PLANS

Of course, what you replace Obamacare with is even more important than repealing it.

One of Obamacare's main flaws was that it set out to make insurance more affordable, but then created so many rules and requirements on insurance plans that it became impossible for insurers to offer truly affordable options.

At the Department of Labor, the Trump administration took a big step toward creating the type of competitive health insurance marketplace that Obamacare failed to create by issuing proposed rules to expand the use of Association Health Plans.

I have been in favor of expanding the use of these plans since I was Speaker of the House. They allow groups of small businesses to band together into a single negotiating block to purchase plans from insurers. The greater numbers give the small businesses greater negotiating leverage with the insurers and spreads the risk over a larger group of people. This drives insurance prices down.

Unfortunately, the rules surrounding these extremely useful plans are so restrictive that they are not currently used to their full potential. For one, they are, at a practical level, very difficult to create across state lines and cannot be fully national in scope. Second, they are not available to the self-employed, which includes groups such as farmers and Realtors.

The Trump administration's proposed rule fixes both those deficiencies, giving small businesses relief and potentially making much lower-cost insurance plans available to an additional 11 million people who do not have access to the benefits of employer-sponsored coverage.

These plans are exempt from some of the more onerous requirements of Obamacare that drive up prices. They do keep some critical protections though. Insurers would still not be allowed to deny coverage based on health status, nor would they be allowed to charge sick people more. This would help prevent plans from "cherry-picking" healthy people into their risk pool to keep prices low, while forcing everyone with serious medical expenses to keep using the individual marketplace, further driving up premiums. Some additional changes to the rules may be necessary to prevent insurers from acting through a broker to achieve the same result.

The plans would also continue to be regulated by the states, which is important to prevent fraud.

The Department of Labor issued the proposed rule changes in January 2018. This was followed by a 60-day comment period, which will lead to the issuing of final rules in the next few months.

LOWERING PRESCRIPTION DRUG PRICES

President Trump has also taken significant steps to lower drug prices. In his State of the Union Address on January 30, 2018, he declared lowering drug prices as one of his main priorities for the year.

One of the most effective ways patients can save money on their prescription drugs is by choosing low-cost generics over name-brand medications. The Trump Food and Drug Administration (FDA), under the leadership of Scott Gottlieb, has made it a priority to maximize the number of generic options available to consumers.

The Trump FDA issued new procedures to shorten the approval process for generics. They are focused particularly on complex, expensive drugs. In addition, Trump's FDA announced that generic drugs whose name-brand alternatives currently have fewer than three generic competitors would receive priority review among generic drug approvals. Studies have shown that multiple generic competitors are necessary to see the full cost-saving benefits of competition.

The Trump FDA has also begun to introduce measures to prevent abuse of the drug approval process rules, by which drug companies unfairly blocked generic competition from entering the marketplace. It also publicly identified the drugs which are the most vulnerable to pricing abuse to encourage drug manufacturers to create more generic alternatives to them. This will help prevent future price gouging scandals, such as when Martin Shkreli increased a long-available AIDS drug from $13.50 a pill to $750 a pill. The Trump administration also announced a new agreement with Mylan, who came under intense criticism for raising the cost of the EpiPen. This deal would give Medicaid programs a substantially larger discount for the critical drug delivery device.

In addition to maximizing the impact generic drugs can have on lowering drug prices, the Trump administration also took needed action to save Medicare patients and taxpayers money on prescription drugs.

The 340B program—named after the section of the Public Health Service Act that created it—was initially designed to help hospitals that serve large populations of poor patients. Under the program, eligible hospitals are entitled to buy Medicare Part B drugs (used to treat cancer and other serious conditions) at a discount from pharmaceutical manufacturers. They are then reimbursed by Medicare at the full rate, allowing them to keep the difference as profit, which they are supposed to use to fund their charitable care.

Since the program's creation it has expanded tremendously. This would be a good thing if it meant more low-income patients were being treated, but that has not been the case. According to a 2014 analysis by the Alliance for Integrity and Reform (a group funded by the pharmaceutical industry) and Avalere Health, fewer than two-thirds of participating hospitals provide charity care at a rate higher than the national average. In January 2018, the *New England Journal of Medicine* published a study showing that, all other factors being equal, hospitals which participate in the program have between 200 and 900 percent more specialty doctors in the areas served by Part B drugs than hospitals that don't.[1] Furthermore, the study showed that these specialty doctors were less likely to serve poor patients than equivalent doctors in hospitals that do not participate in the program.

So, even while the program has grown considerably, patients are not benefiting.

Fortunately, bipartisan legislation has been introduced in Congress which would pause any further expansion of the 340B program and allow Health and Human Services to collect information needed to better police the program against abuse.

The Trump administration, however, is not waiting for Congress. It announced steps to make sure the drug discounts under the program benefit patients, not hospitals' bottom lines. The Centers for Medicare and Medicaid Services (CMS) issued new, reduced Medicare reimbursement rates that more accurately reflect the acquisition costs of the drugs hospitals are receiving under 340B. This will save taxpayers money. Furthermore, CMS is exploring ways to make sure that Medicare patient co-pays, which are usually a percentage of the total cost of a drug, reflect the discounted price rather than the list price. This will save patients a lot of money.

CMS has also introduced a proposed rule in Medicare Part D with the same goal. It would make sure that any discounts drug manufacturers negotiate with pharmacy benefit managers are reflected in the co-pays that seniors pay for drugs. The money would now go to the patients rather than the big pharmacy benefit companies.

Finally, the Trump administration has begun reforming regulatory hurdles that had prevented drug manufacturers and payers, such as insurers and Medicaid programs, from creating payment models based on the effectiveness of drugs. This is an important development in ensuring that patients have access to many new types of highly effective specialty drugs and treatments. These "miracle drugs" may have high up-front costs, but they are so effective that they can save significant amounts of money in the long term. These reforms would allow value-based payment arrangements over a multiyear period based on the ongoing health of patients with expensive diseases. This new process would expand access to patients while not bankrupting state governments or driving up premiums for insurance customers.

THE LEFT'S SINGLE-PAYER DISASTER

I strongly encourage President Trump and Congressional Republicans to continue the strategy of a 1,000-step health reform journey rather than putting everything in one big bill.

However, they do need to communicate their successes and approach better. A properly communicated and properly implemented incremental health care reform focused on commonsense steps will offer a powerful contrast with the Democrats' full-throated embrace of single-payer health care—a solution which, every time it is given serious consideration, is soundly rejected by the American people.

And no wonder. Single-payer health care violates almost every historic American principle which has made our country great and successful.

Most importantly, single-payer is anti-free choice. It puts the bureaucracy at the center of health care instead of the patient and doctor. Under single-payer, there is just one health insurance option (the government, since it eliminates all private insurance) and your choices in treatment are limited by what the government is willing to pay for.

The fact is, if you socialize medical costs, then you must socialize medical decisions. It is unavoidable. Just look at Great Britain, whose National Health System in early 2018 had to delay all nonemergency surgeries due to a flu outbreak. In 2017, the Red Cross declared the British National Health Service a "humanitarian crisis." Rationing is unavoidable in socialized systems—that's why we see the same food lines in Venezuela this century that we did in Soviet countries in the last century.

Single-payer also discourages personal responsibility. The fact is that for most people, their health status is largely determined by personal choices. So, by socializing health costs, you are forcing people who follow healthy lifestyles and have lower medical expenses to pay for the medical expenses of those who don't.

Of course, many medical conditions are the result of bad luck rather than personal choice. Still, according to the Centers for Disease Control and Prevention (CDC), one out of every six health care dollars are spent treating three chronic conditions—cardiovascular disease, diabetes, and cancer. The CDC estimates that nearly 80 percent of heart disease and stroke cases, 80 percent of type 2 diabetes, and 40 percent of cancer cases could be prevented through changes in diet, exercise, and smoking habits.

A reasonable health care system would find ways to encourage healthy living and personal responsibility while creating safety nets for those afflicted with very expensive diseases at little to no fault of their own. Single-payer, socialized medicine makes no such distinction, and most Americans reject the idea that they should be forced to pay for the consequences of other people's lifestyle choices.

Finally, socialized medicine crushes innovation, which has been the cornerstone of America's identity ever since the days of Ben Franklin. This is critically important to understand because innovation—new treatments, cures, breakthroughs— is what saves lives that could never have been saved before.

Socialized health systems are so starved of resources that they lack the capital to produce breakthrough medicines and treatments. That's why as European countries adopted price controls on drugs and further socialized their health care systems throughout the latter half of the twentieth century, the percentage of new drugs (defined as drugs with "new chemical entities," as opposed to a repurposing of an existing medicine) coming from the United States grew from 32 percent in the 1980s to 57 percent in the 2000s. As Europe controlled prices, it began to kill innovation.

Socialized medicine is also exorbitantly and prohibitively expensive—a lesson two liberal states recently learned.

In 2014, Vermont, the state that gives us socialist Bernie Sanders in the Senate, decided it was going to set the example for the rest of the country and adopt a single-payer system. The effort fell apart once the math became clear. Vermont would have to raise its payroll tax to 11.5 percent and set premiums at nearly 10 percent of people's income to afford it. Democratic Governor Peter Shumlin, who initially supported the effort, had to reverse course, admitting that a single-payer health system would bankrupt the state.

A similar story unfolded last year when California sought to enact a single-payer health care bill. Estimates showed the program would cost $400 billion per year, which would require raising the state income tax to 15 percent to raise the additional $200 billion. The bill passed the ultraliberal California Senate, but it was widely known that it was a show vote, so they could claim a victory for their base.

The bottom line is this: A system this expensive, requiring such debilitatingly high taxes will crush the innovation that produces new cures and treatments that save lives in medicine. Furthermore, it will shift power from patients and doctors to Washington bureaucrats.

PRINCIPLES FOR CONTINUING THE HEALTH REFORM JOURNEY

President Trump and Republicans should continue their step-by-step health reform journey toward a twenty-first-century health system by focusing on changes in a number of areas, which I will briefly touch on next.

All of these changes should be made within a framework of reinforcing traditional American values of individual freedom and choice, personal responsibility with compassion, and maximizing innovation.

Americans should expect to have freedom of choice in health care—choice of insurance, choice of doctors, and choice of treatments. Americans should also expect to have access to the type of information necessary to make informed choices.

In addition, a health system consistent with historic American values would reinforce personal responsibility and self-sufficiency.

166 THE GREAT COMEBACK

It is completely reasonable and in line with the type of strongly rooted American values that Trump is tapping into to expect most Americans to be responsible for their own health care expenses— be it through insurance, paying out of pocket, or some other method.

We should also recognize, however, that some people, through no fault of their own, will be hit with diseases that are very expensive to treat. Others simply cannot afford basic insurance. For those who are legitimately priced out of the health system, we should have safety nets in place that make sure nobody slips through the cracks.

This would be a system that reinforces personal responsibility but has compassion for those who get hit with catastrophic health care costs. We can guarantee health care for far less than guaranteeing health insurance.

Meanwhile, the government should not be able to force you to purchase anything as a condition of being alive, even something as important as health insurance. If Americans want to pay for health care out of pocket or decide they will take the risk, they should be allowed to do so.

Of course, with freedom comes personal responsibility. If a person who can afford health insurance chooses not to and then gets sick, he or she should receive the care they need, but should also be expected to pay for it. This may require that the individual pay higher premiums to insurers for a designated period and have a portion of his or her paycheck automatically deducted to compensate the hospitals and doctors. We could also look at additional steps, such as allowing consideration of whether a person has health insurance to be a determining factor in his or her credit rating.

Ultimately, we want to create an incentive structure which, when combined with reforms that drive down the cost of premiums, makes it so financially risky to go without health insurance that few people choose to do so.

Finally, a twenty-first-century health system consistent with historic American values would maximize the rate of medical innovation reaching patients. The faster new cures and treatments are made available, the more lives and money will be saved. According to a study in Health Affairs, for example, the use of statins (a cholesterol lowering drug) has led to a 27 percent decrease in health care costs per patient due to fewer strokes and heart attacks. The same study estimated that between 1987 and 2008, the use of statins generated $1.25 trillion in economic value from years of life saved. During that time, more than $200 billion was spent on statins, meaning statins created a net value of $1 trillion.

Innovation is also critical to the delivery and management of health care. One of the biggest drivers of health inflation is waste and fraud in health care. The Left, with single-payer, tries to address this challenge by putting the supposedly rational and unbiased bureaucracy in charge. Given the rate of fraud in the Medicare system, which we will get into next, this approach clearly does not work.

A truly American system would use new computational capabilities and market-based reforms in transparency to remove inefficiencies and identify ways to improve people's health while saving money.

NEXT STEPS

The following is a brief overview of reforms to get us to a twenty-first-century health system that lowers costs, increases access, and improves health outcomes. Each of these reforms is consistent with the American tradition of preserving individual freedom and choice, encouraging personal responsibility, and maximizing innovation.

INCREASE TRANSPARENCY

One of the primary reasons for health inflation is the hidden nature of health care costs. Few hospitals or providers list their prices because they have different contracts with each different payer. Similarly, while drugs have a "list price," it is almost never the actual cost being paid. The real cost is negotiated separately with a pharmacy benefit manager or directly with an insurer.

The problem is that the hidden nature of health care costs makes it practically impossible for patients to understand what their premiums are paying for. So, they have no way of knowing if they are getting a good bargain from their insurance company. It also makes it difficult for patients to be active participants in their health and be informed consumers.

President Trump and Congress should pass reforms to enable patients to compare the costs of different solutions in real time, so they can make responsible choices.

FIGHT FRAUD IN HEALTH CARE

The FBI estimates that between $100 billion and $300 billion per year in government spending is lost to fraud. Much of that is in Medicare and Medicaid. This is a staggering amount of money. In fact, it is between $1 trillion and $4 trillion over 10 years. Yet, relatively little attention is paid by Washington to solving the health care fraud problem. This is even though virtually all the challenges we face about how to fund health care for the poor through Medicaid and other poverty programs could be solved by eliminating one-third of that theft, all without touching a single honest person's benefits.

By comparison, the rate of fraud in the credit card industry is around one-tenth of 1 percent. The Trump administration and Congress should invite experts from the credit card and other industries that have successfully policed fraud to come in and help design digital systems similar to theirs. Imagine if health care fraud was identified and stopped as rapidly as you get a notice (via a text message or phone call) from your credit card company when there is a suspicious purchase made on your account.

FROM DISABILITIES TO CAPABILITIES

The ratio of working-age adults receiving disability has doubled since 1990, growing to 1 in 20 Americans. Some of this increase is due to an aging population, but a study by the Federal Reserve Bank of San Francisco estimated that at least half of that increase was due to fraud. As the economy changed and manufacturing and other jobs that do not require advanced degrees left the country, many people fraudulently enrolled in disability once their unemployment benefits ran out.

This is not just outrageous; it's tragic. For many Americans, our disability program has become a poverty trap. A *Washington Examiner* study showed that only 13 percent of people who enroll into the program work for pay once they start receiving benefits. Since disability includes Medicare or Medicaid, depending on the program, a person on disability likely receives greater value in benefits from not working than with a minimum wage job earning $15,000 per year.

To fix our disability system, President Trump and Congress should not only insist on tougher enforcement, but they should explore reforms that engender a cultural shift in the way we think about disabilities. Instead of focusing on what a person's disability is, the focus of our programs should be on matching their capabilities to possible employment. Moving from disabilities to capabilities would maximize the number of Americans working and being productive. It would also dramatically increase the lifetime income and choices of people currently trapped in the disabilities system.

VALUE-BASED PURCHASING

The fee-for-service model of health care payment is a big part of America's health inflation problem. The model, which pays providers based on the number of procedures they perform, promotes redundancy and waste while creating a perverse financial incentive to ignore health outcomes in favor of health procedures.

The Medicare system accounts for one out of every five dollars spent in health care, and as such, can be an enormous instigator of reform. President Trump and Congress should expand the pilot programs experimenting in moving away from fee-for-service toward value-based purchasing agreements, which pay based on health outcomes rather than procedures. They should also develop similar programs in the VA, Tricare, Medicaid, Indian Health Service, and other government health programs.

MEDICAL LIABILITY REFORM

Another big driver of waste in our health care system is the constant threat of lawsuits faced by doctors. Estimates show that defensive medicine (when a doctor orders extra tests he or she knows are not necessary just to avoid being sued) costs the health system $46 billion per year.

Medical liability reform will bring down the cost of care, saving patients money, and freeing up time for doctors to see more patients. President Trump and Congress should look at what states have done and at the workmen's compensation boards as models for reform. New Zealand has had enormous success with a workmen's compensation model to replace lawsuits, and it is worth studying as a possible replacement for the current adversarial, lawyer-dominated system.

CREATE HIGH-RISK POOLS

Roughly 5 percent of Americans account for 50 percent of health care spending. These are people with especially expensive diseases that require specialty or ongoing treatment.

One of the biggest reasons why the individual marketplace under Obamacare faced such rapid rises in premiums was that more sick people relative to healthy people enrolled than expected. People who did not qualify for subsidies based on their income were walloped with huge premiums, large deductibles, and no choice but to purchase the plans or pay a tax penalty.

Maine took a different approach. This state flagged the most expensive conditions to treat and, working with insurers, created a separate, heavily subsidized risk pool for patients with those illnesses. The pools are called "invisible" because the patients are unaware they are in separate pools. It is all handled on the back end between the insurers and the state government.

The results have been impressive. Without having to cover the cost of the most expensive conditions, premiums for those in their early 20s have dropped by $5,000. Older customers in their 60s have seen a drop of $7,000.

The program is expensive, but so are the Obamacare subsidies. Congress and the Trump administration should give states the flexibility to convert the Obamacare subsidies into high-risk pool funding. The reason this model is superior to Obamacare's income-based model of subsidization is because it maintains the core ethic of personal responsibility, insisting that most people should be responsible for handling their health care expenses, while creating a safety net for people who are struck with particularly expensive diseases. It creates significantly more savings on premiums for insurance customers while being consistent with an ethos of personal responsibility with compassion, which is at the heart of the American system.

CURING DISEASES BY DRAMATICALLY INCREASING FUNDING FOR SCIENTIFIC RESEARCH

The federal government has an integral role to play in the life cycle of innovation that produces new cures and treatments. While it is true that the clear majority of new medicines are created by the private sector, the basic scientific research that is at the foundation of those breakthroughs is usually funded by the federal government. Medical innovators then take that publicly available basic research and use it as the foundation to create lifesaving new medicines.

This kind of basic research is so speculative and uncertain to result in marketable treatments that few investors would take the risk to fund it. Yet it is essential to producing new medicines. That's why the federal government must step in.

One of the most frustrating tendencies of the Washington budgetary process is to allow short-term budget crises to constrict smart spending in favor of urgent spending. The relative paucity of research investment at the National Institutes of Health (NIH) and the National Science Foundation (NSF) are perfect examples of this phenomenon.

Alzheimer's disease, for example, is a $20 trillion liability over the next four decades. Medicare and Medicaid already spend more than $150 billion per year treating the disease. Yet, NIH is spending only $1.3 billion on research into Alzheimer's disease and dementia, which could produce a cure or other treatments that could delay the onset of the disease. Simply postponing the onset of Alzheimer's disease by five years would save $10 trillion over the next four decades. NSF is similarly underfunded in the field of basic brain research where its research into computing is vital to handle the flood of new data being generated about the workings of the brain.

The booming economy is going to produce more tax revenue than expected in our budget bills. The Trump administration and Congress should dedicate a portion of that extra revenue to effective scientific research at NIH and NSF. They should also look at innovative new ways to fund research beyond the traditional budget, such as the use of Dr. Michael Burgess's "Alzheimer's Bonds," which would pay back the bondholders with money saved by breakthroughs. Cash prizes for breakthroughs should also be explored to focus research on results rather than the grant application process.

NEW METHODS OF PAYING FOR EXPENSIVE DRUGS

The Trump administration should build on the progress they have made in value-based purchasing contracts with additional reforms that allow Medicare, Medicaid, and the private sector to develop methods of arbitraging the cost of expensive breakthrough medicines that produce long-term budget savings.

ACCELERATE THE APPROVAL PROCESS FOR BREAKTHROUGH DRUGS

Recent studies have estimated it takes between $1 billion and $2.6 billion to bring an FDA-approved medication to market. Much of this cost is tied up in the expensive approval process required by the FDA. The 21st Century Cures Act was a big step forward in dealing with this issue. President Trump and Congress should build on this success by giving the FDA more hiring flexibility, so it can keep up with the rapid medical advances of the private sector. Currently, the FDA is trying to evaluate new drugs and treatments it barely understands. This delays the process.

This is just a partial list. There's a lot more we can do to continue the 1,000-step health reform process that President Trump and Congressional Republicans have begun.

To learn more, I recommend reading the health care chapter of my *New York Times* No. 1 best seller *Understanding Trump* and for a 15-year-old look at how little health care has been reformed, look at my 2003 book, *Saving Lives and Saving Money.*

PART TWO

CHALLENGES

President Trump and Republicans face tremendous challenges from virtually every direction. They are being attacked by every facet of the anti-Trump coalition, which controls much of the news media, the Washington establishment, and the cultural Left. At the same time, President Trump is working to solve many of America's toughest problems, such as the opioid epidemic that is devastating communities across our nation. This section confronts these challenges and explains how the president can overcome them.

CHAPTER TEN

FIGHTING FAKE NEWS

The news media aggressively lied about the Tax Cuts and Jobs Act, but this was only part of a much larger campaign of distortion and distraction the media has waged against President Trump.

Trump has had to fight the media on a daily basis because its members are overwhelmingly, bitterly, and actively opposed to him. In fact, the media has reached a point where attacking the president is the default action—no matter what the story is about. It has become muscle memory for reporters, anchors, editors, and producers to go on the offensive.

Yes, President Trump uses strong, sometimes harsh, language when dealing with his opponents (including the media). I am never surprised by the hostile back-and-forth over the president's words and the media's hurt feelings. Yes, the president, as a businessman in politics, doesn't speak or act like a typical politician. After more than two years of getting to know him, you would think the media would be used to this by now. Still, they fill airwaves and news pages with panicked outrage anytime President Trump describes a domestic or foreign issue in blunt, realistic, or indelicate terms.

Clearly, the media is having a hard time adjusting to President Trump's everyday behavior. To give them the benefit of the

doubt, he is a unique commander in chief. However, it is astonishing to see the complete disconnect between the mainstream
media and reality when it comes to the substance and outcomes
of President Trump's policies.

LYING ABOUT THE TRUMP ECONOMY

As I have described in previous chapters, the economy and
stock market have soared during the Trump presidency despite
dire warnings from the media in 2016 that Trump would destroy
our economy if elected.

As Stephen Moore wrote for Townhall.com[1] on January 3,
2018, since President Trump's election, the Dow Jones Industrial Average (DJIA) had gained 35 percent, "making the last 14
months one of the greatest bull market runs in history." In February and March, the markets went through a correction period
amid worries that, due to the strength of the economy, the Federal Reserve would raise interest rates more quickly than expected
and that President Trump's tough posture against China's unfair
trade practices would lead to decreased commerce. However, even
accounting for the correction, the increase in the value of the markets since the election of Donald Trump has been historic.

Media often like to describe stock market gains as only benefiting the wealthiest Americans, however, Moore rightly pointed out
that "some $6 trillion of wealth has been created for Americans—
which is very good news for the 55 million Americans with 401(k)
plans, the 25 million or so who have IRAs, and another 20 million
with company pension plans and employee stock ownership
plans."

Importantly, this historically significant bull market is completely opposite the false reality the liberal media imagined
prior to Trump's election.

Here are just a few of the completely incorrect media pre-
dictions on the economy, which Moore cited:

- The *Washington Post* editorial board wrote on October 5, 2016, that "A President Trump could destroy the world economy."
- Ben White for *Politico*[2] wrote on October 21, 2016, that "Wall Street is set up for a major crash if Donald Trump shocks the world on Election Day and wins the White House. New research suggests that financial markets strongly prefer a Hillary Clinton presidency and could react with panicked selling should Trump deliver a shocking upset on Nov. 8."
- Finally, Paul Krugman of the *New York Times*[3] wrote on November 9, 2016, the day after the election, "It really does now look like President Donald J. Trump, and markets are plunging. When might we expect them to recover? We are very probably looking at a global recession, with no end in sight." The piece was dramatically titled "The Economic Fallout."

These quotes illustrate the level of hostility the media had for President Trump before he even took office. For months before the election, the elite media was desperately trying to persuade the American people not to elect President Trump. Just hours after Americans didn't follow their marching orders, the elite media moved to full-blown scare tactics.

White and Krugman later acknowledged they were wrong. However, Krugman is still warning that the markets should fear President Trump.[4] But they are outliers. Many in the media have never taken the time to acknowledge how completely wrong they have consistently been about President Trump or the economy since his election. In fact, to avoid addressing this elephant in the room, most members of the media have just avoided reporting on the strong and growing economy under President Trump.

For another set of examples, gross domestic product (GDP)

growth has boomed under President Trump—despite claims by so-called media experts that the sluggish sub-2 percent growth under Obama was the new normal.

In May, when President Trump announced his budget plan, the media raced to prove the president wrong when he said that his policies would help drive economic growth beyond the 3 percent mark. Reporters immediately dialed up all the liberal economists they could find to counter President Trump's prediction. Their so-called economic experts said getting to 3 percent economic growth was probably impossible.

CBS News wrote on May 24, 2017,[5] that Trump's claim was unrealistic saying, "many regard the Trump projection—which shows the growth rate advancing from 2.3 percent in 2017 to 3 percent by 2021 and staying at that level until 2027—as far-fetched."

Finance & Commerce wrote,[6] "The Trump team assumes that it can accelerate growth by more than a full percentage point— the equivalent of roughly $200 billion annually in today's dollars. At a time of sluggish worker productivity, an aging workforce and slower spending by consumers, most economists say the promises are far-fetched."

Some so-called experts even said that 3 percent growth would only be possible if the United States doubled its immigrant population over 10 years—or if we nationally adopted one-day weekends. Others said growth at this level would require an unemployment rate of 0 percent. This is completely absurd. Prior to the 2008 recession, U.S. productivity growth had been regularly above 3 percent since the Great Depression.

None of these ridiculous criteria have been met, yet in November 2017, the Commerce Department reported that GDP for the third quarter had grown by 3.3 percent, which Reuters reported[7] was "the quickest pace in three years." That figure was up even from second quarter growth under President Trump, which was at 3.1 percent. Growth slowed slightly in the fourth quarter, and President

Trump's first year ended with 2.6 annualized GDP growth. However, this slowdown was attributed to the wave of late summer hurricanes that battered Texas, Louisiana, and Florida. The storms caused billions of dollars in damage in the southern United States and brought commerce to a near standstill in affected areas.[8]

These growth numbers were still astounding considering President Trump inherited Obama's lethargic economy. In fact, the first quarter's weak growth was the last holdover from the Obama years because Trump's policies were just beginning to go into effect. In fact, the average growth for the last three quarters in 2017 was 2.97. Even with the first quarter included, Trump's first year ended less than half a percentage point away from his goal, which the media had declared impossible.

Trump and his team achieved this terrific increase in our economic growth by enacting his deregulation effort, which was largely ignored by the media. Passage of the Tax Cuts and Jobs Act will help ensure that the United States keeps this pace.

Naturally, those on the Left are trying to claim that the significant gains in the economy during President Trump's first year in office are due to Obama-era policies—or they say Trump is just lucky because the world economy is growing and driving up U.S. productivity. These claims are, of course, absurd.

For a simple visual, type "Dow Jones" in your preferred Internet search engine. A chart will come up in the search results. Select the "five-year" view. There you will see a sudden spike in the stock market value around three-quarters of the way through the chart. Move your mouse to where that spike begins. The sudden jump in value between the week before the 2016 election and the week after, as well as the sustained strong growth since then is a powerful visual indicator of the impact of the Trump presidency on the markets. The growth in the markets is incredibly strong despite a correction in February and March 2018.

The gains made in the United States are a result of President

Trump destroying Obama's regulations and economic policies so businesses can flourish. Government doesn't create wealth or jobs; the private sector does. President Trump knows this.

Finally, in addition to being wrong about or ignoring President Trump's success, members of the media are doing all they can to amplify supposedly bad economic news.

Julia Seymour for the Media Research Center[9] pointed out in a January 9, 2018, article that the three largest broadcast networks in the United States (ABC, CBS, and NBC) went out of their way to report on a less-than-perfect December jobs report by the Commerce Department Bureau of Labor.

Economists had expected 190,000 new jobs in December, yet only 148,000 were gained. Despite this, unemployment remained at a 17-year low and wages grew.

These negative reports came from the three networks after an entire year of ignoring good news under Trump's leadership—such as stock market records, other positive jobs reports, and success in defeating ISIS forces, according to Seymour. In fact, ABC *World News* hadn't reported anything on four previous successful job reports in 2017.

This trend continued when the January jobs report was released. The United States had gained 200,000 jobs—23,000 more than had been predicted.[10]

The media has been consistently wrong about or ignored the success of the Trump economy, and they will likely continue to do so. As Americans continue to see their wages, retirement savings, and job opportunities increase, the ossified media will see its already dwindling influence decrease.

REPORTING GOSSIP, IGNORING SUBSTANCE
Instead of reporting President Trump's achievements, the elite media has decided to scrap journalistic principles to chase rumors and gossip.

The great drama of early 2018 was the release of Michael Wolff's book *Fire and Fury: Inside the Trump White House*. In the book, Wolff wrote many tales attributing odd behavior to the president—and included a host of nasty comments about the president and his family, which were reportedly made by former strategic advisor Steve Bannon.

It was a smear book meant to embarrass the president by calling into question his mental stability and intelligence. Wolff would have us believe the man who built a multibillion-dollar business empire and then defeated 16 formidable Republicans, the Hillary Clinton political machine, and the entire elite media to become president was somehow lacking in mental faculties. Ridiculous.

With enthusiastic media coverage of its unsubstantiated wild claims, the book was a popular left-wing hit piece from the start.

On the *Today Show* on January 5, 2018, Wolff told host Savannah Guthrie that he "said what was necessary to get the story."

Later, when CNN's Michael Smerconish[11] questioned Wolff about this comment—and emails he had sent to the White House that indicated Wolff misrepresented himself and the book in order to get the access he needed, Wolff got flustered and accused Smerconish of "doing the work of the White House." In the emails, Wolff claimed that he "liked" the president and described the book project as an attempt to "humanize" and "change perceptions" about him.

CNN also reported that[12] "while working on the book, [Wolff] also publicly flattered his sources and criticized other news outlets for being too tough on Trump."

Clearly, this was not an honest, scholarly work of journalism. But that didn't stop the mainstream media from treating it as such. Despite the appearance that Wolff misrepresented himself (and despite the media's inability to verify anything he wrote), the elite punditry devoted itself to reporting on the book of gossip and insults as though it was a serious work.

Geoffrey Dickens with the Media Research Center[13] reported on January 10, 2018, that morning and evening shows for ABC, CBS, and NBC had spent more than two hours of combined air time talking about the book from January 3 through January 9.

At the same time, Dickens noted, "other big news, like the FBI re-opening the investigation into the Clinton Foundation scandal (11 minutes, 10 seconds) and the Dow Jones cracking the 25,000 mark (5 minutes, 46 seconds) were swamped by the Wolff book coverage (2 hours, 20 minutes, 5 seconds)."

The left-wing media's treatment of the Wolff book is a model for the way it has reported on the Trump presidency from the start. Real news (especially good news) has taken a back seat to gossip, hearsay, and innuendo. Consider how many times the media has had to walk back inaccurate stories about so-called Russian collusion because overeager reporters and anchors made baseless claims about President Trump. We saw this when ABC's Brian Ross falsely claimed that Trump had directed former national security advisor Michael Flynn to work with Russians during the campaign. Ross was later suspended for four weeks and the network had to issue a "clarification."[14]

The media's blind opposition to the president has led some once-legitimate outlets to become little more than sidewalk tabloids.

PERMANENT OPPOSITION

In my book *Understanding Trump*, which detailed my experience with Donald Trump during the campaign and the early months of his presidency, I described the media as being a part of the permanent opposition.

A year after that book was published, the description remains accurate.

As I'm writing this book, as recently as January 10, 2018, Nicholas Kristof wrote for the *New York Times*[15] that President Trump (and myself) threaten our democracy.

Even anti-Trump bannerman MSNBC's Joe Scarborough has acknowledged that "the entire mainstream media, we are reflexively anti-Trump on all things." According to the Hill[16] news outlet, while Scarborough was speaking with former NBC morning show host Katie Couric on a podcast, he shared the revelation that the media's constant full-court press against the president was a losing fight.

As the Hill reported, Joe's right about the media's bias.

According to a recent report by Pew Research Center,[17] media coverage of President Trump's early administration has been overwhelmingly negative compared to past administrations.

According to Pew:

> Compared with the first 60 days of the Clinton, Bush and Obama presidencies, news outlets' evaluations of Trump's start in office were far more negative and less positive. About six-in-ten news stories about Trump's first 60 days (62%) carried an overall negative assessment of his words or actions. That is about three times more negative than for Obama (20%) and roughly twice that of Bush and Clinton (28% each).

At the same time, only 5 percent of news coverage about Trump has conveyed a positive message, according to Pew. This compares with 27 percent for Bill Clinton, 22 percent for George W. Bush, and 42 percent for Barack Obama.

The Pew study also shows the media's focus on Trump's character rather than his policies. The report found that 69 percent of stories about Trump were about his personality, even though "in previous years, the leadership and character frame never comprised more than half of overall coverage." This focus on covering Trump the person came at the expense of covering his agenda and his achievements. Under past presidencies, about half of the news coverage was devoted to ideology or agenda. For President Trump, that figure was 31 percent, according to Pew.

An earlier survey by Gallup[18] found that the number of Americans who believe the media has a clear political bias is at record levels. In April 2017, Gallup reported 62 percent of Americans say the media favors one political party over another. This is the highest that statistic has been in two decades. Furthermore, 64 percent of those who say the media is biased say news organizations favor the Left.

The media's intense hatred for the president has only amplified its bias for Democrats and set its members into a constant state of frenzy. This mania has caused reporters and anchors to ignore the Trump administration's role in significant military victories in the Middle East, improved relations between North Korea and South Korea, and in creating a better trading climate with China.

Instead, they focus on gossip, the liberal fantasies of so-called economic experts, and anything that could make the president or Republicans look bad.

Piers Morgan describes the media's current pathology as "a new strain of PTSD—Perpetual Trump Shrieking Disorder." He warns as the media's mania gets more and more voracious, Trump will only get stronger.

Morgan wrote for *Daily Mail* on January 10, 2018, that "the less deranged Trump appears, the more deranged many of his more famous critics are starting to appear." Morgan noted that "screaming abuse at everything Trump does or says is self-defeating for his enemies; it simply rallies his base and empowers him more."

Morgan was commenting on a particularly vitriolic speech

made by actor Robert De Niro at the National Board of Review Awards in New York City in which De Niro called the president a "f*****g idiot," a "f*****g fool," and the "baby-in-chief."

Morgan wrote:

> [Robert] de Niro's become one of the first casualties of a new strain of PTSD—Perpetual Trump Shrieking Disorder.
>
> The poor man's been sent doolally by a President who refuses to play by the rules, and infuriates as many people as he delights, but who is starting to deliver, as CNN's Dana Bash said yesterday, what "people who had high hopes for the Trump presidency thought it would be."

The intensity of the media's hostility to President Trump resembles the media reaction to Presidents Andrew Jackson, Abraham Lincoln, and Franklin Delano Roosevelt. When a president comes along who challenges existing orthodoxies and power structures, he or she has to be ready for vicious, intense condemnation from those currently in power. Nothing said about President Trump is worse than comparable scurrilous attacks on Jackson, Lincoln, and FDR.

Like Jackson, Lincoln, and FDR, President Trump is serious about real change, so he is arousing vicious, emotional opposition, which is leading his opponents toward derangement.

However, writer and radio host Erick Erickson offered another view on December 12, 2017.[19]

Erickson suggested that the media is currently grappling with the result of a period of rampant mingling with the Obama administration.

He argues that the revolving door between Washington media, Democratic political offices, liberal think tanks, and lobbying firms has permanently shaped the worldview of many reporters and done irreparable damage to their ability to write objective truth.

Erickson points to the mainstream media's decision to ignore many important details of the Fusion GPS story as evidence of this widespread "incestuousness." Fusion GPS is the Washington, DC, journalist-founded political consulting firm responsible for producing the so-called Steele Dossier. The dossier was created during the campaign by a former British intelligence agent, who was largely fed information by Russian officials. It was paid for by Hillary Clinton's campaign and the National Democratic Party and contained numerous lewd allegations about then candidate Trump that threatened to harm his chances to win the White House. Rumors about the dossier circulated through elite groups in Washington throughout the latter part of the campaign. BuzzFeed.com published the dossier on January 10, 2017, after the election but before Trump's inauguration.

I will write more about Fusion GPS and the entire bogus Russian collusion narrative in the next chapter. However, it's useful to mention here for making Erickson's point.

Erikson wrote:

In fact, the *Washington Post* is now reporting that Fusion GPS used media connections to advance interests of various groups that paid it. It is an ascertainable fact that many reporters have failed to aggressively pursue this story because they have knowingly or unknowingly been used by Fusion GPS to advance the interests of paying clients.

Erickson makes an incredibly valid point here. Members of the Washington, DC, media have moved from news outlets, to administrations, to political firms, and back to media outlets so freely, they have lost any credible ability to remain objective.

Within his piece, Erickson includes a staggering list of people who illustrate his point:

Jay Carney went from *Time* to the White House press secretary's office. Shailagh Murray went from the *Washington Post* to the Veep's office while married to Neil King at the *Wall Street Journal*. Linda Douglass went from ABC News to the White House and then the *Atlantic*. Jill Zuckman went from the *Chicago Tribune* to the Obama administration's Transportation Department. Douglas Frantz went from the *Washington Post* to the State Department and Stephen Barr went from the *Post* to the Labor Department.

Ruth Marcus who heads the *Washington Post* Editorial Board is married to the Obama Administration's former FTC Chairman. Jonathan Allen of NBC News had been at the *Politico* before going to work for Debbie Wasserman Schultz, then back to *Politico* before going to left-leaning Vox. He left Vox and moved to NBC News. Andy Barr worked for the *Politico* before leaving for Democrat politics. Michael Scherer was at both *Salon* and *Mother Jones* before going to *Time*. Laura Rozen was at *Mother Jones* and the *American Prospect* before *Foreign Policy* magazine. Even Nate Silver had started out at Daily Kos. Then, of course, there is Matthew Dowd who worked for scores of Democrats before working for George Bush. That, though he later washed his hands of Bush, bought him street credibility with ABC News to become its senior political analyst alongside George Stephanopoulos, formerly of the Clinton Administration.

Perhaps better than any media poll, Erickson's list shows the clear culture of liberal bias in media today.

TRUMP OWES THEM NOTHING

One of the most puzzling aspects of the media's intense hatred of
President Trump is that he has been incredibly open with his time.

The *Washington Times* reported in December 2017 that
Trump had "engaged in an unprecedented level of interaction
with reporters."

According to the newspaper:

> Mr. Trump allowed pool sprays and other events that
> usually would be relegated to photo ops to become
> impromptu press conferences. He responded to more
> than 500 questions from reporters during these encoun-
> ters, according to a tally by the *Washington Times*.
>
> His walks across the South Lawn to and from
> Marine One routinely become question-and-answer ses-
> sions with reporters along the rope line. He has taken
> questions there on 13 occasions, responding to 42 ques-
> tions during a single session in October.
>
> By comparison, President Obama took questions
> twice when leaving or arriving on the Marine helicop-
> ter, and both times there was a podium placed there for
> the event, according to meticulous lists kept by Mark
> Knoller, White House correspondent for CBS News.

President Trump's willingness to be so open with (and take
abuse from) the press is puzzling because he could just follow in
the footsteps of Obama and ignore them completely.

President Trump must defend the United States Constitution and that includes the First Amendment. A free press is vital
for democracy.

Aside from this defense of their basic First Amendment rights,
however, President Trump owes nothing to the Washington press

corps and elite liberal news media. The First Amendment guarantees that the media can work freely to report the news. It includes no obligation on behalf of the White House to give them full, unfettered access to the president.

As I have written before in my weekly newsletter, President Trump should take a cue from FDR. At President Roosevelt's first press briefing on March 8, 1933, the ground rule was established that no member of the White House Press Corps was free to quote the president outside of a written statement. In fact, most of the conversation was off the record or for background purposes only. This is because the meeting was not about recording gotcha questions or the daily media melee; it was about helping the press understand and communicate the goals and achievements of the administration. Granted, this was a very long time ago, and mass media has drastically changed. However, FDR's ground rules are important for illustrating that the First Amendment's press freedoms were never meant to guarantee unfettered access to the president.

I have learned over the last few years that if President Trump fails to follow sound historic advice, there is often a good reason—and he often has a better idea than I do. I have come to believe that he puts up with the White House Press Corps because he likes fighting with them. He may or may not like them personally, but he likes fighting with them. He spent years being constantly covered by the media in New York City. He learned that noise works, conflict works, getting covered by the press works.

What I didn't understand about the president until late in 2017 was how much he loved fighting reporters and producers. He dislikes Jeff Zucker, the head of CNN (who Trump is convinced got the job leading CNN because of a lunch Trump had with Zucker's future boss). On the other hand, he loves fighting with Zucker. Every time the president tweets or ad libs an attack on CNN, it is pure gold for Zucker. If Trump really wanted to hurt CNN, he would never mention it or its leadership—but that isn't the Trump way.

President Trump has already proven to be an expert in using social media to bypass the elite news media and speak directly with the American people through Facebook, Twitter, YouTube, or other new social media platforms. He could use these skills to connect directly with the American people—much like FDR did with his fireside chats, a series of radio broadcasts he made during his presidency.

President Trump could also move the physical press facility to the Eisenhower Executive Office Building next to the White House, where members of the media could have more room to work without being able to wander the White House looking for opportunities to attack or undermine the president.

President Trump has every right to interact with the American people in any way he wants to, and he has every right to call out the news media for being irresponsible and dishonest. When people go out of their way to lie about the president of the United States, we owe it to the American people to stand up and say we are going to fight back.

When I was Speaker of the House, I learned not to agree to regular on-camera interviews. I had originally set up frequent on-camera interviews with the Capitol Hill press in order to keep my constituents and Americans abreast of goings-on in Congress.

It quickly turned into a weekly sparring match with the press, in which largely uninformed reporters asked erroneous questions they were fed by Democrats in order to shape public opinion and completely undermine what we were trying to do.

These regular, live press gaggles rapidly became so destructive we simply shut them down. The Capitol Hill Press Corps' hostility actually reduced its access to leadership. President Trump should consider doing the same thing.

Perhaps if White House reporters are moved out of their elite gossip circle and forced to start looking for real news from real named sources, the rampant sensationalism in today's media would subside.

I wouldn't count on that happening soon, though.

CHAPTER ELEVEN

THE RULE OF LAW VERSUS THE RULE OF MUELLER

One of the greatest challenges to Trump's America is the rise of Muellerism as a replacement for the rule of law.

Muellerism is the offensive version of Comeyism, which was the desperate effort by former FBI Director James Comey, Attorney General Loretta Lynch, and President Barack Obama to protect Secretary of State Hillary Clinton from answering for wide-ranging violations of the law.

Clinton faced no consequences after she deleted 33,000 emails, then had a staff assistant destroy cell phones and other hardware with a hammer to avoid having them subpoenaed. Her huge foundation continued to operate in the shadows as her husband was paid $500,000 by a Russian bank while she was involved in deciding if the Russians could take control of American uranium. In the midst of the current Mueller frenzy, it is easy to forget just how much then FBI Director Comey was bending or breaking the law on Clinton's behalf.

For myself and many Republicans after the election, it seemed clear that any postelection investigation should focus on the various Clinton cover-ups. If the investigation was going to have a Russian focus, it would be on the Russian-Clinton ties. It was initially difficult for Trump supporters to understand how the national establishment and the deep state could simply skip past the last eight years of illegality and abuse of power and decide to launch a new "Republicans-only" investigation cycle. We had underestimated how much President Trump scared the deep state.

After candidate Trump beat 16 other Republicans and won the nomination, then defeated the elite media and the billion-dollar Hillary Clinton campaign, he thought he would have some legitimacy.

However, the establishment and the deep state were so offended that an "inappropriate," "deplorable" candidate won their presidency, they had to find a new way to frame him as illegitimate. After all, if he was a legitimate president, then their entire world was dying and under siege. They had to find a way to keep him on defense and to keep his legitimacy as president in doubt.

So, the elites decided that Trump could only have done so well with illegitimate help. They determined it had to be the Russians.

The elite media, desperate for a non-Trump future, dutifully adopted a "the Russians did it" theme. Senior elements of the Obama national security team began saying "it might have been the Russians." Democrats in Congress began demanding investigations into the obvious "fact" that Trump and the Russians must have been colluding (how else could you explain deplorables beating Hillary, the great elitist). There was a desperation to these attacks, which intensified every time President Trump tweeted. The Russian collusion was the one thing which was going to save the deep state and the elites from being dramatically changed by the new president.

THE SESSIONS RECUSAL AND MUELLER'S BLANK CHECK

As the Left built into a frenzy, it overwhelmed both Republicans in Congress and Attorney General Jeff Sessions.

I have known and liked Sessions for years. He had great courage as a U.S. senator and routinely defied the Left in the Senate. I had worked with him on the Trump campaign when he had been the only senator willing to work openly for a Trump presidency. His best policy expert, Stephen Miller, had become the new president's top policy advisor and speechwriter (Miller had spent a year on the campaign plane and could channel President Trump on policy and speech language better than anyone else).

Because Sessions is an inherently decent, kind, and friendly person, he thought his former colleagues in the Senate would treat him fairly during his confirmation hearings. He had apparently forgotten that in 1986, Democrats had engaged in a nasty partisan attack to block his nomination by President Reagan to be a federal judge. True to form, after President Trump's election, left-wing senators attacked Sessions over minor discrepancies in his Senate testimony about whether or not he met or contacted any Russians while working on the presidential campaign. In fact, he had spoken with Russians in his normal capacity as a U.S. senator—but not through the Trump campaign. Democrats ignored this important distinction and smeared Sessions in order to hurt Trump.

Sessions tried to appease the Democrats by agreeing to recuse himself on the Russian collusion case and turning supervision of it over to Rod Rosenstein, his deputy attorney general who was a career Justice Department professional. President Trump was livid because he knew there was no Russian collusion with the campaign, and therefore Sessions had no reason to recuse himself.

All of this was occurring in a swirling series of revelations about Comey, who was earning scrutiny for having broken so many rules to protect Secretary Clinton. In fact, early on, it was this mounting pressure that caused him to announce he was reopening the Clinton investigation nearly two weeks before the election. He was trying to cover himself.

On May 16, 2017, President Trump met with former FBI Director Robert Mueller to interview him as Comey's possible replacement. Trump had concluded he wanted someone new. However, the following day, Mueller was instead named by Rosenstein to look into "any links and/or coordination between Russian government and individuals associated with the campaign of President Donald Trump, and any matters that arose or may arise directly from the investigation." It is the last clause which opened the door for the rule of law to be replaced with the rule of Mueller.

Essentially Rosenstein gave Mueller carte blanche to look at anything. What is the limit in the phrase "any matters that arose or may arise"? Of course, week by week, we have watched the Mueller team broaden the scope of its investigation. The original question of whether there was Russian collusion with the Trump campaign seems to have disappeared. Mueller could not find any evidence of collusion. Instead, he is going after Russians for crimes committed while creating propaganda designed to influence our politics and elections. He is going after former Trump campaign workers for tax and banking problems, which preceded the 2016 campaign, and he is going after anyone who gives inconsistent statements to his investigators.

In effect Mueller is setting the stage to go after the Trump family and the president himself by diving into any aspect of his business, taxes, and past statements. This is rapidly becoming an open-ended hunt for guilt with no regard for the limits of the law, the normal limits on an independent counsel, or even the existence of an alleged crime.

Furthermore, Mueller is setting up the threat of an obstruction case against the president, so if he can't get President Trump for any stated violation, he will try to claim Trump interfered with the investigation itself.

NO END IN SIGHT

There is no doubt: Of all the attacks that have been waged upon the Trump presidency, the Mueller investigation is the deadliest.

The investigation stays alive because it is the deep state's last opportunity to stop President Trump from dismantling the bureaucracy and corruption in Washington.

Mueller has assembled a team of more than 15 attorneys. Most of them are Democrats (based on their political donation patterns). These lawyers are high-powered, expensive, and professional. They did not take deep cuts in pay to achieve nothing. They are like a legal wolf pack hunting for big game. When the Russian collusion trail completely dries up, they seek others. If no trail leads them to convictable offenses, they will maneuver until they invent a trail that will. I predict the Mueller team will find someone in the White House to indict for something. That is the pattern of special counsels.

This investigation is especially dangerous because its rules are totally different from anything Trump has experienced. He has been through civil lawsuits. That experience could prove misleading. Prosecutors don't play by the same rules as civil litigators. Every step is a potential land mine. Every statement potentially can be construed as perjury.

More than a dozen really smart prosecutors have been working for a year to assemble facts. They will go into interviews knowing many things that their interviewees do not know. Neither the targets nor their attorneys will have any idea how much the prosecutors have assembled. The one-sided nature of

prosecutorial power makes investigations like this so dangerous. Andrew McCarthy, a former federal prosecutor who tried
the terrorists from the first World Trade Center bombing, has
written extensively on the dangers the Trump team is facing.

I am writing this in the early part of 2018. I cannot predict
how Special Counsel Mueller's boundless investigation will have
proceeded by the time this book is published. However, based
on my observations so far, I can safely bet it will not be any
closer to serving justice or finding truth. These types of special
investigations rarely do. Since the specter of a special investigation into Russian involvement in the 2016 election was raised, I
have warned that it would be an open-ended, unchecked witch
hunt that would not end until someone—specifically someone
connected to President Trump—was convicted of something,
regardless of guilt or innocence. I'm not the only one saying this.
Victor Davis Hanson wrote an excellent article explaining the
following about special investigators for the *National Review* on
December 12, 2017.[1]

In his piece, Hanson wrote:

Special prosecutors, investigators, and counsels are
usually a bad idea. They are admissions that constitu-
tionally mandated institutions don't work—and can be
rescued only by supposed superhuman moralists, who
are without the innate biases inherent in human nature.

The record from Lawrence Walsh to Ken Starr to
Patrick Fitzgerald suggests otherwise. Originally narrow mandates inevitably expand—on the cynical theory that everyone has something embarrassing to
hide. Promised "short" timelines and limited budgets
are quickly forgotten. Prosecutors search for ever new
crimes to justify the expense and public expectations of
the special-counsel appointment.

Hanson is exactly right. Think about it: There is no way, after spending months of time and effort and millions of taxpayer dollars, that any special prosecutor would come before Congress and report that he or she found no evidence of wrongdoing.

Instead, Mueller is dutifully collecting deposition after deposition from as many people in the president's orbit as possible, so he can then recall those people months later and quiz them on what they initially told investigators. Any inconsistencies—no matter how minor—will be aggressively prosecuted as giving false statements, perjury, or obstruction of justice. As Hanson also noted in his piece, "special investigations often quickly turn Soviet, in the sense of 'Show me the man and I'll find you the crime.'"

We have already seen this happen to former National Security Advisor Michael Flynn. Flynn was charged with making false statements[2] to Federal Bureau of Investigation (FBI) agents in January 2017 about a conversation he had with the Russian Ambassador in December 2016.

This is what happened: On December 29, 2016, the Obama administration expelled 35 people it suspected of being Russian spies and sanctioned the country's top intelligence services after U.S. agencies determined Russia was responsible for hacking the Democratic National Committee. The same day, Flynn reportedly spoke to the Russian ambassador and asked him to keep Russian leaders from overreacting to the actions of America's outgoing president. A month later, Flynn didn't accurately relay this conversation to FBI agents. According to court filings, Flynn told the FBI he had not urged Russia to moderate its response to Obama's sanctions and that he didn't recall the ambassador agreeing to do so. Almost 10 months later, Flynn was charged with two counts of giving false statements. Ultimately, Flynn pleaded guilty.

To the layman (thanks in large part to the media's devotion

to casting the Trump administration in a bad light), this all seemed very shady and played into the Trump–Russia narrative. However, what gets lost in this story is the fact that Flynn was perfectly within the law to contact the Russian ambassador and urge him to tone down Russia's response. Flynn was a member of the presidential transition team and had been selected as National Security Advisor. The election was over. Meanwhile, the outgoing Democratic president was trying to cause trouble for the incoming administration. This wasn't an act of collusion. It was diplomacy.

Flynn's mistake was he apparently underestimated just how aggressively the FBI was going to be to draw first blood. He should have kept a much more detailed record of his interactions, so he didn't have to rely on his memory. This would have kept him from losing his job in the White House as well. He wasn't fired because he had conversations with the Russian ambassador. He was fired because he failed to accurately report them to the vice president.

Furthermore, Flynn was faced with the threats of being bankrupted while defending himself and of having his son being drawn into the investigation. His plea was about personal and family survival.

As an example of how dangerous the prosecutors can be, compare Flynn's harsh treatment (after 35 years defending America in uniform) with the Justice Department ignoring all the crimes reportedly committed by Clinton staff.

Justice has ceased to be blind. It keeps its left eye wide open. That is how the rule of law has evolved into the rule of Mueller.

Another example of Mueller's gotcha approach is the indictment and subsequent guilty plea of George Papadopoulos. Now, to be sure, if the FBI's indictment of Papadopoulos[3] is completely accurate, Papadopoulos made some very big mistakes. His first mistake was apparently agreeing to an FBI interview without

an attorney present. His second mistake was apparently trying to outfox investigators by downplaying his contact with
some Russian nationals while he was working for the campaign
overseas—and omitting some contacts entirely.

According to the court filings, Papadopoulos was working
as a foreign policy advisor for the campaign in London. One of
his principle goals was to improve U.S.–Russia relations under
the Trump administration. During the course of this work, he
met with a professor who claimed to have high-level contacts
with the Russian government. In late March 2016, this professor introduced Papadopoulos to a woman who was supposedly
Russian President Vladimir Putin's niece (she wasn't related
to Putin). The two Russians led Papadopoulos to believe they
would introduce him to the Russian ambassador in London
(they did not). The Russians did eventually put Papadopoulos
in contact with someone "who had connections to" the Russian
Ministry of Foreign Affairs (MFA). This person started to work
with Papadopoulos to potentially set up a meeting between
Russian officials and the campaign. More than a month went
by, and the Russian MFA contact apparently extended an invi-
tation for Trump to personally come meet Putin.

This meeting never took place. In a footnote on the indictment,
the FBI acknowledged that top Trump campaign officials had pri-
vately exchanged emails agreeing that "DT is not doing these trips."
Finally, in late April, the professor met with Papadopoulos and told
him Russian officials had "dirt" on Hillary Clinton in the form of
"thousands of emails." Now, the FBI states that Papadopoulos continued to work with the campaign and continued to try to arrange
a meeting between Russia and Trump campaign members—which
he had been doing long before he was told about the "dirt." At no
point does the indictment indicate that Papadopoulos told other
campaign officials about the alleged "dirt" or attempted to use it to
advance Trump's campaign.

By all accounts, it appears Papadopoulos was a low-level advisor in Europe who was trying to make a career for himself by arranging meetings that never happened. It appears nothing he did for the campaign was illegal or even out of the ordinary.

Similar to Flynn, his major mistake was not taking his initial FBI interview seriously. The FBI charged Papadopoulos with giving false statements because he apparently misrepresented *when* his professor contact mentioned the "dirt." He also reportedly failed to disclose his contact with the phony Putin relative and was not honest about the content and frequency of his interactions with Russian nationals overall.

Once again, a Trump staffer was arrested for something he said to the FBI, not for any illegal activity related to Russia or influencing the 2016 election. This is the exact model used to indict and ultimately convict Vice President Cheney's chief of staff Scooter Libby in 2007 over the Valerie Plame CIA scandal. I wrote a newsletter and op-ed for FoxNews.com[4] in April 2017 urging Trump team members to take note of the Libby case and refuse to testify in hearings about the Russia investigation without being assured immunity from prosecution. Here is an excerpt that explains the Libby case—what I consider "the most extraordinary case in my lifetime of process being used to destroy an innocent person." It is useful for understanding the Mueller investigation.

> An independent counsel was appointed to find out who told the press that a woman named Valerie Plame was a covert Central Intelligence Operative in 2003. Her husband was a diplomat who had been critical of the Bush administration. So, the Left (and naturally the media) thought this was a big deal.
>
> The prosecutor targeted Libby, who was Vice President Dick Cheney's chief of staff, because it would be

damaging to the Bush administration before the 2004 election. The prosecutor claimed Scooter had shared government secrets with a Pulitzer Prize winning *New York Times* reporter named Judith Miller. Initially, Miller refused to testify, so—in perhaps the greatest attack on American press freedom in our lifetime—the prosecutor had Miller jailed for 85 days. Finally, she testified that Scooter was the source after he gave her permission to break reporter confidentiality just to get her out of jail.

Libby was ultimately convicted on four counts— but not for leaking information. He was charged with perjury and obstruction of justice because of the way in which he answered questions.

The most relevant part of this story—which shows the investigation was far from an unbiased pursuit of the truth—is Miller never even wrote that Plame was a CIA operative.

Washington Post writer Robert Novak first outed Plame as a member of the CIA in a piece on July 14, 2003. Novak was told by Richard Armitage, the No. 2 person at the State Department. The prosecutor in the Libby case knew this, but he was focused on destroying Libby to hurt Bush—not uncovering the truth. The prosecutor told Armitage to keep quiet in order to continue the investigation. And Armitage—who undeniably leaked the classified information to the public—was never charged.

Mueller and his prosecutors are also scrutinizing every aspect of the lives of Trump's team members, looking for any reasons to accuse them of breaking any laws. It doesn't matter if the alleged crimes have anything to do with the campaign or even Russia.

This is the tactic Mueller used to charge former Trump campaign manager Paul Manafort and his business partner Rick Gates.

The charges against Manafort and Gates[5] are related to allegations that they didn't register as lobbyists for the Ukrainian government and one of its political parties. Importantly, this failure to register is alleged to have happened between 2006 and 2015—prior to the Trump campaign or Manafort's involvement in it. They are also charged with attempting to hide money they allegedly received from the Ukrainians. Gates pleaded guilty to charges of conspiracy and lying to the FBI in late February. Shortly after Gates's plea, a grand jury in Virginia unsealed an indictment of Manafort with new charges related to taxes and alleged bank fraud.

I don't know if any of these allegations against Manafort are true. He pleaded not guilty. However, I'm pretty sure they didn't warrant creating the public spectacle of dragging Manafort out of his home in an armed raid the day after he had voluntarily testified before the Senate Intelligence Committee, which is separately investigating alleged Russian influence in the election.

Clearly, the timing of the Manafort raid was intentional. Mueller raided Manafort's house immediately after Manafort's visit to the Senate to create the impression that the case against Manafort has some vague connection to President Trump—whether any existed or not. Again, compare the careful, courteous approach the FBI and the Justice Department took to the Clinton team during the illegal email server investigation with the secret police-style tactics Mueller used against Manafort.

Put yourself in Manafort's shoes. You are voluntarily cooperating with various congressional investigations. Your attorneys have a positive, practical relationship with the congressional committees. Suddenly, at 3 a.m., your door is kicked in and armed men rush into your bedroom while you and your wife are still in bed in your pajamas. Mueller to this day has not explained why this Gestapo-KGB-police-state raid was necessary. I think it was an effort to scare Manafort into cooperating and to warn others how dangerous this could become.

However, Mueller's secret police tactic failed. In fact, Manafort has filed a lawsuit against the Department of Justice (DOJ) challenging the indictment specifically because the allegations within have nothing to do with the scope of Mueller's supposed mission—to investigate Russian interference in the 2016 elections.

Make no mistake, this is about embarrassing and undermining the president, nothing more.

THE SPECIAL INVESTIGATION SETUP

It is true, when Mueller was first announced as the special counsel to investigate the supposed election influence by Russia, I was heartened. Mueller had an excellent reputation, and I was optimistic that he would allay my fear that the special investigation would be an endless, scattershot, fishing expedition. I genuinely thought that Mueller, who was director of the FBI under Presidents George W. Bush and Barack Obama, would play it straight. My hopes were shaken a month later, however, as soon as I heard testimony by fired FBI Director Comey.[6] On June 8, 2017, Comey admitted to the Senate Intelligence Committee that days after he was fired, he intentionally leaked his confidential notes about private conversations he had with President Trump to a professor at Columbia Law School. Comey asked his professor friend to share the memos with the press specifically because he "thought that might prompt the appointment of a special counsel." He also specified that he didn't do it himself "for a variety of reasons."

Get real. The only reason Comey had a college professor leak these memos was to give Comey's media allies the cover they needed to carry out the vendetta of a disgruntled ex-employee. Naturally, the media used the memos (which represent only Comey's views) to float the absurd story that President Trump attempted to obstruct justice during the investigation of Flynn. Also consider this: Before Comey was fired, he was the head of the FBI. At any point in time, if he had believed a special counsel was needed to investigate alleged Russian interference—or even the president's words or actions—he could have asked Congress to appoint one. Alternatively, he could have approached the attorney general's office with concerns. He didn't do any of this. The absurdity of Comey's testimony was punctuated when Senator Susan Collins, a Republican from Maine, explicitly asked Comey "whether there was any kind of investigation about the President underway" and "was the President under investigation at the time of [Comey's] dismissal on May 9?"

Under oath, Comey answered "no" to both questions.

Comey's answer to Collins's questions revealed the vindictiveness behind his memo-leak ploy. Comey saw no need for a special investigator until after he was canned. This was a clear act of retaliation. He wanted to cause the Trump White House pain, so when he saw an opportunity to do so, he took it.

Another clue that the appointment of Mueller and the special investigation was a thinly veiled effort to undermine the president was the profuse flattery Comey poured on Mueller during his testimony. Over the course of the testimony, Comey referred to Mueller as "one of the finest people and public servants this country has ever produced." He described Mueller as "one of... this country's great, great pros," and he said Mueller was the "right person" to lead the investigation. It all came together for me after the testimony. Comey got fired, so he worked behind the scenes to set up his good friend Mueller as a special counsel to seek vengeance on the man who fired him.

At this point, I realized the special investigation was not

about law and order. It was about a fired employee getting ven-geance and the federal bureaucracy trying to assert its control over a president its members deeply oppose. Remember 97 per-cent of Justice Department employees who made campaign con-tributions during the 2016 election gave to Clinton over Trump.[7]

BUILT-IN BIAS

Despite these revelations about how the special counsel was appointed, a small remainder of my initial optimism that Mueller's investigation might end up being an honest search for truth still remained. That hope was promptly destroyed once Mueller started putting his team together. The web of inherent bias is so thick in Mueller's team, it is difficult to describe in text alone. Many of these attorneys are career Justice Department employees or worked with Mueller at the private law firm WilmerHale. At least one has faced allegations related to overzealous prosecutions and had major con-victions overturned by the Supreme Court.

Many others have overwhelmingly donated to Demo-crats—specifically Hillary Clinton and Barack Obama. Com-bined, Federal Elections Commission records show Mueller's team has donated almost $50,000 to Democratic candidates over the last 12 years. They've given a mere $2,750 to Republi-cans. Some played roles in the investigation into Hillary Clinton's private email server, including the decisions not to put Clinton under oath or charge her with any crimes. Others have more direct financial and political ties to Clinton.

Consider Andrew McCabe: McCabe was the deputy direc-tor of the FBI. He was in charge of the Washington, DC, office as it was carrying out the investigation into Hillary Clinton's private email server.

Judicialwatch.org[8] reported in November 2017 that days after the email server scandal became public, Jill McCabe, Andrew McCabe's wife, was recruited by Democratic Virginia

Governor Terry McAuliffe to run for the Virginia State Senate. McAuliffe is a former Clinton Foundation board member and is close to the Clintons. Shortly after McCabe's wife announced her candidacy, McAuliffe arranged $700,000 in campaign donations for her from the state party and Clinton allies.

Meanwhile, McCabe continued working on the Clinton email server case and didn't recuse himself from the investigation until one week before the 2016 election. Subsequently, McAuliffe is now under investigation for campaign–Clinton Foundation funding issues. McCabe was urged to retire from the FBI in January over this glaring conflict.

Jeannie Rhee is another clear example of pro-Clinton bias. She is a former partner at Mueller's old law firm, WilmerHale, and a former assistant U.S. attorney for the District of Columbia. Prior to this, however, she was an attorney for the Clinton Foundation. Additionally, Rhee donated a total of $5,400 to Hillary Clinton in 2015 and 2016. Before that, she gave a combined $4,800 to Barack Obama in 2008 and 2011.

Then, you have Andrew Weissmann, a career DOJ prosecutor who gave $2,300 to Obama's 2008 campaign and $2,000 to the DNC in 2006. Weissmann is most known for leading the Enron Task Force. During that prosecution, he allegedly intimidated witnesses and hid evidence that he should have disclosed to the defense.

Ultimately, his conviction in the case against the accounting firm Arthur Anderson was overturned 9–0 by the Supreme Court. The high court ruled no crimes had been committed. Still, Weissmann's overzealous prosecution of Arthur Anderson destroyed the company and cost 85,000 people their jobs.

Aside from his history of donating to Democrats, and his attending Hillary Clinton's election night party in 2016,[9] Weissmann expressed his opposition to the Trump administration early on. After acting Attorney General Sally Yates, who was an Obama appointee like Weissmann, ordered DOJ lawyers not to defend against legal challenges to the Trump administration's initial ban restricting travel to and from several terrorism-wracked countries, Weissmann reportedly emailed Yates to congratulate her on refusing to uphold her oath of office.

Early on, Weissmann was hailed as one of Mueller's top lawyers. The *New York Times* referred to him as Mueller's "pit bull." In this case, the *Times* may be right. Weissmann's actions seem more like those of a trained attack dog than an unbiased prosecutor seeking truth.

Another longtime Democrat supporter on the team is James Quarles. A former WilmerHale partner and federal prosecutor who worked on the Watergate case, Quarles has given to Democratic Political Action Committees for decades. He gave more than $7,000 to Obama's campaigns over the last 10 years. However, in 2015, Quarles also donated $2,500 to former Utah Congressman Representative Jason Chaffetz. This list goes on and on. Victor Davis Hanson points out another conflicted attorney on the team: Aaron Zebley, who previously represented the Hillary Clinton IT staffer who reportedly built her illegal home email server—and who smashed her BlackBerries so they couldn't be subpoenaed. Unbiased indeed.

To the best of my knowledge, there are no Trump supporters on the Mueller team.

Each one of these examples calls into question the integrity of Mueller's investigation. However, they are small potatoes compared to other recent examples of profound anti-Trump, pro-Clinton bias at the heart of Mueller's operation.

THE PAGE-STRZOK AFFAIR

As I am writing this book, we are learning more and more about the extraordinary, deep-seated bias shared by two early members of Mueller's team—FBI agent Peter Strzok and FBI lawyer

Lisa Page. Page and Strzok were members of the Mueller investigation, but they were quietly reassigned in the summer of 2017. However, their reassignments later made big headlines. Page and Strzok were also members of the team investigating Clinton's illegal email server in the spring and summer of 2016. The DOJ Office of Inspector General found the two had previously exchanged more than 50,000 text messages, many of which were fiercely anti-Trump and frequently pro-Clinton. Importantly, they exchanged these messages while they were investigating Clinton.

Aside from occasionally bashing Trump with vulgar language, some of the texts apparently referenced sensitive stories which had been leaked to the press, and one referenced an "insurance policy" in case Trump won the election. On August 15, 2016,[10] Strzok sent Page a message saying, "I want to believe the path you threw out for consideration in Andy's office—that there's no way he gets elected—but I'm afraid we can't take that risk. It's like an insurance policy in the unlikely event you die before you're 40."

The "Andy" in this text is reportedly McCabe. The *Wall Street Journal* reported on December 18, 2017,[11] that the "insurance policy" was the then budding idea among FBI leaders to investigate alleged collusion between the Trump campaign and Russia. The implication is that the entire investigation into Trump was hatched by hyper-partisan FBI agents due to their dislike of the incoming president.

Interestingly, in a later text to Page on May 19, 2017,[12] Strzok expressed concern about joining Mueller's team because he thought it might be a waste of time. "You and I both know the odds are nothing. If I thought it was likely, I'd be there no question. I hesitate in part because of my gut sense and concern that there's no big there there," Strzok wrote. This shows Strzok clearly only cared about this investigation if he "thought it was likely" to be able to take down Trump. We have already learned that Strzok is not above influencing important FBI decisions more directly. In fact, when it became clear that the 2016 election would be between Trump and Clinton, he texted Page saying, "Now the pressure really starts to finish MYE."

MYE is reportedly the acronym for "midyear exam,"[13] the FBI code name for the Clinton email case.

Further, during the FBI's probe into Clinton's private emails—and specifically her handling of classified information—Strzok reportedly changed language in Comey's statement describing Clinton's actions[14] from "grossly negligent" to "extremely careless."

This change is significant. Gross negligence is a specific legal term that carries a specific meaning. Cornell Law School's Legal Information Institute defines gross negligence as:

A lack of care that demonstrates reckless disregard for the safety or lives of others, which is so great it appears to be a conscious violation of other people's rights to safety. It is more than simple inadvertence and can affect the amount of damages.

This is a term that could clearly lead to the prosecution of Clinton. "Extreme carelessness" apparently could not. An FBI investigator would know that.

This language change perhaps sheds light on why Strzok said in a July 1, 2016, text message to Page that then Attorney General Loretta Lynch, knew "no charges will be brought" against Clinton in the email scandal a full four days before Comey made public his decision not to prosecute Clinton.

It's unclear if Strzok was able to influence the early Russia investigation the way he reportedly influenced the outcome of the Clinton email probe. This uncertainty is compounded by the fact that the FBI is claiming it failed to retain texts from

Strzok's phone over a five-month span due to a technical glitch. Conveniently, that five-month gap goes from December 14, 2016 to May 7, 2017—the first three months of the Trump presidency, when the so-called Russian collusion story was being covered full tilt.

Attorney General Sessions announced in late January that he was going to investigate this supposed gap in information and turn whatever he found over to Congress for review. Sessions told Fox News that,[15] "We will leave no stone unturned to confirm with certainty why these text messages are not now available to be produced and will use every technology available to determine whether the missing messages are recoverable from another source."

While you are considering all this, remember that 97 percent of DOJ employees who made campaign donations supported Clinton in the 2016 election. If these texts can be recovered, it will provide very interesting insights into the depth of Trump resistance at the top of the FBI establishment.

REAL COLLUSION

For those of us in Trump's America, the bitter ironies behind the Russian collusion narrative are that our own government attempted to influence our 2016 election far more than Russia ever could, and the overwhelming evidence shows that the Clinton campaign colluded with Russia to undermine Trump, not vice versa.

These two facts are unassailable.

The real story of Russian collusion starts with the so-called Trump dossier produced by Fusion GPS, a Washington-based research firm that was started by former *Wall Street Journal* reporters. During the primary, the *Washington Free Beacon* reportedly hired the firm to do opposition research on Trump when he was a candidate. Once he won the nomination, the

Democratic National Committee retained Fusion GPS via the law firm Perkins Coie to do the same research. In the course of its work, Fusion GPS hired a former British Intelligence agent named Christopher Steele to do research on Trump's businesses overseas. The firm paid this ex-spy roughly $160,000, according to testimony[16] Fusion GPS co-owner Glenn Simpson gave before the House Intelligence Committee. According to Simpson, Steele didn't actually go to Russia—that would have been dangerous since he was an outed former MI6 agent. So, instead, Steele reached out to his sources in Russia.

Simpson declined to share Steele's Russian sources with the Committee, citing security reasons, however, he did say he "knew generally where they're positioning. In other words, we would discuss generally where that person sat in relation to a senior government official or, you know, what other position they held."

Based on information from these Russian sources, Steele developed an extraordinarily salacious, controversial dossier on candidate Trump. Steele then turned that over to Fusion GPS, and ultimately decided it was so damning he needed to share it with the FBI. Interestingly, Simpson acknowledged at the time that he "wasn't convinced of the facts of anything in terms of—I wasn't convinced that there was a specific crime that occurred."

From there, the illicit (unverified and likely unverifiable) dossier floated around Washington, piquing the interest of the anti-Trump coalition, and quietly fanning the flames of the Russian collusion narrative, which heated up once the DNC's computers had reportedly been hacked. Despite this, President Trump won the election.

At some point after this—the timeline is unclear—Simpson and Steele met with Bruce Ohr, who is yet another member of Mueller's team of witch hunters.

According to CNN, Fusion GPS had "contracted with

Nellie Ohr [Ohr's wife] to help with its 'research and analysis of Mr. Trump,' and that Simpson met with Bruce Ohr, 'at his request, after the November 2016 election to discuss our findings regarding Russia and the election.'" Forget partisan bias for a moment, how is Bruce Ohr supposed to take an objective view of his wife's work? The most flabbergasting thing about this entire Russian collusion story is the anti-Trump coalition's willingness to ignore facts that are in plain view.

Here's what we know for sure:

The DNC (which was under Hillary Clinton's control) paid for some exceptionally damning opposition research on Donald Trump that was sourced from Russians. Then this Clinton-financed, Russian-sourced dossier of damning information was shared with the FBI as evidence that Trump was colluding with Russians to get damning evidence about Hillary Clinton—and the FBI is taking it seriously.

GOING FORWARD

At this time the president has agreed to be interviewed by Mueller under oath, although lawyers are working out conditions.

The first thing Trump's lawyers should do is ask Mueller what crime he is investigating. Then, following the spirit of the Manafort lawsuit, they should agree only to sit for questions about alleged Russian collusion in the 2016 election. They should make Mueller put his case on the table.

If, as I suspect, the Russian collusion trail has produced nothing, then the burden should be on Mueller to define what grounds he has for taking up the president of the United States' time—and using the American taxpayers' dollars.

Make no mistake. Mueller's out-of-control special prosecutor investigation is the greatest threat President Trump faces. He should meet with Scooter Libby to understand that being innocent isn't enough if a prosecutor sets out to get you. The president needs to focus on this and prepare for it as the mortal threat it is.

National Review editor Andrew McCarthy has a few more pointed questions, which he wrote about in a column on February 17, 2018.[17] He suggests that Trump's lawyers ask the Justice Department's Office of Legal Counsel two questions:

- "Why is there a special counsel in the Russia investigation?"
- "May the president of the United States be charged with obstruction based on non-criminal discretionary acts that are unquestionably within his constitutional authority as chief executive?"

The heart of McCarthy's argument is that in the United States, law enforcement officers have to actually have evidence that a crime has been committed before they bring a case. As McCarthy puts it, "in the absence of such evidence, a prosecutor should never be assigned to investigate whether an American may have committed some unknown crime."

The Russian collusion investigation is a counterintelligence probe—not a criminal investigation. Further, alleged links between President Trump or any of his former team members are not illegal, McCarthy argues.

In this case, Mueller is an illegitimately appointed prosecutor looking for crimes for which to convict people. The presumption of innocence at the heart of the American justice system is entirely absent.

We are literally swinging in the balance between the rule of law and the rule of Mueller. These are very important months for our constitutional Republic.

CHAPTER TWELVE

DRAINING THE SWAMP

The Washington swamp is vast. It has been steadily growing since the city became our nation's permanent capital in December 1800 and President Jefferson moved there from Philadelphia in early 1801.

The swamp is a natural habitat for a large swath of the anti-Trump coalition.

Legions of lawyers, lobbyists, and media members have been attracted to this elite ecosystem. They seek to influence the movements of the federal government, steer lawmakers toward decisions that benefit their fellow swamp denizens, and—most importantly—achieve their goals by sidestepping the American people and manipulating the government.

However, there is a core to the swamp that binds the entire biome together—the entrenched federal bureaucracy.

Without the bureaucrats, the lawyers and lobbyists would have a harder time getting their words woven into legislation, and the members of the media would have a harder time getting the leaked documents and insider gossip on which they thrive.

This ability to almost invisibly shape law and political opinion is a tremendous power, which the members of the bureaucracy wield with vigor. The bureaucracy works with many branches of the anti-Trump coalition.

For the left-wing factions of the coalition, the bureaucracy provides a way to impose a radical worldview on Americans without having to win elections or pass laws in Congress. If you want to change the behavior of Americans, you simply start proposing myriad federal rules that incrementally block whatever behavior you are trying to stop—energy exploration, logging, certain agricultural practices, or the consumption of sugary drinks, for example.

For the orderly institutionalist branch of the anti-Trump coalition, the bureaucracy provides all the speed bumps one could wish for to slow-walk or completely halt reforms proposed by an "upstart" president or lawmaker.

For the elite wing of the anti-Trump coalition, the bureaucracy provides a back channel to make sure your interests are protected from new rules governing business, commerce, or some other sector.

Finally, some in the anti-Trump coalition like the bureaucracy because it keeps them from having to do real work. It is far simpler for politicians to delegate fact-finding and analysis to federal agencies than to do the research themselves. Furthermore, this carries the added benefit of being able to use whatever the agency finds as cover for not being able to deliver on campaign promises or other pledges.

For all of these reasons, the people of Trump's America despise the bloated bureaucracy.

Hardworking Americans in agriculture, construction, and other blue-collar fields constantly grapple with unnecessary, costly regulations that force them to spend more time filling out paperwork than plying their trade. Some of these unlucky Americans only interact with federal bureaucrats when they learn that they have unwittingly broken some obscure federal regulation and are required to pay a fine.

Similarly, those in Trump's America who are being harmed by unreasonable regulations and are desperate for change see the bureaucracy as a slow-moving, inefficient, broken machine that is keeping them from resolving their problems.

Naturally, the small business owners who are part of Trump's America are fed up with big business insiders getting deals from their bureaucratic relationships that tilt the playing field or eliminate competition by regulation.

Moreover, virtually everyone in Trump's America rejects the notion that the federal government can impose rules and restrictions upon the American people without any accountability or recourse. The people of Trump's America believe wholeheartedly that government requires the consent of the governed. For them, the bureaucracy is government growing beyond the reach and control of the people.

This is why Americans responded so positively to President Trump's campaign promise to drain the swamp and bring its inhabitants into the light of day. Since Trump took office, he has been doing just that in the most effective way possible—by limiting the power of the bureaucracy. Through deregulation, and smart use of his appointment powers, President Trump has been fighting a battle against the bureaucracy since day one.

And the bureaucrats have been fighting back.

THE FOURTH BRANCH OF GOVERNMENT

We can learn a great deal about our federal bureaucracy by watching the 1980s British sitcom, *Yes, Minister.*

The very first episode introduces the story of the newly appointed Right Honorable James Hacker, MP, Minister for Administrative Affairs, and his pursuit to uphold and abide by his values of having a transparent, open government system.

At every turn, this well-intentioned but naive politician is comically manipulated by members of the British bureaucracy—

especially via the tactful string-pulling of the clever political puppeteer Sir Humphrey Abbleby, the minister's senior-ranking chief bureaucrat.

When the minister enters his new office for the first time, he meets Sir Humphrey, who briefs the minister on the structure of the department he will be overseeing. Here's how it goes:

> Minister: Who else is in this department?
>
> Sir Humphrey: Well briefly, sir, I am the Permanent Under Secretary of State, known as the Permanent Secretary. Woolley here is your Principal Private Secretary. I too have a Principal Private Secretary and he is the Principal Private Secretary to the Permanent Secretary. Directly responsible to me are ten Deputy Secretaries, 87 Under Secretaries and 219 Assistant Secretaries. Directly responsible to the Principal Private Secretaries are plain Private Secretaries, and the Prime Minister will be appointing two Parliamentary Under-Secretaries and you will be appointing your own Parliamentary Private Secretary.
>
> Minister: Can they all type?
>
> Sir Humphrey: None of us can type, Minister. Mrs. Mackay types: she's the secretary.

This is a satirical show, and it is meant to be funny. However, like all good satire, it exposes an important truth. This excerpt clearly illustrates how vast, complicated, inefficient, and deeply entrenched bureaucracies perpetuate themselves and persist through changes in elected government.

This exact same model, without the humor, exists in the United States in the bureaucracy. Our bureaucracy has ballooned along with the federal government itself over the last century. Just like Sir Humphrey, the members of the bureaucracy are accountable to no one, they pursue their own agendas regardless of the will of "we the people" as expressed through elections, and they work tirelessly to undermine administrations they oppose.

Aside from being a large, inefficient model that produces unnecessary regulations, the bureaucracy poses a fundamental threat to our constitutional system of government, our liberty, and the rule of law.

The permanent continuation of the swamp, specifically the bureaucracy, threatens the foundation of our democracy by taking power away from American voters and placing it in the hands of unelected career bureaucrats in Washington.

In the U.S. government in 1790, there were just 1,000 non-military workers, but today, there are about 2.8 million.[1]

This dramatic surge in employees and the creation of the modern bureaucracy has essentially led to the establishment of a "fourth branch of government," that "now has a larger practical impact on the lives of citizens than all the other branches combined," according to Jonathan Turley, the Shapiro professor of public interest law at George Washington University.[2]

Members of this fourth branch of government answer only to their bureaucratic bosses and colleagues who are equally entrenched in the Washington swamp. They don't answer to elected officials or the American people.

As such, bureaucrats have implemented thousands of rules and regulations in efforts that undermine the legislative, judicial, and executive branches.

In fact, today, instead of laws strictly being made by Congress, most federal actions, which any normal American would consider laws in the practical sense, are issued by the bureaucracy in the form of rules and regulations. According to Turley, in 2007, Congress successfully enacted 138 laws. However, that same year, federal agencies finalized 2,926 rules including 61 major regulations. With how rapidly these agencies are putting these changes into effect, and with the now 2.8 million bureaucrats,[3] there's no possible way that Congress could effectively oversee the bureaucracy's efforts.

Not only do these agencies effectively make laws without Congress, they enforce them and rule on their validity in administrative courts that sidestep the judiciary. As a result, Turley writes that Americans are 10 times more likely to be tried by an agency than an actual court of law.

Administrative judgments are made every day about alleged infractions. As bureaucracies get used to making decisions about citizens' lives, they become more empowered.

This is a mockery of due process. Professor Gary Lawson of the Boston University School of Law explained in his 1994 article "The Rise and Rise of the Administrative State" how these courts operate:

> Consider the typical enforcement activities of a typical federal agency—for example, of the Federal Trade Commission. The Commission promulgates substantive rules of conduct. The Commission then considers whether to authorize investigations into whether the Commission's rules have been violated. If the Commission authorizes an investigation, the investigation is conducted by the Commission, which reports its findings to the Commission. If the Commission thinks that the Commission's findings warrant an enforcement action, the Commission issues a complaint. The Commission's complaint that a Commission rule has been violated is then prosecuted by the Commission and adjudicated by the Commission. This Commission adjudication can either take place before the full Commission or before a semi-autonomous Commission administrative law judge. If

the Commission chooses to adjudicate before an administrative law judge rather than before the Commission and the decision is adverse to the Commission, the Commission can appeal to the Commission. If the Commission ultimately finds a violation, then, and only then, the affected private party can appeal to an Article III court. But the agency decision, even before the bona fide Article III tribunal, possesses a very strong presumption of correctness on matters both of fact and of law.

And just as the Fourth Branch strips power from the legislative and judicial branches, it serves to undermine the authority of the president as well. President Harry Truman said, "I thought I was the president, but when it comes to these bureaucrats, I can't do a damn thing."[4] And how could he, when such a small slice of federal positions are filled by executive appointees. Especially since these appointees serve for as few as two to as many as seven years?

The power of presidential appointees is further weakened by the very time-consuming process of finding them, getting them through the White House selection process and the FBI clearance, and then getting them through the Senate confirmation process. There are presidential appointee positions which have been vacant for well over a year and a half. If a frustrated nominee withdraws, the vacancy remains until another person can go through the same vetting process. When K.T. McFarland concluded the Senate Democrats would never allow her to become ambassador to Singapore, she withdrew. The job had already been open for 13 months. Now, the White House will have to find a new candidate and go through the same process. At the earliest, Singapore will see a new American ambassador only after an 18-month vacancy.

Even when people are confirmed, they often find the long

hours, the limited pay (most presidential appointees are taking a pay cut to serve their country, some are losing millions of dollars in order to be helpful citizens), the frustration with the red tape, the exhaustion from interagency fighting, the constant struggle with the White House staff, all lead to a very short retention. On average, appointees serve for two and a half years, while a quarter stay on fewer than 18 months.[5]

Given this constant churning and long periods of vacancy it is little wonder the Pentagon term for the presidential appointees is "the summer help."

This process strengthens the permanent state and weakens the ability of the American people to insist on change through the election process.

THE CONSTITUTIONAL MODEL

Allowing the bureaucracy to undermine the three branches of government directly contradicts the system of checks and balances that were put in place by our Founders. They were concerned primarily with ensuring individual liberty, peace, and prosperity through limited government made up of three co-equal branches, which could be held accountable to the American people.

Laws were to derive from the elected legislative branch—not agencies. Most importantly, the Founders believed that the American government could not rule without the consent of the governed.

Nowhere in the Constitution does it call for a fourth branch of government comprised of unelected bureaucrats.

As the late Justice Antonin Scalia has written, "Too many important decisions of the Federal Government are made nowadays by unelected agency officials…rather than by the people's representatives in Congress."[6]

Even liberal Justice Stephen Breyer acknowledged, "[T]he

public now relies more heavily on courts to ensure the fairness and rationality of agency decisions."[7]

This fact is fundamentally antithetical to the constitutional model of our government and gives bureaucrats control of the destiny and future of our country.

This is exactly what James Madison warned against in "Federalist No. 47" when he wrote, "The accumulation of all powers, legislative, executive, and judiciary, in the same hands, whether of one, a few, or many, and whether hereditary, self-appointed, or elective, may just be pronounced the very definition of tyranny."[8]

The threat of tyranny and unchecked, opaque power that is unconstitutionally vested in the bureaucracy threatens the well-being of our nation. It will lead to nothing but abuse and inevitable corruption.

THE FAILURE OF THE BUREAUCRACY

Another gem from *Yes, Minister* illustrates a quality that entrenched bureaucrats also use to their advantage—the ability to hide their mistakes.

As the top bureaucrats are sitting in an opulent room discussing their plans to undermine the new minister's goal to make government more open, one of them points out, "If people don't know what you're doing, they don't know what you're doing wrong."

Unfortunately, prior to the election of President Trump, this perfectly described the American bureaucratic system.

Consider the Department of Veterans Affairs (VA) scandal that broke in 2014. Were it not for whistleblowers who uncovered blatant neglect shown toward our nation's heroes by a system charged with providing them the health care they need and deserve, many more veterans would have suffered.

Unreasonably long wait times and false record-keeping by VA officials at facilities across the country resulted in thousands of veterans not receiving the vital care they needed. Shockingly,

1,700 veterans were specifically kept on waiting lists and waited an average of 115 days for an initial primary care appointment at a VA medical center in Phoenix.[9]

The *National Review* published an article in 2016 that outlined that despite two years of hearings, investigations, testimonies, and increases of funding, conditions had not improved for veterans seeking treatment since the scandal broke.[10]

The *National Review* reported that wait times for care had even increased in some places and records of these wait times had continued to be manipulated. The article cites the wait times for those applying for disability claims had stayed at an average of 389 days for first-time applicants. The figure was more than 770 days for applicants in Baltimore and 630 days for those in Boston.

Backlogged disability claims had declined in number, but the number of backlogged appeals claims at the time the article was published was more than 255,000. Many of these veterans had sadly been waiting for their health issues to be addressed for more than three years.

Further, the article asserts that those responsible for the despicable treatment of our country's heroes were not being adequately held accountable for their unjustifiable behavior and the irreparable damage they caused.

According to the *National Review*:

Efforts to hold negligent or dishonest—sometimes even criminal—VA officials accountable have also met a brick wall. VA accountability rules aimed at senior managers were part of the same 2014 legislation [Veterans Access, Choice, and Accountability Act], but less than a handful of VA officials have actually been fired. The VA refuses to use this and other accountability tools, even against officials who defrauded the department of hundreds of thousands of dollars. Unsurprisingly, top VA officials and their Beltway enablers are opposed to stronger accountability legislation, which remains stalled in the Senate. Perhaps worst of all, the whistleblowers who exposed the scandal in the first place continue to be marginalized, targeted, and even spied on, as the *Washington Examiner* reported in January this year.[11]

It is nothing short of unfathomable as to why these VA administrators were not being properly held accountable for their actions under President Obama.

In fact, the *Washington Post* exposed how far the bureaucracy went to protect its members from repercussions. According to one *Post* article:

> More than 2,500 employees at the Department of Veterans Affairs were placed on paid leave for at least a month [in 2014], and the agency acknowledges it didn't track the details and why they were sent home.…
>
> The total tab in salary alone for these absences—ranging from 30 days to more than a year for 46 employees—came to $23 million, according to a report provided to several congressional Republicans.[12]

And this was just one example.

USA Today reported that Sharron Helman, the Phoenix VA Health Care System director during the wait times scandal, was on paid leave for six months.[13]

Also, Lance Robinson, associate director at the Phoenix VA hospital, was put on paid leave for 19 months after the scandal broke, then got put back to work[14] for two months before being given a termination notice in 2016.[15]

According to the Daily Caller, David Houlihan, a doctor and chief of staff at the Tomah VA known as the "Candy Man," was on paid leave for 10 months during an investigation into drugging veterans with massive amounts and dangerous combinations of opioid painkillers.[16] He eventually surrendered his medical license to avoid further investigation into his activities.

Finally, the *Clarion Ledger* wrote that Jose Bejar, a neurologist at the Topeka, Kansas, VA, received more than $330,000 while on paid leave for two years after five women accused him of sexual misconduct. He finally pleaded no contest to the charges.[17]

It is surprisingly difficult to discipline, or even to terminate, these members of the bureaucracy. The bureaucracy is currently entitled to lengthy and expensive appeals processes, during which employees receive their salaries. President Trump has been working to empower his cabinet members with more authority to discipline bad employees, and he has already seen some success.

This utter public failure of the VA was horrible, but it served an important purpose in exposing the corrupt bureaucracy. The 2016 Forrester Research Customer Experience Index found the federal government was ranked last by survey respondents out of 21 major industries. In fact, of the 319 brands tested, 5 out of the 8 of the worst performing brands were run by the federal government.[18] And according to Pew, just 20 percent of Americans believe that government programs are "well run."[19]

This failure of the bureaucracy proved to be a big motivator for Americans in the 2016 election, and Donald Trump seemed to be the only candidate truly willing to take on the swamp.

TRUMPING THE BUREAUCRATS AND DRAINING THE SWAMP

Indeed, President Trump has been working to strike at the heart of the bureaucracy and counteract the wrongdoing and corruption that has been allowed to fester throughout the Washington swamp.

First, the president has appointed judges who will uphold

the rule of law and provide a much-needed check on the bureaucracy's rogue attempts to sidestep the Constitution.

He has also put in place serious reformers like VA Secretary David Shulkin, who has already overseen tremendous improvements in care at VA hospitals and clinics.

In June 2017, President Trump signed the Department of Veterans Affairs Accountability and Whistleblower Protection Act[20] as a positive step toward helping Secretary Shulkin in reforming the VA. According to the Government Executive, this "law will give VA Secretary David Shulkin the authority to fire any employee, lower the threshold to prove the action was justified and expedite the appeal process. Trump said it would help [the] VA remove employees involved in recent scandals involving waitlists and patient data manipulation."[21]

More specifically:

> The bill would allow the department's secretary to fire, suspend or demote an employee with only 15 days' notice. Employees would be able to appeal to the Merit Systems Protection Board in an expedited timeframe. MSPB would have 180 days to issue a decision, with the law designed to make it easier for VA to prove a negative personnel action was warranted. Employees would maintain the right to appeal an MSPB decision to federal court.
>
> Unionized and Senior Executive Service employees would each have distinct, internal grievance processes that would have to be completed within 21 days. VA could revoke bonuses from employees found to have engaged in misconduct or poor performance prior to the award and dock retirement benefits from workers found guilty of a felony that could have affected their work.[22]

The appointment of Office of Management and Budget Director Mick Mulvaney, who is committed to bringing bureaucracies under control, was also a critical step in reigning in the bureaucracy. Importantly, Mulvaney is also serving as acting director of the previously out-of-control Consumer Finance Protection Bureau, which I discussed previously.

At his first State of the Union Address on January 30, 2018, President Trump called on Congress to change the laws that protect federal employees who do not do their jobs, saying:

> I call on Congress to empower every cabinet secretary with the authority to reward good workings and to remove federal employees who undermine the public trust or fail the American people.

This is important because there is only so much the president can do on his own. Congress must enact serious civil service reform by getting rid of the protective language the bureaucracy has been able to weave into our laws.

President Trump and the Republican Congress have made historic strides toward giving American citizens the open, honest, fair, accountable, and lawful government that they deserve. However, there is still much more to be done.

As Inez Feltscher Stepman with the Federalist pointed out on January 31, 2018, "in November 2016, Washington was abuzz with talk of 'landing teams,' as though transitioning from a Democratic administration to a Republican one was akin to landing at Omaha Beach. After Trump's election, bureaucratic employees in the executive branch openly declared their intention to 'resist' by undermining his policies."[23]

This is what President Trump is facing—a bureaucracy that is prepared to fight a war. We have to make sure the bureaucrats lose.

CHAPTER THIRTEEN

LET'S TRUMP ADDICTION

On October 15, 2016, then candidate Donald Trump stepped onto a stage in Portsmouth, New Hampshire, to address a state ravaged by opioid addiction. It proved to be one of the defining moments of his campaign.

New Hampshire has been one of the states hardest hit by the nationwide opioid epidemic. When Trump visited, the state had lost nearly 500 people in 2016 alone to opioid overdose. Families were being torn apart, and the suffering was enormous. The state's leadership, public health officials, and first responders were grappling with how to deal with this growing crisis.

In front of more than 2,000 granite staters, Trump noted, "Recovery medications have the potential to save thousands and thousands of lives. We prescribe opioids like OxyContin freely, but when patients become addicted to those drugs, we stop doctors from giving patients the treatments they medically need."

This direct acknowledgment of a clear problem was textbook Trump.

In 2016, most of the country was affected by the opioid crisis, and the response from the Obama administration—as well as virtually every candidate for office, save for Trump—was lacking in fundamental ways. The Obama White House knew the scope of the crisis at hand but lacked the will and energy to address it head on.

The Obama administration passed the problem to the Surgeon General. The outcome—one more government report was issued in October of an election year. This was not exactly meeting urgency with urgency.

By contrast, Trump's intentional effort to face the opioid epidemic directly led to his wide support in counties with the highest rates of opioid overdose deaths. This was a remarkable aspect of the 2016 race because these counties had previously been carried by Democrats or carried with a much lower percent by Romney in the 2012 election. Some have dubbed these election deciders the oxy-electorate.

The opioid crisis in their communities was just another reason they felt forgotten by the Obama administration and Democrats for the previous eight years. It compounded frustrations caused when high-paying manufacturing and mining jobs were replaced by lower-wage service jobs. These are the communities where "Make America Great Again" was not just a mantra but a daily prayer.

President Trump did not forget them.

One year after Trump's New Hampshire speech, he and First Lady Melania Trump brought the weight of the White House to the crisis. The First Family jointly addressed the country from the East Room with advocates, members of Congress, and families of those suffering through this crisis in attendance. The First Lady clearly expressed the wide reach this crisis has had, saying:

> Drug addiction can take your friends, neighbors, or your family. No state has been spared, and no demographic has been untouched, which is why my husband

and this administration has dedicated itself to combating this health crisis by using every resource available.

It was here that President Trump then outlined his bold agenda to expand treatment to evidence-based medicine, break down outdated barriers to treatment, and initiate a massive public awareness campaign. He declared the epidemic a nationwide public health emergency.

Unlike his predecessor, Trump didn't stop with words.

In Trump's first 100 days as president, the Department of Health and Human Services (HHS) initiated a new plan for fighting the opioid crisis. Shortly after that, President Trump handpicked New Jersey Governor Chris Christie to lead the Commission on Combating Drug Addiction and the Opioid Crisis.

The Commission was instructed to outline what the federal response to the opioid crisis should involve—from parity enforcement to expanded use of medication-assisted treatments.

To be sure, this problem is far from solved. However, President Trump has undeniably done more in his first year to address this crisis than President Obama did in eight—as the epidemic exploded under his watch.

However, the president cannot do this on his own. Trumping the opioid crisis is going to take a truly bipartisan American spirit to work at the speed this crisis—and the loss of American lives—requires. This is why I've joined with former congressman and addiction survivor Patrick Kennedy and criminal justice reformer Van Jones to form Advocates for Opioid Recovery (opioidrecovery.org).

THE GATHERING STORM IN AMERICA

Before the 1990s, the use of prescription opioids was sparse, episodic, and mostly limited to clinical settings. But when new, highly addictive, easy-to-use drugs like oxycodone came to the market, America was a prime target.

"Physicians and medical professionals were bombarded with advertisements and educational materials that touted opioid-based treatments." Doctors, under pressure to treat pain more seriously, bought into the messaging and prescribed opioids in massive amounts.

Peaking in 2012, U.S. physicians wrote 255 million prescriptions for opioid painkillers—enough to give a bottle of pills to every adult in the country.[1] The United States now leads the world in opioid consumption. As a point of comparison, Americans are prescribed about six times as many opioids per capita as the French or Portuguese.

As a result, the overdose and opioid addiction epidemic is disproportionately American. A recent United Nations report indicated America makes up roughly 4 percent of the world's population but accounts for 27 percent of the world's drug overdose deaths.[2] Opioids are driving this statistic.

Here are some other grim facts being driven by opioid abuse:

- On average, 175 Americans die every day from overdoses;
- A person dies every eight minutes from an opioid addiction;
- Overdoses kill more people than gun violence or car crashes;
- In 2017, more people died of an unintentional drug overdose than in the entire 20-year Vietnam War conflict.[3]

This is an absolute crisis. And it is in danger of becoming worse.

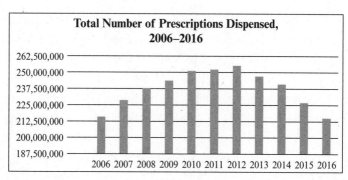

From the Center for Disease Control and Prevention Prescribing Rates[4]

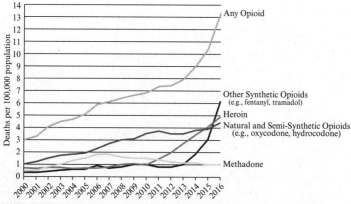

SOURCE: CDC/NCHS, National Vital Statistics System, Mortality. CDC WONDER, Atlanta, GA: US Department of Health and Human Services, CDC; 2016. https://wonder.cdc.gov/.

New types of opioid drugs are finding their way onto our streets. Fentanyl, a synthetic version of heroin, is among the worst offenders. At 100 times the potency of morphine or heroin, a dose of fentanyl the size of a grain of salt can kill a person.[5,6] As a result, the death rate from synthetic opioids (including fentanyl) increased dramatically in 2015.

China has played a significant role in causing fentanyl and other synthetic opioids to become commonplace. Chinese exporters are finding ways to mail them into the United States directly and through Canada and Mexico. Some efforts have been made to cooperate with U.S. authorities[7] to shut down the imports, but President Trump should apply serious trade pressure on Chinese President Xi Jinping to cut this industry off at its knees. It's time we communicate with President Xi in the economic terms he understands.

THE MEDICAID PROBLEM

Another contributing factor to the epidemic are the loopholes in our own health care systems.

A recent report by U.S. Senator Ron Johnson (R-WI), chairman of the Senate Homeland Security and Governmental Affairs Committee, showed that low patient cost sharing from Medicaid have played an unintentional role in driving the opioid crisis.[8] For some opioids, such as oxycodone, the Medicaid beneficiary co-pay is $1 for 240 pills. Meanwhile, the street value for those pills could be $4,000 or more.

For some cash-strapped Medicaid beneficiaries, the temptation to defraud the system by presenting phantom pain to multiple doctors, gathering the pills, and selling them on the street is just too much to resist. Enterprising criminals also quickly organize beneficiaries to do their bidding.

We know Medicaid is a factor because this problem has been spreading more rapidly in states that extended their Medicaid programs. The committee report sites internal HHS data, which indicates that between 2013 and 2015, death rates due to drug overdoses rose nearly twice as fast in Medicaid expansion states than in states that did not expand Medicaid. This is supported by Centers for Disease Control and Prevention (CDC) data, which shows in 2015 the five states with the highest rates of overdose deaths were all Medicaid expansion states: West Virginia, New Hampshire, Kentucky, Ohio, and Rhode Island.

Government agencies must crack down on health care fraud. The Trump administration must find and deal with all who are trying to profit from this system at the cost of American lives.

And fraud is not Medicaid's only problem.

Outdated laws make it nearly impossible for residential treatment facilities with more than 16 beds to treat Medicaid patients for opioid addiction. This law, the Medicaid Institutions for Mental Diseases exclusion, has been part of the Medicaid program since its creation in 1965. This exclusion was meant to favor community-based care and protect mental health patients from overcrowded and under-resourced facilities, but it has become an artificial barrier keeping Medicaid patients from getting treatment at these facilities.

President Trump boldly announced his administration's intent to overcome this troubling exclusion and is using executive authority through a waiver program to do just that. However, Congress must provide a permanent legislative solution.

OPIOID ADDICTION IS UNIQUE

The American health care system has always given mental health a lower priority than physical health. Some progress has been made, but mental health remains undertreated and brain science is still underfunded and underappreciated.

This poses serious challenges for dealing with opioid addiction since it is a mental illness.

Most people living with addiction are not receiving any medical treatment. Even many of those who are getting treated are not receiving the most effective care. Only about one in ten people with a substance use disorder receive any type of treatment.[9]

Worse, our current system for opioid addiction treatment is antiquated. It uses old information and perceptions about addiction and treatments. Furthermore, it doesn't take into account that opioid addiction is unique.

Behavioral approaches like traditional therapy and abstinence-based rehabilitation are indeed successful options for many types of addiction and can be part of the solution for this crisis.

For people living with opioid addiction, however, abstinence-only and talk therapy often fails and can be deadly. Opioid misuse, even for a short time, changes the brain's chemistry. When a patient tries to stop using opioids, the body starts the withdrawal process.

If the individual later relapses and attempts to take the same dose of opioids he or she is used to, the brain often can't handle it, the body shuts down from the overdose, and the person dies. In fact, a person is more likely to overdose and die after going to an abstinence-only, in-patient rehabilitation center than if they never sought treatment at all.

Even if they do not overdose, 80 percent or more of those in traditional treatment for addiction relapse.[10]

Despite these crushing facts, the United States still pours resources into abstinence-only rehabilitation and expects a different result. This not only fits the definition of insanity—it is deadly.

MEDICATION-ASSISTED TREATMENT, FIGHTING BIAS

There is a better way. The research is unequivocal that behavioral therapy combined with recovery medications, such as methadone, buprenorphine, and Suboxone, is the most effective way to treat opioid addiction.

Evidence shows this combination of treatment can cut the mortality rate among addiction patients by half or more.[11] It also leads to improved health and functioning. Behavioral therapy helps people develop support systems and coping mechanisms to stay on their road to recovery. At the same time, opioid recovery medications help patients better weather the withdrawal process and curb cravings.

The effectiveness of medication-assisted treatment is supported by the World Health Organization, the United Nations Office on Drug Policy, the CDC, the National Institute on Drug Abuse, and the American Society of Addiction Medicine. However, only 41 percent of treatment programs offer any kind of medication-assisted treatments. Even if such treatments are offered, many patients don't receive the medications.

Shockingly, fewer than 3 percent of treatment programs offer all three of the medications available to help fight opioid addiction.[12] This is a problem because each of the three recovery medications in the market has its own benefits and drawbacks. There is not a one-size-fits-all opioid addiction medication.

Breaking down barriers that keep medication-assisted treatment away from patients will save lives.

Imagine if our health care system told a heart attack survivor that talk therapy and exercise was their only medical option to prevent a second heart attack. What if insurance companies did not cover insulin for diabetics until a patient experienced a diabetic-induced coma at least twice? These situations would be absurd, illegal, and unethical. Yet, this is how the health system treats most people with opioid addiction in the United States today.

People suffering from addiction are frequently denied medicine that would help them cope with and eventually conquer their addictions. And many insurance companies do not cover opioid recovery medications until someone has overdosed multiple times.

These barriers exist for various reasons, but a main one is simple bias.

Stigma around addiction and the belief that someone can "will themselves out of it" keeps our society trapped in a vicious, deadly, wasteful cycle of relapse and overdose.

This bias exists at the highest levels of public and private bureaucracy and continues to shape insurance coverage, dictate policy, and perpetuate regulations not based on evidence.

Widespread bias even exists in the recovery and medical community itself. Faith-based and abstinence-only programs—such as Alcoholics Anonymous—have helped millions of people, including many close personal friends of mine. However, opioid addiction and alcohol addiction are fundamentally different.

Proponents of abstinence-only support group programs believe them to be the only legitimate way to treat opioid addiction. To them, the use of a recovery medication is just "replacing one drug with another." Tragically, patients getting medication-assisted treatment would not be welcome in these support groups, if they were honest about their treatments.

Imagine being an opioid-addicted patient in the early days of recovery. While you are battling the disease minute by minute, you build up the courage to attend your first support group meeting. After standing up and discussing your treatment plan (which includes a recovery medication), the leadership tells you that you are really not in recovery at all because you are getting medication-assisted treatment—essentially cheating.

At this critical time when peer support and encouragement are most needed, you feel shame, embarrassment, and confusion. This is no way to help someone who is suffering from opioid addiction.

Widespread bias isn't the only major barrier to curing opioid addiction today. Our own rules are in the way.

Currently, any health care provider can prescribe an opioid for pain management, but when it comes to prescribing two of the three opioid recovery medications that exist, special circumstances and training requirements must be met. These requirements are contributing to the massive shortage of medication-assisted treatment providers.

For example, a law passed by Congress in 2000 (known as DATA-2000) forced health care providers to pass an eight-hour course and meet other qualifications to be granted a special waiver to treat people battling opioid addiction with buprenorphine. Congress's rationale was that because buprenorphine was opioid-based, it needed to be closely monitored to ensure it would not be used for unintended illegal use, which law enforcement refers to as diversion.

Think about this: Buprenorphine—which is designed to help get people off of opioids—is held to a stricter standard than the multitude of pain management opioids that have an unlimited capacity for abuse and helped cause this epidemic.

Furthermore, this law arbitrarily capped the number of patients that physicians can treat at any one time. The Obama administration did raise the cap from 100 to 275 in 2016, and the Republican-controlled Congress extended the eligible prescribers to include nurse practitioners and physician assistants through 2021. However nonphysician providers still have a 100-patient cap.

Fundamentally, this cap makes no sense. No other medications have such restrictions—including the pain management opioid prescriptions that have helped cause this problem.

Our rules also keep methadone—the oldest, most researched, and most inexpensive recovery drug—out of the hands of most patients. It must be administered in federally regulated facilities called opioid treatment programs. Patients must visit their opioid treatment program for a daily dose. This daily disruption to their family and work routine puts this option out of reach for many people with opioid addiction. The facilities are often too far away

242

242 CHALLENGES

to visit for patients to maintain their jobs, or they cannot find transportation. Again, the current situation is absurd. Methadone can be prescribed for home use to treat pain, but when used for addiction treatment, it needs special oversight and more stringent regulatory control.

TRUMPING ADDICTION WITH MEDICATION-ASSISTED TREATMENT

The unintended consequences of these well-intentioned, but misguided, policies are significant. The current treatment capacity falls far short of the number of Americans suffering from substance use disorders.

For example, 60 percent of rural counties in America lack physicians who have DATA-2000 waivers to prescribe buprenorphine. The same is true for more than a quarter of urban counties.

Even in areas that appear to have providers able to prescribe medication-assisted treatments, some providers are at capacity and other providers are not treating for various reasons—one being that doctors doubt patients have access to the behavioral counseling and social support necessary for successful recovery.[13]

Similarly, there are simply not enough opioid treatment programs in the United States. Although there has been a 26 percent increase in the number of opioid treatment facilities from 2003 to 2015 and a nearly 60 percent increase in the number of patients being treated,[14] the opioid overdose death numbers have grown more than 250 percent in the same time frame. Clearly, we are still badly under-resourced.[15]

We would never consider keeping proven medications away from patients suffering from diabetes or cancer. There is no reason we should cap the number of people who can be helped with opioid recovery medications. President Trump and Republicans must act swiftly to end treatment caps for physicians, physician assistants, and nurse practitioners who are authorized to treat opioid addiction with medication.

The administration should also work to make treatment available to those in underserved areas through technology.

With too few licensed clinics and too few doctors with medication-assisted treatment waivers, rural communities face the highest barriers for access to treatment.

Telemedicine could help us immediately close part of this gap.

Telemedicine, also referred to as telehealth, allows people to consult their doctors remotely through videoconferencing or other technologies. Federal agencies should review and revise regulations and reimbursement policies to make telemedicine more available for opioid addiction treatment.

At the same time, we should offer incentives for providers to use the technology. While telemedicine has limitations, the greater availability and advancement of this kind of technology has the potential to expand access to care.

THE PARITY PROBLEM

When I was Speaker of the House, we took the first step toward mental health equality in passing the Mental Health Parity Act of 1996.[16] It was improved upon in 2008 with the Paul Wellstone and Pete Domenici Mental Health Parity and Addiction Equity Act, which sought to ensure that insurance companies cover treatments for mental illness and addiction the same as they would treatments for physical ailments.

Under this law, a patient provided unlimited doctor visits for a chronic condition like diabetes would also be offered unlimited visits for a mental health condition such as depression or schizophrenia.

Lack of insurance parity is contributing to the opioid epidemic by limiting access to both medications and providers.

Each of the three recovery medications in the market have varying degrees of availability.

Many insurance plans don't cover all three medications. Additionally, some plans that do cover all three impose dangerous fail-first protocols, onerous and frequent prior authorization requirements, and dosage and lifetime limits.

When it comes to the opioid epidemic and enforcing insurance parity, the first step President Trump and Republicans should take is to fix the government-sponsored health plans Americans pay for.

Take Medicare for example:

Medicare, the insurance program for America's seniors, is the largest single health insurance program in the country. Despite the clear public health endorsement of medication-assisted treatment, Medicare does not cover all three recovery medications.

Individuals who have successfully stayed in recovery with methadone reach the age of 65 and panic that they cannot continue their treatment. This is more common than you would think.

According to data from the CDC's National Health and Nutrition Examination Survey, nearly four in ten people above age 65 use five or more prescriptions,[17] which increases the risk of drug misuse or abuse.[18]

In 2016, one out of every three Medicare beneficiaries received at least one prescription opioid through Medicare Part D, but Part D does not cover all three of the recovery medications.

Strangely, methadone, the cheapest of the three, is not paid for by Medicare for opioid addiction recovery—only as a pain treatment. It has fallen through the cracks of the bureaucracy—a victim of the siloed Medicare billing system. It can't be covered as a recovery drug under Part D because you can't get it at the pharmacy.

. Further, it is not covered in Medicare Part B because it is administered through outpatient opioid treatment program (OTP) centers, and Part B only covers inpatient drugs.

This system's failure means that Americans who may have been treated at an OTP for years are forced to switch to more expensive medication and lose the OTP services when they are Medicare eligible. It's nonsensical and destructive.

Considering that insurance coverage parity is the law of the land and the administration and every major public health organization supports medication-assisted treatment, it is shocking that Medicare does not cover these treatments. The oversight is so irrational and the solution so undeniable that fixing this disparity will be a litmus test on the seriousness of any effort to combat this epidemic.

Congress should review Medicare, Medicaid, Veterans Health, the Military Health System, the Indian Health Program, and the Federal Employee Health Benefits Program. They should modify policies to ensure that these insurance programs support access to all three recovery medications and are using evidence-based treatment guidelines.

Additionally, every governor should audit his or her Medicaid program to see if it provides for meaningful medication-assisted treatment coverage for all three medications. Aggressive clinical management practices such as arduous prior authorizations, and dosage and lifetime limits may make sense for insurance actuaries and bureaucrats, but they have no place in a serious response to solving this crisis.

The Trump administration should also enforce parity in reimbursement rates by insurance companies.

Millikan, Inc., published a report that was released by a

group of American's top mental health and addiction treatment organizations in December 2017. The report found that insurance companies in 46 states have been paying physical health care providers about 20 percent better than they were paying addiction and mental health providers for the same types of services. In many states, the disparities in payment rates were two to three times greater.[19] Additionally, the report showed people seeking addiction and mental health treatment had to use "out-of-network" providers far more often than patients seeking treatments for physical ailments. This results in higher costs to patients and indicates the networks are much narrower for addiction treatment services.

Existing addiction and mental health care providers won't stay in business very long if they don't get properly paid for their work. This will put treatment further out of reach for those battling opioid addiction.

A key recommendation by President Trump's Commission on Combating Drug Addiction and the Opioid Crisis was to fully enforce the parity law. President Trump should ensure the Department of Labor has real authority and resources to enforce this law, audit violators, and impose fines.

DECRIMINALIZE ADDICTION: MORE PATIENTS, FEWER PRISONERS

According to the Surgeon General's report, substance use disorder costs the country $442 billion annually in health care costs, criminal justice spending, and lost productivity.[20]

The criminal justice system is often the first institution to encounter those suffering from addiction. As a result, jails have become warehouses for those struggling with mental illness and substance use disorders.

To relieve prison populations and keep people with addictions or mental illness out of jail, we should invest more in treatment courts and ensure they are using evidence-based treatments. These courts are already profoundly successful in some states for combating addiction and keeping jail populations low. These courts offer people in need of long-term help a far better option than incarceration and can help them find the best treatment programs. These programs also provide people with addictions or mental illness a path of accountability, compassion, and assistance in getting the treatment they need.

Georgia Governor Nathan Deal has achieved tremendous success using treatment courts to help people with drug addictions stay out of jail and get the help they need.

As the *Atlanta Journal-Constitution* (AJC) reported on January 25, 2018, Governor Deal's focus on treatment courts, along with a lowered crime rate and a legislative push to adjust the state's property crime laws, have made a significant impact.[21]

The overall incarceration rate has dropped by 19 percent in the last eight years—and the incarceration rate for African Americans in Georgia has fallen by 30 percent to the "lowest level in decades," according to the AJC.

However, medication-assisted treatment is only used in half of drug courts operating around the country. This means that these jurisdictions are wasting money. Diversion programs favor evidence-based treatment over incarceration save more than $2 for every dollar spent.[22]

Courts that do not support medication-assisted treatments often cite the potential for diversion. However, if these courts are properly funded and staffed, they could easily put accountability measures in place and support evidence-based treatments.

The criminal justice system can hold people accountable for their actions, but it can also help them become productive and healthy members of society. Isn't that the point of a corrections system?

DOLLARS AND SENSE

The opioid epidemic is larger and more devastating than any natural disaster we have seen. Leaders have a moral imperative to help solve it.

When Hurricane Harvey hit, $15 billion was quickly approved in the weeks to follow. Yet, Congress has only allotted $1 billion over two years to combat the opioid crisis. This is not enough. For those who are unmoved by the moral argument, it also makes economic sense to invest in fighting this epidemic. Every dollar we invest saves money:

- $1 for brief primary care addiction intervention saves $27 across the system;
- $1 for addiction intervening at a hospital saves over $36, or $9 in the emergency room;
- $1 for treating substance abuse saves $4 in overall health care costs, and $7 in criminal justice costs by preventing the cycle of recidivism that often accompanies addiction.[23]

As current funding is appropriated and new funding is granted, Congress should ensure the funding is going toward evidence-based treatments. This will help ensure taxpayer money is being spent on treatments that work.

Now, to summarize:

Addiction is not a moral failing or a lack of strong will. It is not a choice, it is a disease.

No healthy person would willingly put themselves and their families through the horror and destruction caused by opioid addiction.

If opioid addiction wasn't such a stigmatized illness, immediate action would be taken to address this clear public health emergency. Instead, many of our policies and programs have been based on the flawed stigma.

This must change.

Americans seeking treatment should be supported for their efforts, not shamed and dismissed.

Real, evidence-based treatments must become more widely available, or the death toll will continue to rise. If we fail, people all over the world will look back in 10 years and say a generation of Americans died because their fellow Americans refused to help them.

That America would be far from great.

CHAPTER FOURTEEN

HELPING AMERICANS RETURN TO WORK

The keys to reaching President Trump's goal of a sustained 3 to 4 percent economic growth are for the United States to dramatically ramp up its productivity and expand its workforce.

Through the passage of the Tax Cuts and Jobs Act and the administration's massive deregulation efforts, President Trump and Republicans have already laid the groundwork for companies to be able to expand and create more jobs. A vital second step will be passing a significant infrastructure bill that will create jobs at nearly every skill level in virtually every state and infuse local communities with commerce.

However, unemployment is already at 4.1 percent—a 17-year low. This is certainly a good thing, but it creates a key hurdle for boosting productivity. To fill all the jobs that the Trump economy is creating, we need an ample supply of Americans willing and able to work. And as new technology and new productivity tools become available, we will need a lot of retraining for the workforce to achieve its full potential.

President Trump, as someone who has employed thousands of people in a wide range of jobs, thoroughly understands the importance of job training and vocational education. President Trump combines a desire to get everyone working with a clear understanding that we need dramatically better vocational education and far more apprenticeship programs if we are to match up the workforce with emerging job opportunities. The men and women of Trump's America also seek a concerted policy shift across the entire American system, so it favors honest work over dependency and illegal economies.

This is radically different from the Obama-Left system. President Obama and his left-wing base were comfortable with the largest number of Americans in history being dependent on government. They viewed large enrollment in food stamps as a positive, not a negative. Getting more people dependent on Medicaid was a sign of progress to them.

President Trump and the men and women of Trump's America will only be comfortable when a booming economy has drawn the largest number of Americans possible out of dependence and into the workforce.

Those are diametrically opposed visions of how America should operate.

President Trump can break us out of the decay of the Obama-Left model, solve our workforce problems, and revamp our nation's infrastructure by pushing reforms and innovation on several tracks: removing hurdles for career and vocational training, reforming welfare, and fixing our broken criminal justice system.

WHY INFRASTRUCTURE NOW?

A large-scale infrastructure plan would create well-paying jobs in virtually every state in the Union. This would include jobs at every skill level. It would give relief to many Americans who have been looking for work—and provide an entry point for young Americans looking to start careers in construction, engineering, or other skilled trades. It would also make our economy more efficient and more competitive in the world market. The economic impact would be felt nationwide.

Critics of the president—and even some who generally support him—question whether we should focus on passing a large-scale infrastructure bill before we see more of the benefits from the tax cuts and deregulation efforts.

The first reason is simple: Our national infrastructure is already falling apart in many areas, and those bridges, locks, dams, and roadways are going to keep eroding regardless of whether it is politically convenient to fix them.

The American Society of Civil Engineers (ASCE) gave America's infrastructure a D+ in 2017.[1]

According to the ASCE, 40 percent of our 614,387 bridges are 50 years old or older. In 2016, 56,007 were found to be structurally deficient, yet, on average, they were still crossed by traffic 188 times a day. The current backlog of work to fix our bridges is estimated at $123 billion, according to ASCE.

On average, the 90,580 dams in the United States are 56 years old. Almost 15,500 of those dams have "high-hazard potential" and about 2,170 of those high-hazard dams are also deficient. What American wants their family to live or work near one of these more than 2,000 deficient dams?

Traffic delays on our nation's urban interstates cost the United States roughly $160 billion in 2014, according to ASCE, and one in five miles of our roadways nationwide are reportedly in poor condition. This is not just about dealing with bumps and potholes. Rundown roads are dangerous. According to the engineering association, traffic fatalities jumped by 7 percent from 2014 to 2015, up to 35,092 deaths.

As a final example, many of the one million miles of water pipes in our country were first laid in the 1950s. They are only meant to last 75 to 100 years, according to ASCE. After the catastrophe in Flint, Michigan, where thousands contracted lead poisoning from deteriorating pipes and insufficient filtration, we all know how devastating unsafe drinking water can be.

Frankly, Congress and past administrations have passed the buck on infrastructure for too long. Yes, fixing infrastructure is expensive. Yes, it doesn't get as much media attention as other more exciting issues. However, it is a lot cheaper to maintain infrastructure than to fix it when it breaks—and when it breaks, and people are hurt or killed, the media always looks to elected officials to find out why. "It was too expensive" and "it wasn't politically smart" are never acceptable answers.

President Trump and the Republican Congress should move to a major infrastructure plan now. It is an opportunity to show the American people that the Republican majority and the Republican White House can and will do what is necessary to keep America prosperous and safe.

Specifically, they should follow the model President Trump proposed in early February.[2] Trump's plan calls for leveraging $200 billion in federal dollars in order to generate $1.5 trillion worth of infrastructure investment. The plan would achieve this by making federal money available to state and local governments, which would match the dollars four to one by partnering with private investors. The main idea here is to give states, local governments, and industries more control over the infrastructure projects important to their communities.

President Trump's plan to get $1.5 trillion worth of results is totally different than the typical bureaucratic idea of having $1.5 trillion of taxpayers' money to spend. Instead, President Trump's program would divide the $200 billion in federal dollars into categories for important national projects, rural block grant programs, federal infrastructure loan programs, and other projects. Each category would then dispense money to state and local governments based on certain criteria that depended on what type of project was being built.

Not all of this matching money must come from governments. A significant share of funding for projects could also come from the private sector. President Trump can help states and local governments find these investors by leveraging his relationships with people in the private sector to create public–private partnerships on large infrastructure projects that benefit entire communities. The president's decision to go to the World Economic Forum in Davos in January 2018 was an excellent step toward maintaining and building those relationships and moving in this direction. I have spoken with leaders in Canada where this method has been put to the test. It is entirely possible that 10 to 20 percent of the investments for major infrastructure projects could come from private companies rather than government coffers.

In addition to restructuring how federal dollars are used, President Trump's plan also calls for dramatically streamlining the federal process for approving infrastructure projects. The goal is to cut the time it takes for issuing a permit to no more than two years. In some cases, federal permitting currently can take up to a decade. As I described in an earlier chapter, the administration has already made great strides in this area and will continue to do so. As a lifelong builder, President Trump understands how burdensome regulations can slow down projects and increase costs. When work gets delayed by regulations or hiccups in the bureaucratic process, companies either have to pay workers to do nothing or tell them to go home and rehire them later. This costs companies money—but it also puts tremendous economic uncertainty and burdens on workers and their families.

Trump will direct his agencies to specifically look for regulations that slow down large infrastructure projects and either streamline them or get rid of them. This includes onerous environmental regulations, expensive or burdensome permitting rules, and others that hinder work. Reducing the cost of compliance with regulations will provide an immediate savings for private-sector companies and state and local governments, which can dramatically reduce the final price tag for the infrastructure plan. President Trump should also consider including provisions to allow governors to waive some regulations. Governors such as Pete Wilson, Arnold Schwarzenegger, Mike Leavitt, Mitch Daniels, and John Kasich have already demonstrated that replacing the standard government model can save a lot of time and money.

All five of these governors have used emergency or executive powers in various ways to make sure large infrastructure projects in their states were completed on time and under budget. Many also created performance plans that incentivized private contractors to finish work on, or ahead of, schedule.

In fact, Governors Daniels and Kasich greatly reduced government involvement altogether to achieve goals for their states.

Daniels contracted with a private company to manage part of the state's interstate system and then used payments from that contract to fund other infrastructure projects. Governor Kasich was able to ignore federal rules by funding road improvements with state money from leasing state-owned liquor stores. In both cases, the result was more infrastructure, faster, for less money.

Finally, President Trump should also focus on projects that use twenty-first-century technology that will save money in the long run. Things which are as simple as switching street and highway lighting over to a hybrid system that combines solar power and traditional electricity to power LEDs, installing smart traffic and water management devices, and upgrading our electrical grid with more efficient systems can save tremendous amounts of money. Those savings can then be reinvested to continue the infrastructure improvements and create a virtuous cycle of savings and investment in infrastructure.

Politically speaking, the infrastructure bill will also put Democrats in yet another spot where they either have to vote with Republicans to improve America or explain to their constituents why their streets, bridges, dams, and ports were less important than partisan politics. This will be particularly difficult for Democrats who are up for reelection in states that President Trump won.

It's a win-win play.

BRIDGING THE SKILLS GAP

However, creating jobs does no good if there aren't Americans prepared to take them. President Trump's infrastructure plan also calls for prioritizing federal work study funding for job training.

For years, companies have noticed a skills gap in the American workforce. As experienced employees of a certain age retire, there are fewer Americans with comparable skills to replace them. At the same time, our education system has moved away from focusing on vocational and skilled trade programs. For instance, the Department of Labor reported in January 2018 that there were 5.9 million unfilled jobs in the United States. Many of those remain open because companies cannot find qualified workers to fill them. This is creating big problems for manufacturing and construction sectors—which will be critical to completing the work created by the infrastructure bill.

The Trump administration has already started work to close the skills gap by ending enforcement of the Obama-era Gainful Employment Rule, which I discussed previously. This is one step toward reversing the war Obama waged on private, for-profit institutions that offer needed vocational and career training in the United States.

The Obama administration fought tooth and nail to destroy the private vocational school industry. Under his reign, ITT Technical Institutes were shut down despite having trained American workers for more than 50 years. Roughly 40,000 students and 8,000 employees were left out to dry by Obama, according to a September 20, 2016, *Washington Post* editorial.

Just before Obama left office, the Department of Education also revoked accrediting authority from the Accrediting Council for Independent Colleges and Schools. This was devastating for private vocational schools—as well as career and job training nationwide.

President Trump has been working to undo much of the damage caused by the elitist Obama-era Education Department, which heavily prioritized college over the vocational training our workforce desperately needs.

In June 2017, President Trump also issued a significant executive order[3] aimed at rebuilding apprenticeship programs in the United States. The order directed the Labor Department to work with private companies, trade associations, and unions to establish broad vocational and job training programs through which Americans seeking to gain new skills can learn—and be paid—on the job.

At the same time, according to *U.S. News and World Report*, President Trump urged companies and schools (mainly high schools and community colleges) to work together to develop meaningful vocation training programs, so students who are not interested in college still learn applicable, marketable skills.

In the course of developing these new programs with the private sector, Trump's Labor Department is also reviewing and analyzing all 43 of the existing federal job training programs to weed out ineffective or duplicative programs that are wasting taxpayer dollars. According to *U.S. News and World Report*, these programs are spread across many parts of the federal government and currently account for $16.7 billion of the annual federal budget.

Focusing that money on programs that work could help train millions of Americans (young and old) with the skills they need to fill twenty-first-century jobs. The Higher Education Act will need to be renewed in 2018 or 2019. It would be a good opportunity to reorient our federal higher education focus toward skills training.

WELFARE REFORM

To achieve growth targets, President Trump, working with Congress, can also tap a large section of the workforce that is currently on the sidelines, trapped in a welfare system of dependency and idleness.

Consider these startling figures:

In the last 18 years, the number of Americans who receive food stamps, also known as Supplemental Nutrition Assistance Program (SNAP) benefits, ballooned from 17 million to 42 million.[4] For perspective, that exceeds the entire population of the state of California, which has 39 million people. It is also higher than the populations of all of Canada (36 million) and Australia (24 million).

In the same time frame, enrollment for Medicaid has also grown to 75 million people (more than two Canadas). Nearly one-fifth of the people in our country are drawing Medicaid benefits—this includes able-bodied adults. Most alarming: 52 percent of these working-age, capable Americans enrolled in the program do not work.[5]

We see a similar trend in our Social Security Disability program. The *Washington Post* reported in March 2017[6] that the number of working-age adults in the program almost doubled from 7.7 million to 13 million from 1996 to 2015. In a period when workplaces became safer, more people found ways to get on the disabilities program.

Now, these enrollment numbers are staggering, but the cost figures are devastating. Nationwide annual spending on the SNAP program is $70 billion.[7] Meanwhile, states on average devote about 30 percent of their budgets to funding bloated Medicaid programs. These programs are not sustainable or good for America. They are also harmful to the people they are meant to help. The Trump administration has thankfully returned to the Reagan-era belief that employment is always superior to welfare, and that the success of welfare programs should be measured by the number of people who get out of the system, rather than the number of people who become trapped in it.

President Trump and Republicans will greatly grow the American workforce by putting in place work requirements for many of these programs. We already know this works. A recent experiment in Maine led by then Health and Human Services Commissioner Mary Mayhew (who is now running for governor) showed the speed with which workforce participation could dramatically change.

Like many states, Maine had been allowing able-bodied adults without children to participate in its food stamp program. As a result, a high number of these able-bodied adults avoided work and simply depended on the taxpayers to take care of them.

When Mayhew instituted a strong work/study requirement to receive food stamps in the state, the program's rolls plummeted—and wages for those who used to be on food stamps soared.

In an interview Mayhew gave to *Forbes Magazine*,[8] the interviewer even commented that "a year after work requirements

for able-bodied adults who receive food stamps were put into
effect in October 2014...the number of able-bodied adults on
the program has fallen from 16,000 to 4,500." This represented
an almost 72 percent reduction in dependency in this population. According to *Forbes'* Jared Meyer, the 11,500 people who
reentered the workforce in Maine saw their incomes double on
average, which "more than offset the lost welfare benefits."

Mayhew responded by acknowledging that many lawmakers have approached welfare programs with backward thinking.

Policymakers often talk about the American dream, but
poorly designed welfare programs can trap people in a
nightmare of poverty and despair. Maine, like too many
other states, measured welfare programs' successes by
ever-increasing caseloads instead of by the number of
individuals who successfully transitioned off the programs by increasing their earnings....

We were up against fierce resistance while reestablishing work requirements for able-bodied, child-
less adults between the ages of 19 and 49. The work
requirements we instituted include working a minimum
of 20 hours per week, being in a vocational training program, or volunteering for about 24 hours per month.
Putting in place these common-sense requirements led
to an 88 percent drop in SNAP enrollment and a 114
percent spike in average wages, which more than offset
lost SNAP benefits. Kansas implemented similar policy
reforms and experienced the same positive results.

If the Mayhew model is applied nationwide, millions of
Americans who have been excluded from unemployment reports
for decades would suddenly move back into the workforce.

This is similar to the reforms we accomplished when I was

Speaker of the House. We included strong work requirements, time limits, and a host of other accountability measures to welfare programs that incentivized people to work rather than depend on the government. As a result, enrollment dropped by 60 percent as Americans who had been trapped in dependency rejoined the workforce. These families saw on average a 25 percent increase in their incomes and children were raised out of poverty at a record level.

However, the Obama administration diligently worked to undo many of our successful reforms. As a result, a lot more people are depending on the government. Most current welfare programs have no work requirement for able-bodied individuals. Also, there is no time limit for how long someone can benefit from subsidized housing, so there is never an incentive to make more money and exit the subsidized housing system.

So, in addition to his early actions to reverse Obama's push for more government dependency, President Trump has his work cut out for him.

Today, the United States has the lowest workforce percentage for men age 25 to 54 of any economically developed country except Italy.

This is alarming, and it is antithetical to the ideas on which America was founded. America was based on the idea that you could have big dreams, but you have to work to make them come true. All of the Founding Fathers thought work was absolutely essential to America's success, and all of them would be appalled at the number of people that are now dependent on the government—and the structure of the bureaucracy that encourages them to be dependent.

America was founded on the importance of the work ethic. If you work hard, study, and learn, you'll rise because you will have earned it. Those in Trump's America still believe this is the essential principle for success in America. The Left side of the anti-Trump coalition, however, would rather convince the public that work is unnecessary and that people should simply be dependent on the government for their daily needs. After all, in 2014 after the Congressional Budget Office found that Obamacare would greatly reduce work hours in America—to the tune of 2.5 million full-time jobs—Nancy Pelosi said it was a goal to help people "not be job-locked, but to follow their passion." Keep in mind, the jobless rate at the time was at 6.7 percent and 10.5 million Americans did not have jobs.[9] If Trump and the Republican Congress can implement sensible reforms to our national dependency programs, the American workforce will easily be able to sustain a 3 to 4 percent GDP.

CRIMINAL JUSTICE REFORM

The final piece of the puzzle for solving America's workforce problems (as well as helping solve a number of human and community problems) is through serious, thoughtful criminal justice reform. I discussed some of these ideas in the previous chapter dealing with the opioid epidemic, but they are useful for building the workforce as well.

First, the numbers: At the end of 2016, there were 1.51 million people locked up in state and federal prisons nationwide. This is far from normal. As Senator Rand Paul of Kentucky noted in March 2015, "Though only 5 percent of the world's population lives in the United States, it is home to 25 percent of the world's prison population.... Not only does the current overpopulated, underfunded system hurt those incarcerated, it also digs deeper into the pockets of taxpaying Americans."

Senator Paul is exactly right.

The most recent estimate from the Federal Bureau of Prisons indicates that it costs roughly $32,000 a year per prisoner to house these inmates. That comes out to more than $48 billion a year. And this estimate may be modest. The Prison Policy

Initiative[10] estimates the total cost to U.S. taxpayers for the U.S. prison system at every level is roughly $182 billion annually.

At the same time, according to the Bureau, roughly 15 percent of state prisoners are jailed for nonviolent drug offenses, while 47 percent of the federal inmates incarcerated are nonviolent drug offenders. Some of these prisoners may be drug dealers who should be dealt with strictly, but some are people with addictions who do not necessarily belong in prison.

Another significant portion of the incarcerated population suffers from some form of mental illness. We can't know for sure how large this subset is, as the Department of Justice Office of the Inspector General reported in July 2017 that, among other problems, the Bureau of Prison's "mental health staff do not always document inmates' mental disorders."

People who have drug addictions and mental illness don't need to be in prison—they need to be in treatment programs. If these Americans can get the help they need, some can overcome their personal hurdles and return to being productive members of society.

Finally, there are many other low-risk, nonviolent inmates who possibly deserved to be convicted for theft or other property crimes, but who have received overly harsh sentences. One thing we have learned from the 1980s, when the federal government started heavily utilizing mandatory minimum sentences, is that long sentences do not make Americans safer, nor do they help those who commit crimes change their lives.

In fact, research shows low-risk, nonviolent offenders who receive overly tough sentences often become more serious offenders later. This is partly because they spend a significant time in prison with serious criminals. When they are eventually released, these once low-risk offenders are often behind the times in terms of technology, applicable skills, and education. They have been schooled by hardened criminals rather than potential employers. For them, crime seems like a more lucrative and realistic career choice.

Had they instead received a sentence that more reasonably fit their crime, they might have been incarcerated for a shorter time, been able to participate in a work program, or been able to get a job and work off their debt to society while on probation.

For these reasons, I have been troubled by Attorney General Jeff Sessions's decisions to pursue harsh sentences for drug crimes and other nonviolent offenses. I appreciate Sessions's position. He is the attorney general and is responsible for seeing that our laws are enforced as they are written, but I don't think the steps he is taking will help lower crime or boost productivity.

President Trump should work with Congress to put in place reasonable, common sense, criminal justice reforms, and provide the opportunity of a much brighter future for many Americans who are incarcerated. Republicans can look to reforms that have worked in Texas and Georgia for guidance. Texas implemented sweeping criminal justice reform a decade ago, and this year it has seen the lowest crime rates in more than a century. More recently, in 2012, Georgia Governor Nathan Deal worked with the state legislature to pass a set of reforms that redesigned sentencing guidelines for nonviolent property crimes and drug offenses, so low-risk offenders weren't being turned into hardened criminals after spending years in prison. Long sentences were replaced with substance abuse courts, accountability programs, and other diversionary systems, which ultimately led to fewer victims of crime, lower costs to the justice system, and less recidivism by offenders.

As an example, from 2007 to 2016, parole revocations in Georgia declined by 35 percent. This is remarkable because it means a significant number of men and women who went to prison in Georgia and were then released on parole decided to live lawful, peaceful lives instead of returning to their old ways.

Applying this Georgia model to the federal system could have a tremendously positive impact on America as a whole by making it a safer, more law-abiding country. And it could also mean a large number of Americans could rejoin the workforce. Many of these men and women are smart, talented people who either struggle with addiction, mental illness, or simply made bad decisions.

We would all be better off if they had the opportunity to be responsible, healthy, citizens—and help the United States remain the most productive country on the planet along the way.

CHAPTER FIFTEEN

REACHING BEYOND THE STARS

Perhaps more than any other initiative, President Trump's commitment to revive American leadership in space will have enormous, long-lasting outcomes that will help ensure the United States remains a global superpower for decades to come. Even more importantly, if the Trump administration can build on the emerging commercial launch systems Americans will lead people throughout the solar system and freedom will be the banner of space travel.

Right now, we are at an incredibly exciting—potentially revolutionary—moment when it comes to space travel. At the time I am writing this, it has been only a few weeks since SpaceX successfully launched its Falcon Heavy rocket for the first time from the Kennedy Space Center in Cape Canaveral, Florida. This was truly a historic moment for American space flight. The Falcon Heavy is the most powerful rocket launched since the Apollo era, and it is the biggest rocket ever made by a private company. This was a clear signal that the commercial sector is ready to take on challenges in space that conventional wisdom has for decades claimed can be met only by government.

Just as important, the Falcon Heavy launch was a blazing signal of inspiration for young people across America. Young Americans throughout our nation watched Musk's rocket blast into space and catapult into orbit a red Tesla Roadster piloted by "Starman" (a mannequin dressed in a spacesuit). They then watched streaming video online of Starman as he and his sports car floated above our planet before being sent further into space. This symbol let every one of these young American students know that a career in the American space industry was just as real and attainable as a career in medicine, engineering, or any other occupation that requires hard work and dedication. In this way, SpaceX was able to rekindle a sense of patriotic, American intrepidness that has not been felt since millions of Americans watched astronaut Neil Armstrong take his "one small step" on the surface of the Moon.

President Trump and Vice President Pence have a tremendous opportunity to foster more of this activity in the commercial sector—and help launch the American space industry into a new era of adventure and prosperity.

Furthermore, from the standpoint of human history, the Trump-Pence space initiative will ensure that the principles of freedom, the rule of law, private property, and free enterprise become the core values that define humans in space.

Do not be complacent. A Russian- or Chinese-defined spacefaring system will carry dictatorship and the subordination of people to the state into space. There are very large historic reasons for making sure the dynamic leadership in colonizing the solar system is based on freedom.

As I write this book, it has been nearly a year since President Trump signed the order reestablishing the National Space Council and designating Vice President Pence as its leader. In that time, I have had the opportunity to work with Vice President Mike Pence on strategic planning for America in space.

When President Trump announced he would revive this important institution, he challenged us to profoundly rethink American activities in space. His words on June 30, 2017, were simple and direct; America must start thinking big again:

> With the actions we are launching today, America will think big once again. Important words: Think big. We haven't been thinking so big for a long time, but we're thinking big again as a country. We will inspire millions of children to carry on this proud tradition of American space leadership—and they're excited—and to never stop wondering, hoping, and dreaming about what lies beyond the stars.

Three months later, on the eve of the first meeting of the National Space Council, Vice President Pence outlined a focus for President Trump's challenge that we "think big." In the *Wall Street Journal*,[1] the vice president wrote that "America will lead in space again." He went on to say:

> We will refocus America's space program toward human exploration and discovery. That means launching American astronauts beyond low-Earth orbit for the first time since 1972. It means establishing a renewed American presence on the moon, a vital strategic goal. And from the foundation of the moon, America will be the first nation to bring mankind to Mars.
>
> We will renew America's commitment to creating the space technology needed to protect national security. Our adversaries are aggressively developing jamming and hacking capabilities that could cripple critical military surveillance, navigation systems, and communication

networks. In the face of this threat, America must be as dominant in the heavens as it is on Earth.

We will promote regulatory, technological, and educational reforms to expand opportunities for American citizens and ensure that the U.S. is at the forefront of economic development in outer space. In the years to come, American industry must be the first to maintain a constant commercial human presence in low-Earth orbit, to expand the sphere of the economy beyond this blue marble.

To achieve these goals, the National Space Council will look beyond the halls of government for insight and expertise.

Thinking big and achieving big in American space exploration and commercialization will require a lot more drive, mental toughness, and determined implementation than anything we have seen in space since the Apollo program, which put us on the moon.

Unfortunately, the speed, creativity, risk-taking, and technological and managerial innovation born out of the Apollo period from 1961 to 1969 has been replaced by bureaucracies, lobbyists, entrenched old systems, and narrowly defined ways of thinking and measuring success.

Many of these old bureaucracies, old systems, and old interest groups are working overtime to redefine their activities to fit the Trump-Pence vision. In other words, they are trying to put new paint jobs on 50-year-old cars and pitching them as new.

If the old guard succeeds, we will have another eight years of rope-a-dope with slow moving, expensive, safe bureaucratic activities that achieve very little.

Real change in American space activities will be controversial. It will stir up opposition from entrenched bureaucracies, large corporations, and congressional pork barrel vested interests. If you don't see or hear about this resistance, you can assume it is because the old guard has successfully minimized the amount of change coming, and instead of thinking big, we are acting small.

MEETING THE TRUMP-PENCE STANDARD

At the first meeting of the National Space Council, Vice President Pence outlined the following clear goals based on President Trump's directive:

1. Refocus America's space program toward human exploration and discovery—launching American astronauts beyond low-earth orbit for the first time since 1972;
2. Establishing a renewed American presence on the moon to build a foundational system for space activities beyond earth's reach. The moon will be a stepping-stone, a training ground, a venue to strengthen our commercial and international partnerships as we refocus America's space program toward human space exploration;
3. From the moon as a foundation, America will be the first to bring mankind to Mars;
4. Renew America's commitment to creating the space technology to protect national security. America must be as dominant in space as it is on earth;
5. Promote regulatory, technological, and educational reforms to expand opportunities for American citizens and ensure that the U.S. is at the forefront of economic development in outer space;
6. American industry must be the first to maintain a constant commercial human presence in low-earth orbit expanding the economy beyond the planet.

We'll strengthen our economy, as we unlock new
opportunities, new technologies, and new sources of
prosperity;

7. We'll inspire our children to seek education in science,
technology, engineering, and math.

8. Our nation will bring American values to this infinite
frontier. We will renew the American spirit itself and
rekindle our belief that America can accomplish
anything.

If we insist on the scale of change these eight goals will
require, we will have an amazingly dynamic and popular program in space by 2020. Furthermore, we will be poised to make
even greater leaps during a second Trump-Pence administration.

A major key to succeeding in this effort is recognizing this
level of advancement is vastly more complex than the Apollo
program. Apollo was an engineering project with the full force
of political-governmental support that could be managed by a
bureaucracy with adequate resources. The Trump-Pence goals,
on the other hand, require a series of cultural, political, economic, and technological changes that transcend any single
bureaucracy or manageable, measurable system.

This new system requires fundamental shifts in virtually
every current space-focused activity in our society.

First, the federal government must break out of its old funding
paradigm and embrace public–private partnerships. To be clear,
I'm not talking about the traditional partnership, where government puts up a ton of taxpayer money, assumes virtually all the
risk, and hopes that its private-sector partners succeed at building a launch vehicle or other spacecraft. The federal government
needs to develop models for partnering with space-based entrepreneurs as investors—who can get returns on its investments.

Entrepreneurs already have ideas about what they could do

if frequent journeys to low-Earth orbit were possible and afford-able. Operating in zero gravity provides significant opportu-nities for drugmakers, advanced material manufacturing, and other important fields of science. There are companies right now that want to mine near-earth asteroids for precious met-als, water, and other resources. Imagine a system in which the government enabled—and drew dividends from—a new U.S.-led space economy.

An aggressive public–private partnership regime could help close government budget shortfalls and bring entrepreneurial drive and risk-taking into government programs. This would normally take years at the pace of traditional bureaucracies. The development of this system should be approached more like a wartime project with real deadlines and real efforts to cut through red tape and get a variety of partnerships moving.

If you think this might be overkill, consider that our global competitors, such as China, are aggressively leveraging the power of their governments to beat the United States so they can dominate space.

It should be possible to get 40 to 60 percent more resources in the short run with public–private partnerships. By 2020, the United States should have more private money than pub-lic money going into implementing the Trump-Pence vision of America in space.

We must also create an environment for military-civilian space cooperation that emulates, and complements, established relationships in our naval and aerial sectors. These partnerships are part of the reason the United States was able to achieve and maintain supremacy in the air and sea. For the sake of our nation's current and future security, we must have supremacy in space, as well.

We must do all we can to drastically increase the speed and scale of innovation in our American aerospace sector and reallocate our federal resources to achieve new goals. For too long, the United States has lacked a focused mission when it comes to space. Exploration and observation is important, but it is not enough. The United States should do all it can to enable American industry to commercialize space and create a new economy.

This means Congress should create a "Thinking Big Space Caucus" in the House of Representatives and the Senate dedicated to writing the necessary new laws and passing expanded appropriations to revive our dominance in space.

Further, change on this scale requires leadership at the top, constant action, a willingness to fail and to correct mistakes quickly, and constant pressure to focus on a bold future. Finally, the federal bureaucracy must be taught—or forced—to change current activities so it can achieve that future.

EMPOWERING INDUSTRY AND DEFENSE

The world market for space activities is continuing to grow.

The Space Foundation estimated the 2015 total worldwide activity in space was $323 billion.

According to the Foundation, 76 percent of this activity was commercial ($243 billion). Meanwhile, U.S. government space spending was estimated at around $45 billion (defense and civilian combined).

In a decade, commercial space will likely grow to over $300 billion. Of course, if the cost of getting to orbit collapses as much as Elon Musk and Jeff Bezos suggest, there could be a dramatically bigger market. The economic activity of the American space industry might even reach $500 billion a year by 2024, according to one study.

United States domination in this global market would carry with it enormous national security, economic, and prestige value. For the last 70 years, the United States has dominated the airliner business. This has provided huge foreign earnings,

American jobs, and a technologically advanced manufacturing base of tremendous value to our national security.

America must establish the same dominance in the world market for space activities. This will require expediting bureaucratic requirements, rethinking some of the export control regime, matching foreign subsidies, and having the president possibly discuss coordinating with allied countries to join U.S.-led space activities. All these efforts must be focused on empowering the American space industry. It's a matter of economic success, but also of our future security.

In 2015, General John Hyten, who was then the commander of Air Force Space Command, gave a speech often referred to as a "call to arms" for military space. His concern was that foreign nations are rapidly developing and deploying anti-satellite capabilities, ballistic weapons that cover vast distances by transiting space, and weapon systems that could carry the next war into orbit. Since then, North Korea has aggressively developed nuclear weapons and an ability to launch them through space at the United States.

What if the response of the United States was to leverage the technologies already being developed in the commercial sector? What if we developed reusable launch vehicles able to reconstitute our communications and intelligence satellite constellations within hours? What if we enabled reusable hypersonic global aircraft, which could carry 100 special forces anywhere on the world in hours—or minutes? What if we took advantage of the myriad communication and observation satellite constellations currently being deployed by the commercial sector?

We created the world's finest Navy and Air Force by building on American commerce. This is how we won World War II and collapsed the Soviet Union in the Cold War. Building on the great engine of American industry is also how we will protect and maintain peace on the twenty-first-century space frontier.

For instance, hypersonic flight could be the biggest breakthrough in technology and transportation of the next 20 years. It
could also be a significant military breakthrough. Hypersonic aircraft that can achieve a speed beyond Mach 5 (roughly a mile per
second) are already at the development level. I have spoken to several companies operating in this arena that are developing engines,
weapons, and passenger vehicles, which could potentially reach
anywhere on the globe in four hours.

As this technology develops—and if it is provided an environment to develop—Mach 5 engines could become a stepping-
stone to even more powerful propulsion systems. With enough
investment and research, we could eventually develop reusable
systems that could take off from runways and achieve Mach
25—the speed necessary to exit the Earth's gravity well. This
could render traditional vertical lift rockets obsolete for trans-
porting all but the very largest payloads into space. This is con-
ceivable in the not too distant future.

However, I have no illusions: Reaching Mach 25 from a
runway will require a robust research program, many years of
advancements in engineering, and rigorous trial-and-error testing. The jump from the Wright Brothers' tiny first airplane to
the first militarily usable aircraft took about 10 years. A decade
of robust research in hypersonics would yield enormous results.

Hypersonic flight technologies are an especially good area
to empower investment because hypersonic vehicles and weapons give the United States a wide range of military capabilities,
which would allow us to dominate in virtually every combat
arena.

This technology also creates breakthrough potential in
commercial aviation. A flight from New York to Singapore
could suddenly be a short (four-hour) trip in a hypersonic aircraft. This would produce a huge positive impact for passenger
and freight air travel alike.

Hypersonic flight may also eventually become the most convenient and lowest-cost way of getting people and smaller cargos into space.

For these reasons, research and development of hypersonic systems should be a major investment priority for both defense and commercial applications.

In addition to boosting research that enables the private sector, the military should be directed to maximize the use of services in space rather than paying for hardware. The military has a very substantial budget for space, and it currently maximizes old hardware systems which it can control.

Shifting the military's purchasing power toward paying for launches, research, or material manufacturing and other space-based commercial endeavors rather than large, expensive spacecraft would spur growth in the industry and help create a base for prolonged commercial activity. For example, the Wright Brothers built the first military airplane in response to a U.S. Army proposal. The contract they signed with the army enabled them to keep improving their aircraft.

Further, if the Trump administration insisted that the military operate within the National Space Council, it would be a real sign of dramatic change. The scale of the military's actual space activity can be tremendous. Consider the following example from the 1980s—when President Reagan was proposing the Strategic Defense Initiative for space-based missile defense.

In 1987, in response to a question from Senate NASA authorizers Don Riegle and Larry Pressler, the Government Accountability Office (GAO) wrote a fact sheet called "Space Funding: NASA's Appropriations and DOD's Funding Estimates for Space Programs."

The GAO looked at the period from 1981 to 1985 and came up with those years' "space-only" numbers. (The NASA figures exclude spending for aeronautics, so they are different from the top line agency appropriation. The Department of Defense [DOD] figures were compiled from the armed services, Defense Agencies, SDI, and classified programs.)

1981 NASA: $4.996B—DOD: $4.828B
1982 NASA: $5.504B—DOD: $6.575B
1983 NASA: $6.289B—DOD: $8.551B
1984 NASA: $6.651B—DOD: $10.195B
1985 NASA: $6.925B—DOD: $12.768B

Clearly, if the Trump administration can engage the DOD in helping create a bigger commercial market in space, it could have a huge impact. Remember how important government subsidized airmail was in growing the American commercial airlines business.

The latest National Defense Authorization Act proposal for a DOD "czar" on space may facilitate this step. However, as a prerequisite for the appointment, any "czar" chosen should agree to transition toward more military purchases of services.

MODERN SPACE REGULATIONS

There are currently 58,622 employees of the Department of Transportation (DOT). Only 100 of these employees work on space regulatory activities. That represents 0.17 percent of the DOT workforce. Furthermore, these employees are buried within the Federal Aviation Administration (FAA).

Instead of waiting for the next budget cycle, as people retire DOT should transfer 100 more positions to space-oriented work to double the number of staff focused on space. Similarly, the president should consider reversing the Clinton administration's decision to bury space regulatory activities in the FAA. Instead, the Secretary of Transportation's office should directly handle space regulations. The administration already did something similar with the Office of Space Commerce. Vice President Pence directed Commerce Secretary Wilbur Ross to move the space commerce office directly under his jurisdiction and appoint a new director of the office during the second National Space Council meeting in February 2018. This will help to enable a forgiving, streamlined, fast-fail, risk-taking approach that will allow industry to innovate and build an American commercial sector in space.

To this end, the goal should be modernizing regulations for space—not reforming them. The difference is important. Modernizing requires regulators to consider the scale of launches over the next 20 years assuming the Trump-Pence goals are met. Modern regulations should account for commercial space activities, lunar colonization, missions to Mars, asteroid mining, tourism, and manufacturing in space. At the same time, terrestrial regulators should consider the robust increase in America's capacity to defend itself once a fully functioning space economy is realized.

This doesn't simply require a few reforms of a system designed for a slow, small cottage industry of occasional launches. This requires conceptualizing many different approaches to making entrepreneurial and commercial space viable. Genuine innovators must not be crushed by government regulators. Commercial operations ought to have greater and greater autonomy as they prove more and more reliable. Eventually, we should get to a permissive, "file and fly" system for approving space launches, similar to what we have in the air travel industry. This scale of change means that regulatory modernization must be an ongoing process. There will not be a final breakthrough moment. Thought must be given to creating a flexible system that is capable of adapting at a rate that is inconceivable to most bureaucracies.

This will also require convincing Congress to adopt new models of flexible regulatory evolution. This approach of continuous modernization must be broadened to include use of the electromagnetic spectrum, export controls, and other regulations which hinder our development in space. A continuous dialogue between users and the regulatory system must lead to continuous improvement in a timely way.

Another way Congress could help bring more resources into the system would be to turn five smaller National Aeronautics and Space Administration centers into Federally Funded Research and Development Centers (FFRDC). There are currently 42 such centers across the government. The five NASA centers that could fit this model are:

- Ames Research Center in Mountain View, California
- Armstrong Flight Research Center at Edwards Air Force Base in California
- Glenn Research Center in Cleveland, Ohio
- Goddard Institute for Space Studies in New York City, New York
- Langley Research Center in Hampton, Virginia

These five centers could increase the entrepreneurship and flexibility of NASA activities and bring much needed private resources into the system. This FFRDC approach has worked incredibly well at the Jet Propulsion Laboratory, which collaborates with the California Institute of Technology, and could accelerate the tempo of development across the U.S. space sector.

EXECUTING CLEAR STRATEGIC VISION

A small working group should outline the key areas that must be developed to implement the Trump-Pence vision of a dynamic American future in space. It is important that this comprehensive visionary outline be developed as quickly as possible because it will shape much of what the Trump administration will be able to achieve in space—as well as lay the foundation for future activity in the next term.

The past mismatch between words and budgets, combined with resistance from bureaucrats, lobbyists, and congressional special interests explain why most former presidential goals for space have remained merely words and led to virtually no change.

Only by explaining and then imposing a clear road map into space—then exciting the American people and growing support in Congress—can real change occur that will turn "big thinking" into "big actions." If this isn't done quickly, the machinery of government and bureaucracy will force near-endless delays.

To that end, if we are going to think big and act big, we need a much stronger, more dynamic National Space Council. The National Space Council should be more like the National Security Council—in both staffing and clout. It must be able to spur real change in government, provide real leadership for the private sector, and maximize presidential and vice-presidential communications efforts. This will enable the National Space Council to excite the American people, grow a grassroots pro-space movement, build a network of space activists and companies, and develop a strong legislative caucus in the House and Senate to sustain the legislation and appropriations necessary to think big and act big in space.

The National Space Council needs full-time, dedicated employees. These should not be loaned from other areas of government. The Council also should have sufficient funds to pay for travel, conferences, public events, and grants. The Council must be able to plan, monitor, and empower a wide range of actions. While that is a big jump from the current operation, it should be remembered that the U.S. government spent $31.458 billion on space in Fiscal Year 2016 (not counting classified programs). Surely, in that context, this proposal for the National

Space Council is modest. However, it is a necessary down payment on thinking big and acting big.

Finally, the newly empowered Trump administration National Space Council must remember the adage: "you get what you inspect, not what you expect." Someone must be in charge of each zone with a clear set of metrics for success. If the National Space Council is going to be the vice president's operating arm for space, it must have the resources and authority to force movement. If the National Space Council is going to be primarily a policy developing agency, then other people must be tasked and held accountable. Since 1969, there have been a lot of good speeches and intentions about space—which disappeared into the bureaucratic, lobbying, parochial interest swamp.

Breaking through that will require hard work and real accountability.

But this work will be worth it. In 20 years, if the United States is as dominant in space as it has been in the sea and in the air, America will be at a tremendous economic, political, and security advantage. And the future of the human race in space as a free people will be dramatically more likely.

CHAPTER SIXTEEN

THE COMEBACK IS NOT GUARANTEED

Once again America finds itself in a period of turbulent, intense creativity and conflict with no guarantee about the outcome.

We have been here before, and—as long as we remain a free, dynamic, entrepreneurial society—we will be here again in the future.

The key for Trump's America in 2018 and beyond is to recognize we are in the fight of our lives against a well-financed, heavily organized, extremely militant coalition of people who despise us and the country for which we stand.

Doing nothing guarantees America is taken over by this militant left-wing, establishment coalition that will use mob violence, news media propaganda, and government power to coerce the rest of us into submitting to their worldview.

This struggle is profound and deeply felt. It is a countrywide cultural civil war. We should expect the fight to be remarkably intense. This is not a time of compromise. This is a time of winning or losing. Each of us must decide if the America we love is worth fighting for. Our individual decisions will add up to victory or defeat.

Fortunately, this is not a new experience. We can learn a great deal about today's struggle by studying American history. One of the amazing things about the American story has been our ability to reinvent ourselves again and again. The depth of the struggle which produced the Jacksonian Revolution may be the most useful parallel to the rise of Trump and Trump's America.

America's government started as an orderly Federalist system dominated by southern aristocrats and Yankee gentlemen of wealth. That group dominated society and government from the Declaration of Independence in 1776 through the election of 1820.

However, as Gordon Wood has reported in numerous books, the flexibility and openness of American society undermined the power of the wealthy establishment. Inventors were creating the steamship, the cotton gin, the assembly line production of guns, and a host of new goods and services. Meanwhile, there were rural farmers and blue-collar urban workers who had contempt and hostility—instead of respect and affection—for the establishment.

The tension between the dynamic America that was growing and the orderly America that wanted to keep its stability and control grew greater and greater. That tension found an explosive spark in the form of Andrew Jackson. General Jackson won the battle of New Orleans in 1815, beating the British and restoring American pride. Jackson then went on to become a two-term governor of Tennessee.

In 1824, Jackson put together a unique coalition of rural farmers and urban working men during his run for the presidency. He was as favored in Philadelphia working-class precincts as he was in rural small towns. His aggressive campaign seemed to pay off with 99 electoral votes and 153,544 popular votes.

However, Jackson won a plurality—not a majority. John Quincy Adams, the son of our second president, received 84 electoral votes and 108,740 popular votes. William Crawford came in third in the electoral college with 41 electoral votes but was fourth in popular vote with 41,032 votes. Henry Clay was fourth in electoral votes at 37 electoral votes but passed Crawford with 47,545 popular votes.

In short, the election was a mess. Jackson had 41.36 percent of the popular vote. Adams had 30.92 percent. Crawford and Clay had 11.21 percent and 12.99 percent, respectively. However, Jackson got fewer electoral votes per popular vote than his opponents.

What made things even worse was that the weakest electoral college candidate, Clay, was the Speaker of the House. He would preside over the House picking the president since the electoral college had failed to produce a majority.

The House then selected John Quincy Adams to be president. President Adams, in turn, promptly appointed Speaker Clay to be Secretary of State. This had important symbolism in 1824 because the last four presidents had all been Secretary of State. In effect, Adams was signaling Clay would be the president after him.

To the already angry Jacksonians, this was the establishment stealing success from their hero. They knew exactly what had happened. There had been a "corrupt bargain" between Adams and Clay. These two members of the establishment had cheated America of its hero through petty personal ambition. The anger was instant and exploded months before the inauguration, which back then was held in March.

Jackson was an energetic, naturally hostile figure. He had been a fighter since childhood (a British soldier slashed his face with a saber when he was 13, leaving him with a scar and a deep desire for vengeance against the British). For Jackson, all of life was passionate and personal.

After the 1824 election, he was offended and enraged.

Long before Adams was sworn in, the Jacksonians were blanketing the country with their shocking story of the "corrupt bargain." They became so well organized they set the record for using franking privilege to send postage-free mail. Jackson's supporters in the House and Senate took every anti-Adams newspaper and mailed them far and wide at taxpayer expense.

In rural America, Jacksonian campaigners attacked and defamed Adams for four years straight. When Adams said America needed an observatory, the Jacksonians sensed a big mistake. All across rural America, Jacksonians pulled people out of taverns, pointed to the stars and said things like, "Can you see them for free?" When their constituents would nod, the Jacksonians would point out Adams had grown so European he wanted to spend their money to have the government look at their free stars. The ridicule sank in.

As Robert V. Remini outlines in his book, *The Election of Andrew Jackson*, the Adams-Clay forces couldn't match the intensity, the anger, the organization, or the maniacal determination of the Jacksonians. It is a remarkable book, which we studied in designing the Contract with America campaign in 1994.

After four years of daily assaults, the election of 1828 was decisive. Jackson won the Electoral College 178–83. He won the popular vote 642,553 to 500,897 (56 percent to 43.6 percent).

Jackson governed tumultuously against various strong forces. He destroyed the Bank of the United States, the largest financial institution in America. Yet, he governed so frugally, the United States was briefly out of debt shortly after he left office.

Jackson built a system, the Democratic Party, which elected his vice president for one term, lost an election to the opposition, and then elected President James K. Polk—another former governor of Tennessee. In fact, until 1860 and the election of Abraham Lincoln, the Jacksonians were the dominant force in

America. It is worth noting, too, in 1860, Lincoln got a smaller percentage of the total vote than Jackson but because his multiple opponents were split in a unique way, he had a decisive majority in the Electoral College. Lincoln actually fought and won the Civil War starting from a narrower base than Jackson had.

The Trump system is very much like the Jacksonian system. It is trying to replace a deeply entrenched establishment. It is trying to defeat the cultural, academic, and news media elites. It is trying to drain the swamp and root out the deep state. None of these opposing forces are going to go quietly. They understand that this is life and death for their values and their interest groups.

The bitterness, meanness, and ferocity of the Senate Democrats in methodically blocking every Trump appointee is so destructive of government, it is putting partisanship above patriotism. Watch a week or two of the lockstep blocking of people whose lives are on hold. This is a cynical, deliberate strategy made even more effective because the permanent bureaucrats running things while appointees are blocked are overwhelmingly liberal and part of the anti-Trump coalition.

As Jackson had his Jacksonians, President Trump needs the people of Trump's America if America's great comeback is to continue. The fight will go on. I think we will win. With your help, I am a lot more certain. This is the real test of Trump's America, and 2018 is the decisive battle.

Acknowledgments

Trump's America was a challenging project, and I am grateful to the remarkable team of people who helped me think it through.

Conceptualizing and writing *Trump's America* was made unusually complicated by the fact that Callista became the American Ambassador to the Holy See, and I was spending 70 percent of my time in Rome, Italy. Many pages of this book were written and edited on trans-Atlantic airplane flights at very odd hours. Callista's support and encouragement was essential in this complicated process. In addition, Bess Kelly made an enormous difference in our ability to both serve the United States and remain productive.

Here at home, I have to thank the team at Gingrich Productions who helped think through and research the wide-ranging topics. Louie Brogdon took the leading role in developing the ideas. He was assisted at every turn by Joe Desantis, Claire Christensen, and Anne Woodbury. As he has for more than 30 years, Joe Gaylord offered invaluable advice. Randy Evans, who is my close friend and a brilliant lawyer, once again helped focus us, as he did so successfully with *Understanding Trump*. My daughter, Kathy Lubbers, once again represented us as our agent. My other daughter, Jackie Cushman, discussed with me many of the ideas that ended up in this book. Woody Hales did an excellent job scheduling and keeping me focused and on time. Audrey Bird did a remarkable job marketing *Understanding Trump* and gave us confidence we would reach a lot of people with *Trump's America*. Christina Maruna does an amazing job of managing our social media and digital projects, including experiments like our "What If?" series of alternative histories that is now approaching 50,000 followers on Facebook. She has been critical to growing our more than 2 million followers on Twitter and more than a million followers on Facebook. Taylor Swindle keeps all the finances straight, and John Hines simply keeps the system running and supports what I am doing in an endless number of ways. Of course, I would also like to thank our three hardworking interns—Miracle Parish, Cameron Bosch, and Casey Ryan—who were a great help every step of the way. It is a great team, and it gives me confidence to undertake projects like *Trump's America*.

Kate Hartson was once again a great partner and editor in this, our fifth book together. Her enthusiasm and encouragement made it a lot easier to stay focused.

No one has done more to expose the corruption of the deep state than Sean Hannity, and his insights, hard work, network of reporters, and persistence shaped a lot of my thinking about just how sick the system has become. Andy McCarthy's years as a federal prosecutor and his intense focus on the distortions in the Justice Department process were a significant factor in my writing about the investigatory system. So was my friendship with Scooter Libby, who remains a vivid example of injustice and the power an independent counsel can wield to deliberately trap an innocent person. Scooter's experience informs a great deal of my suspicion about putting too much power in one lawyer's hands. Conversations with Leonard Leo of the Federalist Society, along with Evans, helped further clarify the legal situation.

Vince Haley and Ross Worthington used to work at Gingrich Productions but are now speechwriters for President Trump. Chatting with them and swapping ideas substantially improved my own thinking. Their colleague, Tony Dolan, brought to this process his own depth of experience as chief speechwriter for both President Ronald Reagan and Secretary of Defense Don Rumsfeld, and his extraordinary career as a Pulitzer Prize-winning investigative journalist. He is a national treasure.

The insights of David Winston and Myra Miller from their years of polling expertise helped me think about what is happening to the American people.

On the political side, the insights of Republican National Committee Chair Ronna McDaniel, and experienced strategists like Mike and Katie Shields, Corry Bliss, Governor Haley Barbour, Barry Casselman, and Johnny DeStefano enriched my thinking. Emily Schillinger and the staff at the House Ways and Means Committee were also incredibly helpful in helping me understand the details of the Tax Cuts and Jobs Act.

On national security and America's role in the world, I first have to acknowledge the extraordinary achievement of Dr. Nadia Schadlow in developing a wide consensus for the National Security Strategy. The seven-month development of this document beginning in May 2017 was a major achievement and educated all of us who were privileged to participate. I am confident this book would have been much narrower without Dr. Schadlow's extraordinary work.

For years, I have also looked to Herman Pirchner, Ilan Berman, Cliff May, Kiron Skinner, and General Jack Keane for national security advice.

On the opioid crisis, Anne Woodbury, Patrick Kennedy, and Van Jones played major roles.

Pat Nolan also helped me better understand this crisis and continues to be invaluable on criminal justice reform. Pete Earley, with whom I write fiction books, was also enormously helpful on issues of mental illness and the prison system.

For getting a grasp on current economics, Stephen Moore, Kevin Hassett, Larry Kudlow, Alfredo Ortiz, Steve Hantler, Ken Kies, and John Mauldin were all helpful.

In understanding how to approach writing the "Helping Americans Return to Work" chapter, Mary Mayhew of Maine has provided an excellent model as the leading reformer in the country. The leaders of America Works in New York City also have a long, distinguished career of helping people move from dependency to work.

On the great potential of American leadership in space, I have been working with Representative Bob Walker for over 30 years. Jim Muncy, Tony Tether, General Pete Worden, Bill Brunner, Lynn Rothschild, Mark Lewis, Scott Pace, Dan Golden, Sean O'Keefe, and the leadership of Blue Origin, SpaceX, Sierra Nevada Corporation, United Launch Alliance, Stratolaunch, and others have been inspirational. A morning with Jeff Bezos discussing his personal $1 billion-a-year investment in space was extraordinary. We are on the verge of great breakthroughs, and these are the kind of people who can make it happen.

Each one of these wonderful people played an important role in making *Trump's America* a useful, interesting book. Any mistakes are, of course, mine.

Remarks by President Trump
to the People of Poland

July 6, 2017
Krasiński Square
Warsaw, Poland

Thank you very much. That's so nice. The United States has many great diplomats, but there is truly no better ambassador for our country than our beautiful First Lady, Melania. Thank you, Melania. That was very nice.

We've come to your nation to deliver a very important message: America loves Poland, and America loves the Polish people. Thank you.

The Poles have not only greatly enriched this region, but Polish-Americans have also greatly enriched the United States, and I was truly proud to have their support in the 2016 election.

It is a profound honor to stand in this city, by this monument to the Warsaw Uprising, and to address the Polish nation that so many generations have dreamed of: a Poland that is safe, strong, and free.

President Duda and your wonderful First Lady, Agata, have welcomed us with the tremendous warmth and kindness for which Poland is known around the world. Thank you. My sincere—and I mean sincerely thank both of them. And to Prime Minister Syzdlo, a very special thanks also.

We are also pleased that former President Lech Walesa, so famous for leading the Solidarity Movement, has joined us today, also.

On behalf of all Americans, let me also thank the entire Polish people for the generosity you have shown in welcoming our soldiers to your country. These soldiers are not only brave defenders of freedom, but also symbols of America's commitment to your security and your place in a strong and democratic Europe.

We are proudly joined on stage by American, Polish, British, and Romanian soldiers. Thank you. Thank you. Great job.

President Duda and I have just come from an incredibly successful meeting with the leaders participating in the Three Seas Initiative.

To the citizens of this great region, America is eager to expand our partnership with you. We welcome stronger ties of trade and commerce as you grow your economies. And we are committed to securing your access to alternate sources of energy, so Poland and its neighbors are never again held hostage to a single supplier of energy.

Mr. President, I congratulate you, along with the President of Croatia, on your leadership of this historic Three Seas Initiative. Thank you.

This is my first visit to Central Europe as President, and I am thrilled that it could be right here at this magnificent, beautiful piece of land. It is beautiful. Poland is the geographic heart of Europe, but more importantly, in the Polish people, we see the soul of Europe. Your nation is great because your spirit is great and your spirit is strong.

For two centuries, Poland suffered constant and brutal attacks. But while Poland could be invaded and occupied, and its borders even erased from the map, it could never be erased from history or from your hearts. In those dark days, you have lost your land but you never lost your pride.

So it is with true admiration that I can say today, that from the farms and villages of your countryside to the cathedrals and squares of your great cities, Poland lives, Poland prospers, and Poland prevails.

Despite every effort to transform you, oppress you, or destroy you, you endured and overcame. You are the proud nation of Copernicus—think of that—Chopin, Saint John Paul II. Poland is a land of great heroes. And you are a people who know the true value of what you defend.

The triumph of the Polish spirit over centuries of hardship gives us all hope for a future in which good conquers evil, and peace achieves victory over war.

For Americans, Poland has been a symbol of hope since the beginning of our nation. Polish heroes and American patriots fought side by side in our War of Independence and in many wars that followed. Our soldiers still serve together today in Afghanistan and Iraq, combatting the enemies of all civilization.

For America's part, we have never given up on freedom and independence as the right and destiny of the Polish people, and we never, ever will.

Our two countries share a special bond forged by unique histories and national characters. It's a fellowship that exists only among people who have fought and bled and died for freedom.

The signs of this friendship stand in our nation's capital. Just steps from the White House, we've raised statues of men with names like Pułaski and Kościuszko. The same is true in Warsaw, where street signs carry the name of George Washington, and a monument stands to one of the world's greatest heroes, Ronald Reagan.

And so I am here today not just to visit an old ally, but to hold it up as an example for others who seek freedom and who wish to summon the courage and the will to defend our civilization. The story of Poland is the story of a people who have never lost hope, who have never been broken, and who have never, ever forgotten who they are.

Such a great honor. This is a nation more than one thousand years old. Your borders were erased for more than a century and only restored just one century ago.

In 1920, in the Miracle of Vistula, Poland stopped the Soviet army bent on European conquest. Then, 19 years later in 1939, you were invaded yet again, this time by Nazi Germany from the west and the Soviet Union from the east. That's trouble. That's tough.

Under a double occupation the Polish people endured evils beyond description: the Katyn forest massacre, the occupations, the Holocaust, the Warsaw Ghetto and the Warsaw Ghetto Uprising, the destruction of this beautiful capital city, and the deaths of nearly one in five Polish people. A vibrant Jewish population—the largest in Europe—was reduced to almost nothing after the Nazis systematically murdered millions of Poland's Jewish citizens, along with countless others, during that brutal occupation.

In the summer of 1944, the Nazi and Soviet armies were preparing for a terrible and bloody battle right here in Warsaw. Amid that hell on earth, the citizens of Poland rose up to defend their homeland. I am deeply honored to be joined on stage today by veterans and heroes of the Warsaw Uprising.

What great spirit. We salute your noble sacrifice and we pledge to always remember your fight for Poland and for freedom.

This monument reminds us that more than 150,000 Poles died during that desperate struggle to overthrow oppression.

From the other side of the river, the Soviet armed forces stopped and waited. They watched as the Nazis ruthlessly destroyed the city, viciously murdering men, women, and children. They tried to destroy this nation forever by shattering its will to survive.

But there is a courage and a strength deep in the Polish character that no one could destroy. The Polish martyr, Bishop Michael Kozal, said it well: "More horrifying than a defeat of arms is a collapse of the human spirit."

Through four decades of communist rule, Poland and the other captive nations of Europe endured a brutal campaign to demolish freedom, your faith, your laws, your history, your identity—indeed the very essence of your culture and your humanity. Yet, through it all, you never lost that spirit. Your oppressors tried to break you, but Poland could not be broken.

And when the day came on June 2nd, 1979, and one million Poles gathered around Victory Square for their very first mass with their Polish Pope, that day, every communist in Warsaw must have known that their oppressive system would soon come crashing down. They must have known it at the exact moment during Pope John Paul II's sermon when a million Polish men, women, and children suddenly raised their voices in a single prayer. A million Polish people did not ask for wealth. They did not ask for privilege. Instead, one million Poles sang three simple words: "We Want God."

In those words, the Polish people recalled the promise of a better future. They found new courage to face down their oppressors, and they found the words to declare that Poland would be Poland once again.

As I stand here today before this incredible crowd, this faithful nation, we can still hear those voices that echo through history. Their message is as true today as ever. The people of Poland, the people of America, and the people of Europe still cry out "We want God."

Together, with Pope John Paul II, the Poles reasserted their identity as a nation devoted to God. And with that powerful declaration of who you are, you came to understand what to do and how to live. You stood in solidarity against oppression, against a lawless secret police, against a cruel and wicked system that impoverished your cities and your souls. And you won. Poland prevailed. Poland will always prevail.

You were supported in that victory over communism by a strong alliance of free nations in the West that defied tyranny. Now, among the most committed members of the NATO Alliance, Poland has resumed its place as a leading nation of a Europe that is strong, whole, and free.

A strong Poland is a blessing to the nations of Europe, and they know that. A strong Europe is a blessing to the West and to the world. One hundred years after the entry of American forces into World War I, the transatlantic bond between the United States and Europe is as strong as ever and maybe, in many ways, even stronger.

This continent no longer confronts the specter of communism. But today we're in the West, and we have to say there are dire threats to our security and to our way of life. You see what's happening out there. They are threats. We will confront them. We will win. But they are threats.

We are confronted by another oppressive ideology—one that seeks to export terrorism and extremism all around the globe. America and Europe have suffered one terror attack after another. We're going to get it to stop.

During a historic gathering in Saudi Arabia, I called on the leaders of more than 50 Muslim nations to join together to drive out this menace which threatens all of humanity. We must stand united against these shared enemies to strip them of their territory and their funding, and their networks, and any form of ideological support that they may have. While we will always welcome new citizens who share our values and love our people, our borders will always be closed to terrorism and extremism of any kind.

We are fighting hard against radical Islamic terrorism, and we will prevail. We cannot accept those who reject our values and who use hatred to justify violence against the innocent.

Today, the West is also confronted by the powers that seek to test our will, undermine our confidence, and challenge our interests. To meet new forms of aggression, including propaganda, financial crimes, and cyberwarfare, we must adapt our alliance to compete effectively in new ways and on all new battlefields.

We urge Russia to cease its destabilizing activities in Ukraine and elsewhere, and its support for hostile regimes—including Syria and Iran—and to instead join the community of responsible nations in our fight against common enemies and in defense of civilization itself.

Finally, on both sides of the Atlantic, our citizens are confronted by yet another danger—one firmly within our control. This danger is invisible to some but familiar to the Poles: the steady creep of government bureaucracy that drains the vitality and wealth of the people. The West became great not because of paperwork and regulations but because people were allowed to chase their dreams and pursue their destinies.

Americans, Poles, and the nations of Europe value individual freedom and sovereignty. We must work together to confront forces, whether they come from inside or out, from the South or the East, that threaten over time to undermine these values and to erase the bonds of culture, faith and tradition that make us who we are. If left unchecked, these forces will undermine our courage, sap our spirit, and weaken our will to defend ourselves and our societies.

But just as our adversaries and enemies of the past learned here in Poland, we know that these forces, too, are doomed to fail if we want them to fail. And we do, indeed, want them to fail. They are doomed not only because our alliance is strong, our countries are resilient, and our power is unmatched. Through all of that, you have to say everything is true. Our adversaries, however, are doomed because we will never forget who we are. And if we don't forget who we are, we just can't be beaten. Americans will never forget. The nations of Europe will never forget. We are the fastest and the greatest community. There is nothing like our community of nations. The world has never known anything like our community of nations.

We write symphonies. We pursue innovation. We celebrate our ancient heroes, embrace our timeless traditions and customs, and always seek to explore and discover brand-new frontiers.

We reward brilliance. We strive for excellence and cherish inspiring works of art that honor God. We treasure the rule of law and protect the right to free speech and free expression.

We empower women as pillars of our society and of our success. We put faith and family, not government and bureaucracy, at the center of our lives. And we debate everything. We challenge everything. We seek to know everything so that we can better know ourselves.

And above all, we value the dignity of every human life, protect the rights of every person, and share the hope of every soul to live in freedom. That is who we are. Those are the priceless ties that bind us together as nations, as allies, and as a civilization.

What we have, what we inherited from our—and you know this better than anybody, and you see it today with this incredible group of people—what we've inherited from our ancestors has never existed to this extent before. And if we fail to preserve it, it will never, ever exist again. So we cannot fail.

This great community of nations has something else in common: In every one of them, it is the people, not the powerful, who have always formed the foundation of freedom and the cornerstone of our defense. The people have been that foundation here in Poland—as they were right here in Warsaw—and they were the foundation from the very, very beginning in America.

Our citizens did not win freedom together, did not survive horrors together, did not face down evil together, only to lose our freedom to a lack of pride and confidence in our values. We did not and we will not. We will never back down.

As long as we know our history, we will know how to build our future. Americans know that a strong alliance of free, sovereign and independent nations is the best defense for our freedoms and for our interests. That is why my administration has demanded that all members of NATO finally meet their full and fair financial obligation.

As a result of this insistence, billions of dollars more have begun to pour into NATO. In fact, people are shocked. But billions and billions of dollars more are coming in from countries that, in my opinion, would not have been paying so quickly.

To those who would criticize our tough stance, I would point out that the United States has demonstrated not merely with words but with its actions that we stand firmly behind Article 5, the mutual defense commitment.

Words are easy, but actions are what matters. And for its own protection—and you know this, everybody knows this, everybody has to know this—Europe must do more. Europe must demonstrate that it believes in its future by investing its money to secure that future.

That is why we applaud Poland for its decision to move forward this week on acquiring from the United States the battle-tested Patriot air and missile defense system—the best anywhere in the world. That is also why we salute the Polish people for being one of the NATO countries that has actually achieved the benchmark for investment in our common defense. Thank you. Thank you, Poland. I must tell you, the example you set is truly magnificent, and we applaud Poland. Thank you.

We have to remember that our defense is not just a commitment of money, it is a commitment of will. Because as the Polish experience reminds us, the defense of the West ultimately rests not only on means but also on the will of its people to prevail and be successful and get what you have to have. The fundamental question of our time is whether the West has the will to survive. Do we have the confidence in our values to defend them at any cost? Do we have enough respect for our citizens to protect our borders? Do we have the desire and the courage to preserve our civilization in the face of those who would subvert and destroy it?

We can have the largest economies and the most lethal weapons anywhere on Earth, but if we do not have strong families and strong values, then we will be weak and we will not survive. If anyone forgets the critical importance of these things, let them come to one country that never has. Let them come to Poland. And let them come here, to Warsaw, and learn the story of the Warsaw Uprising.

When they do, they should learn about Jerusalem Avenue. In August of 1944, Jerusalem Avenue was one of the main roads running east and west through this city, just as it is today.

Control of that road was crucially important to both sides in the battle for Warsaw. The German military wanted it as their most direct route to move troops and to form a very strong front. And for the Polish Home Army, the ability to pass north and south across that street was critical to keep the center of the city, and the Uprising itself, from being split apart and destroyed.

Every night, the Poles put up sandbags amid machine gun fire—and it was horrendous fire—to protect a narrow passage across Jerusalem Avenue. Every day, the enemy forces knocked them down again and again and again. Then the Poles dug a trench. Finally, they built a barricade. And the brave Polish fighters began to flow across Jerusalem Avenue. That narrow passageway, just a few feet wide, was the fragile link that kept the Uprising alive.

Between its walls, a constant stream of citizens and freedom fighters made their perilous, just perilous, sprints. They ran across that street, they ran through that street, they ran under that street—all to defend this city. "The far side was several yards away," recalled one young Polish woman named Greta. That mortality and that life was so important to her. In fact, she said, "The mortally dangerous sector of the street was soaked in the blood. It was the blood of messengers, liaison girls, and couriers."

Nazi snipers shot at anybody who crossed. Anybody who crossed, they were being shot at. Their soldiers burned every building on the street, and they used the Poles as human shields for their tanks in their effort to capture Jerusalem Avenue. The enemy never ceased its relentless assault on that small outpost of civilization. And the Poles never ceased its defense.

The Jerusalem Avenue passage required constant protection, repair, and reinforcement, but the will of its defenders did not waver, even in the face of death. And to the last days of the Uprising, the fragile crossing never, ever failed. It was never, ever forgotten. It was kept open by the Polish people.

The memories of those who perished in the Warsaw Uprising cry out across the decades, and few are clearer than the memories of those who died to build and defend the Jerusalem Avenue crossing. Those heroes remind us that the West was saved with the blood of patriots; that each generation must rise up and play their part in its defense— and that every foot of ground, and every last inch of civilization, is worth defending with your life.

Our own fight for the West does not begin on the battlefield—it begins with our minds, our wills, and our souls. Today, the ties that unite our civilization are no less vital, and demand no less defense, than that bare shred of land on which the hope of Poland once totally rested. Our freedom, our civilization, and our survival depend on these bonds of history, culture, and memory.

And today as ever, Poland is in our heart, and its people are in that fight. Just as Poland could not be broken, I declare today for the world to hear that the West will never, ever be broken. Our values will prevail. Our people will thrive. And our civilization will triumph.

So, together, let us all fight like the Poles—for family, for freedom, for country, and for God.

Thank you. God Bless You. God bless the Polish people. God bless our allies. And God bless the United States of America.

Thank you. God bless you. Thank you very much.

Remarks by President Trump to the 72nd Session of the United Nations General Assembly

September 19, 2017
United Nations
New York, New York

Mr. Secretary General, Mr. President, world leaders, and distinguished delegates: Welcome to New York. It is a profound honor to stand here in my home city, as a representative of the American people, to address the people of the world.

As millions of our citizens continue to suffer the effects of the devastating hurricanes that have struck our country, I want to begin by expressing my appreciation to every leader in this room who has offered assistance and aid. The American people are strong and resilient, and they will emerge from these hardships more determined than ever before.

Fortunately, the United States has done very well since Election Day last November 8th. The stock market is at an all-time high—a record. Unemployment is at its lowest level in 16 years, and because of our regulatory and other reforms, we have more people working in the United States today than ever before. Companies are moving back, creating job growth the likes of which our country has not seen in a very long time. And it has just been announced that we will be spending almost $700 billion on our military and defense.

Our military will soon be the strongest it has ever been. For more than 70 years, in times of war and peace, the leaders of nations, movements, and religions have stood before this assembly. Like them, I intend to address some of the very serious threats before us today but also the enormous potential waiting to be unleashed.

We live in a time of extraordinary opportunity. Breakthroughs in science, technology, and medicine are curing illnesses and solving problems that prior generations thought impossible to solve.

But each day also brings news of growing dangers that threaten everything we cherish and value. Terrorists and extremists have gathered strength and spread to every region of the planet. Rogue regimes represented in this body not only support terrorists but threaten other nations and their own people with the most destructive weapons known to humanity.

Authority and authoritarian powers seek to collapse the values, the systems, and alliances that prevented conflict and tilted the world toward freedom since World War II.

International criminal networks traffic drugs, weapons, people; force dislocation and mass migration; threaten our borders; and new forms of aggression exploit technology to menace our citizens.

To put it simply, we meet at a time of both immense promise and great peril. It is entirely up to us whether we lift the world to new heights, or let it fall into a valley of disrepair.

We have it in our power, should we so choose, to lift millions from poverty, to help our citizens realize their dreams, and to ensure that new generations of children are raised free from violence, hatred, and fear.

This institution was founded in the aftermath of two world wars to help shape this better future. It was based on the vision that diverse nations could cooperate to protect their sovereignty, preserve their security, and promote their prosperity.

It was in the same period, exactly 70 years ago, that the United States developed the Marshall Plan to help restore Europe. Those three beautiful pillars—they're pillars of peace, sovereignty, security, and prosperity.

The Marshall Plan was built on the noble idea that the whole world is safer when nations are strong, independent, and free. As President Truman said in his message to Congress at that time, "Our support of European recovery is in full accord with our support of the United Nations. The success of the United Nations depends upon the independent strength of its members."

To overcome the perils of the present and to achieve the promise of the future, we must begin with the wisdom of the past. Our success depends on a coalition of strong and independent nations that embrace their sovereignty to promote security, prosperity, and peace for themselves and for the world.

We do not expect diverse countries to share the same cultures, traditions, or even systems of government. But we do expect all nations to uphold these two core sovereign duties: to respect the interests of their own people and the rights of every other sovereign nation. This is the beautiful vision of this institution, and this is foundation for cooperation and success.

Strong, sovereign nations let diverse countries with different values, different cultures, and different dreams not just coexist, but work side by side on the basis of mutual respect.

Strong, sovereign nations let their people take ownership of the future and control their own destiny. And strong, sovereign nations allow individuals to flourish in the fullness of the life intended by God.

In America, we do not seek to impose our way of life on anyone, but rather to let it shine as an example for everyone to watch. This week gives our country a special reason to take pride in that example. We are celebrating the 230th anniversary of our beloved Constitution—the oldest constitution still in use in the world today.

This timeless document has been the foundation of peace, prosperity, and freedom for the Americans and for countless millions around the globe whose own countries have found inspiration in its respect for human nature, human dignity, and the rule of law.

The greatest in the United States Constitution is its first three beautiful words. They are: "We the people."

Generations of Americans have sacrificed to maintain the promise of those words, the promise of our country, and of our great history. In America, the people govern, the people rule, and the people are sovereign. I was elected not to take power, but to give power to the American people, where it belongs.

In foreign affairs, we are renewing this founding principle of sovereignty. Our government's first duty is to its people, to our citizens—to serve their needs, to ensure their safety, to preserve their rights, and to defend their values.

As President of the United States, I will always put America first, just like you, as the leaders of your countries will always, and should always, put your countries first.

All responsible leaders have an obligation to serve their own citizens, and the nation-state remains the best vehicle for elevating the human condition.

But making a better life for our people also requires us to work together in close harmony and unity to create a more safe and peaceful future for all people.

The United States will forever be a great friend to the world, and especially to its allies. But we can no longer be taken advantage of, or enter into a one-sided deal where the United States gets nothing in return. As long as I hold this office, I will defend America's interests above all else.

But in fulfilling our obligations to our own nations, we also realize that it's in everyone's interest to seek a future where all nations can be sovereign, prosperous, and secure.

America does more than speak for the values expressed in the United Nations Charter. Our citizens have paid the ultimate price to defend our freedom and the freedom of many nations represented in this great hall. America's devotion is measured on the battlefields where our young men and women have fought and sacrificed alongside of our allies, from the beaches of Europe to the deserts of the Middle East to the jungles of Asia.

It is an eternal credit to the American character that even after we and our allies emerged victorious from the bloodiest war in history, we did not seek territorial expansion, or attempt to oppose and impose our way of life on others. Instead, we helped build institutions such as this one to defend the sovereignty, security, and prosperity for all.

For the diverse nations of the world, this is our hope. We want harmony and friendship, not conflict and strife. We are guided by outcomes, not ideology. We have a policy of principled realism, rooted in shared goals, interests, and values.

That realism forces us to confront a question facing every leader and nation in this room. It is a question we cannot escape or avoid. We will slide down the path of complacency, numb to the challenges, threats, and even wars that we face. Or do we have enough strength and pride to confront those dangers today, so that our citizens can enjoy peace and prosperity tomorrow?

If we desire to lift up our citizens, if we aspire to the approval of history, then we must fulfill our sovereign duties to the people we faithfully represent. We must protect our nations, their interests, and their futures. We must reject threats to sovereignty, from the Ukraine to the South China Sea. We must uphold respect for law, respect for borders, and respect for culture, and the peaceful engagement these allow. And just as the founders of this body intended, we must work together and confront together those who threaten us with chaos, turmoil, and terror.

The scourge of our planet today is a small group of rogue regimes that violate every principle on which the United Nations is based. They respect neither their own citizens nor the sovereign rights of their countries.

If the righteous many do not confront the wicked few, then evil will triumph. When decent people and nations become bystanders to history, the forces of destruction only gather power and strength.

No one has shown more contempt for other nations and for the well-being of their own people than the depraved regime in North Korea. It is responsible for the starvation deaths of millions of North Koreans, and for the imprisonment, torture, killing, and oppression of countless more.

We were all witness to the regime's deadly abuse when an innocent American college student, Otto Warmbier, was returned to America only to die a few days later. We saw it in the assassination of the dictator's brother using banned nerve agents in an international airport. We know it kidnapped a sweet 13-year-old Japanese girl from a beach in her own country to enslave her as a language tutor for North Korea's spies.

If this is not twisted enough, now North Korea's reckless pursuit of nuclear weapons and ballistic missiles threatens the entire world with unthinkable loss of human life.

It is an outrage that some nations would not only trade with such a regime, but would arm, supply, and financially support a country that imperils the world with nuclear conflict. No nation on earth has an interest in seeing this band of criminals arm itself with nuclear weapons and missiles.

The United States has great strength and patience, but if it is forced to defend itself or its allies, we will have no choice but to totally destroy North Korea. Rocket Man is on a suicide mission for himself and for his regime. The United States is ready, willing and able, but hopefully this will not be necessary. That's what the United Nations is all about; that's what the United Nations is for. Let's see how they do.

It is time for North Korea to realize that the denuclearization is its only acceptable future. The United Nations Security Council recently held two unanimous 15–0 votes adopting hard-hitting resolutions against North Korea, and I want to thank China and Russia for joining the vote to impose sanctions, along with all of the other members of the Security Council. Thank you to all involved.

But we must do much more. It is time for all nations to work together to isolate the Kim regime until it ceases its hostile behavior.

We face this decision not only in North Korea. It is far past time for the nations of the world to confront another reckless regime—one that speaks openly of mass murder, vowing death to America, destruction to Israel, and ruin for many leaders and nations in this room.

The Iranian government masks a corrupt dictatorship behind the false guise of a democracy. It has turned a wealthy country with a rich history and culture into an economically depleted rogue state whose chief exports are violence, bloodshed, and chaos. The longest-suffering victims of Iran's leaders are, in fact, its own people.

Rather than use its resources to improve Iranian lives, its oil profits go to fund Hezbollah and other terrorists that kill innocent Muslims and attack their peaceful Arab and Israeli neighbors. This wealth, which rightly belongs to Iran's people, also goes to shore up Bashar al-Assad's dictatorship, fuel Yemen's civil war, and undermine peace throughout the entire Middle East.

We cannot let a murderous regime continue these destabilizing activities while building dangerous missiles, and we cannot abide by an agreement if it provides cover for the eventual construction of a nuclear program. The Iran Deal was one of the worst and most one-sided transactions the United States has ever entered into. Frankly, that deal is an embarrassment to the United States, and I don't think you've heard the last of it—believe me.

It is time for the entire world to join us in demanding that Iran's government end its pursuit of death and destruction. It is time for the regime to free all Americans and citizens of other nations that they have unjustly detained. And above all, Iran's government must stop supporting terrorists, begin serving its own people, and respect the sovereign rights of its neighbors.

The entire world understands that the good people of Iran want change, and, other than the vast military power of the United States, that Iran's people are what their leaders fear the most. This is what causes the regime to restrict Internet access, tear down satellite dishes, shoot unarmed student protesters, and imprison political reformers.

Oppressive regimes cannot endure forever, and the day will come when the Iranian people will face a choice. Will they continue down the path of poverty, bloodshed, and terror? Or will the Iranian people return to the nation's proud roots as a center of civilization, culture, and wealth where their people can be happy and prosperous once again?

The Iranian regime's support for terror is in stark contrast to the recent commitments of many of its neighbors to fight terrorism and halt its financing.

In Saudi Arabia early last year, I was greatly honored to address the leaders of more than 50 Arab and Muslim nations. We agreed that all responsible nations must work together to confront terrorists and the Islamist extremism that inspires them.

We will stop radical Islamic terrorism because we cannot allow it to tear up our nation, and indeed to tear up the entire world.

We must deny the terrorists safe haven, transit, funding, and any form of support for their vile and sinister ideology. We must drive them out of our nations. It is time to expose and hold responsible those countries who support and finance terror groups like al Qaeda, Hezbollah, the Taliban and others that slaughter innocent people.

The United States and our allies are working together throughout the Middle East to crush the loser terrorists and stop the reemergence of safe havens they use to launch attacks on all of our people.

Last month, I announced a new strategy for victory in the fight against this evil in Afghanistan. From now on, our security interests will dictate the length and scope of military operations, not arbitrary benchmarks and timetables set up by politicians.

I have also totally changed the rules of engagement in our fight against the Taliban and other terrorist groups. In Syria and Iraq, we have made big gains toward lasting defeat of ISIS. In fact, our country has achieved more against ISIS in the last eight months than it has in many, many years combined.

We seek the de-escalation of the Syrian conflict, and a political solution that honors the will of the Syrian people. The actions of the criminal regime of Bashar al-Assad, including the use of chemical weapons against his own citizens—even innocent children— shock the conscience of every decent person. No society can be safe if banned chemical weapons are allowed to spread. That is why the United States carried out a missile strike on the airbase that launched the attack.

We appreciate the efforts of United Nations agencies that are providing vital humanitarian assistance in areas liberated from ISIS, and we especially thank Jordan, Turkey and Lebanon for their role in hosting refugees from the Syrian conflict.

The United States is a compassionate nation and has spent billions and billions of dollars in helping to support this effort. We seek an approach to refugee resettlement that is designed to help these horribly treated people, and which enables their eventual return to their home countries, to be part of the rebuilding process.

For the cost of resettling one refugee in the United States, we can assist more than 10 in their home region. Out of the goodness of our hearts, we offer financial assistance to hosting countries in the region, and we support recent agreements of the G20 nations that will seek to host refugees as close to their home countries as possible. This is the safe, responsible, and humanitarian approach.

For decades, the United States has dealt with migration challenges here in the Western Hemisphere. We have learned that, over the long term, uncontrolled migration is deeply unfair to both the sending and the receiving countries.

For the sending countries, it reduces domestic pressure to pursue needed political and economic reform, and drains them of the human capital necessary to motivate and implement those reforms.

For the receiving countries, the substantial costs of uncontrolled migration are borne overwhelmingly by low-income citizens whose concerns are often ignored by both media and government.

I want to salute the work of the United Nations in seeking to address the problems that cause people to flee from their homes. The United Nations and African Union led peacekeeping missions to have invaluable contributions in stabilizing conflicts in Africa. The United States continues to lead the world in humanitarian assistance, including famine prevention and relief in South Sudan, Somalia, and northern Nigeria and Yemen.

We have invested in better health and opportunity all over the world through programs like PEPFAR, which funds AIDS relief; the President's Malaria Initiative; the Global Health Security Agenda; the Global Fund to End Modern Slavery; and the Women Entrepreneurs Finance Initiative, part of our commitment to empowering women all across the globe.

We also thank—we also thank the Secretary General for recognizing that the United Nations must reform if it is to be an effective partner in confronting threats to sovereignty, security, and prosperity. Too often the focus of this organization has not been on results, but on bureaucracy and process.

In some cases, states that seek to subvert this institution's noble aims have hijacked the very systems that are supposed to advance them. For example, it is a massive source of embarrassment to the

United Nations that some governments with egregious human rights records sit on the U.N. Human Rights Council.

The United States is one out of 193 countries in the United Nations, and yet we pay 22 percent of the entire budget and more. In fact, we pay far more than anybody realizes. The United States bears an unfair cost burden, but, to be fair, if it could actually accomplish all of its stated goals, especially the goal of peace, this investment would easily be well worth it.

Major portions of the world are in conflict and some, in fact, are going to hell. But the powerful people in this room, under the guidance and auspices of the United Nations, can solve many of these vicious and complex problems.

The American people hope that one day soon the United Nations can be a much more accountable and effective advocate for human dignity and freedom around the world. In the meantime, we believe that no nation should have to bear a disproportionate share of the burden, militarily or financially. Nations of the world must take a greater role in promoting secure and prosperous societies in their own regions.

That is why in the Western Hemisphere, the United States has stood against the corrupt and destabilizing regime in Cuba and embraced the enduring dream of the Cuban people to live in freedom. My administration recently announced that we will not lift sanctions on the Cuban government until it makes fundamental reforms.

We have also imposed tough, calibrated sanctions on the socialist Maduro regime in Venezuela, which has brought a once thriving nation to the brink of total collapse.

The socialist dictatorship of Nicolas Maduro has inflicted terrible pain and suffering on the good people of that country. This corrupt regime destroyed a prosperous nation by imposing a failed ideology that has produced poverty and misery everywhere it has been tried. To make matters worse, Maduro has defied his own people, stealing power from their elected representatives to preserve his disastrous rule.

The Venezuelan people are starving and their country is collapsing. Their democratic institutions are being destroyed. This situation is completely unacceptable and we cannot stand by and watch.

As a responsible neighbor and friend, we and all others have a goal. That goal is to help them regain their freedom, recover their country, and restore their democracy. I would like to thank leaders in this room for condemning the regime and providing vital support to the Venezuelan people.

The United States has taken important steps to hold the regime accountable. We are prepared to take further action if the government of Venezuela persists on its path to impose authoritarian rule on the Venezuelan people.

We are fortunate to have incredibly strong and healthy trade relationships with many of the Latin American countries gathered here today. Our economic bond forms a critical foundation for advancing peace and prosperity for all of our people and all of our neighbors.

I ask every country represented here today to be prepared to do more to address this very real crisis. We call for the full restoration of democracy and political freedoms in Venezuela.

The problem in Venezuela is not that socialism has been poorly implemented, but that socialism has been faithfully implemented. From the Soviet Union to Cuba to Venezuela, wherever true socialism or communism has been adopted, it has delivered anguish and devastation and failure. Those who preach the tenets of these discredited ideologies only contribute to the continued suffering of the people who live under these cruel systems.

America stands with every person living under a brutal regime. Our respect for sovereignty is also a call for action. All people deserve a government that cares for their safety, their interests, and their well-being, including their prosperity.

In America, we seek stronger ties of business and trade with all nations of good will, but this trade must be fair and it must be reciprocal.

For too long, the American people were told that mammoth multinational trade deals, unaccountable international tribunals, and powerful global bureaucracies were the best way to promote their success. But as those promises flowed, millions of jobs vanished and thousands of factories disappeared. Others gamed the system and broke the rules. And our great middle class, once the bedrock of American prosperity, was forgotten and left behind, but they are forgotten no more and they will never be forgotten again.

While America will pursue cooperation and commerce with other nations, we are renewing our commitment to the first duty of every government: the duty of our citizens. This bond is the source of America's strength and that of every responsible nation represented here today.

If this organization is to have any hope of successfully confronting the challenges before us, it will depend, as President Truman said some 70 years ago, on the "independent strength of its members." If we are to embrace the opportunities of the future and overcome the present dangers together, there can be no substitute for strong, sovereign, and independent nations—nations that are rooted in their histories and invested in their destinies; nations that seek allies to befriend, not enemies to conquer; and most important of all, nations that are home to patriots, to men and women who are willing to sacrifice for their countries, their fellow citizens, and for all that is best in the human spirit.

In remembering the great victory that led to this body's founding, we must never forget that those heroes who fought against evil also fought for the nations that they loved.

Patriotism led the Poles to die to save Poland, the French to fight for a free France, and the Brits to stand strong for Britain.

Today, if we do not invest ourselves, our hearts, and our minds in our nations, if we will not build strong families, safe communities, and healthy societies for ourselves, no one can do it for us.

We cannot wait for someone else, for faraway countries or far-off bureaucrats—we can't do it. We must solve our problems, to build our prosperity, to secure our futures, or we will be vulnerable to decay, domination, and defeat.

The true question for the United Nations today, for people all over the world who hope for better lives for themselves and their children, is a basic one: Are we still patriots? Do we love our nations enough to protect their sovereignty and to take ownership of their futures? Do we revere them enough to defend their interests, preserve their cultures, and ensure a peaceful world for their citizens?

One of the greatest American patriots, John Adams, wrote that the American Revolution was "effected before the war commenced. The Revolution was in the minds and hearts of the people."

That was the moment when America awoke, when we looked around and understood that we were a nation. We realized who we were, what we valued, and what we would give our lives to defend. From its very first moments, the American story is the story of what is possible when people take ownership of their future.

The United States of America has been among the greatest forces for good in the history of the world, and the greatest defenders of sovereignty, security, and prosperity for all.

Now we are calling for a great reawakening of nations, for the revival of their spirits, their pride, their people, and their patriotism.

History is asking us whether we are up to the task. Our answer will be a renewal of will, a rediscovery of resolve, and a rebirth of devotion. We need to defeat the enemies of humanity and unlock the potential of life itself.

Our hope is a word and—world of proud, independent nations that embrace their duties, seek friendship, respect others, and make common cause in the greatest shared interest of all: a future of dignity and peace for the people of this wonderful Earth.

This is the true vision of the United Nations, the ancient wish of every people, and the deepest yearning that lives inside every sacred soul.

So let this be our mission, and let this be our message to the world: We will fight together, sacrifice together, and stand together for peace, for freedom, for justice, for family, for humanity, and for the almighty God who made us all.

Thank you. God bless you. God bless the nations of the world. And God bless the United States of America. Thank you very much.

Remarks by President Trump in State of the Union Address

January 30, 2018
U.S. Capitol
Washington, D.C.

Mr. Speaker, Mr. Vice President, Members of Congress, the First Lady of the United States, and my fellow Americans:

Less than one year has passed since I first stood at this podium, in this majestic chamber, to speak on behalf of the American people and to address their concerns, their hopes, and their dreams. That night, our new administration had already taken very swift action. A new tide of optimism was already sweeping across our land.

Each day since, we have gone forward with a clear vision and a righteous mission—to make America great again for all Americans.

Over the last year, we have made incredible progress and achieved extraordinary success. We have faced challenges we expected, and others we could never have imagined. We have shared in the heights of victory and the pains of hardship. We have endured floods and fires and storms. But through it all, we have seen the beauty of America's soul, and the steel in America's spine.

Each test has forged new American heroes to remind us who we are, and show us what we can be.

We saw the volunteers of the Cajun Navy, racing to the rescue with their fishing boats to save people in the aftermath of a totally devastating hurricane.

We saw strangers shielding strangers from a hail of gunfire on the Las Vegas strip.

We heard tales of Americans like Coast Guard Petty Officer Ashlee Leppert, who is here tonight in the gallery with Melania. Ashlee was aboard one of the first helicopters on the scene in Houston during the Hurricane Harvey. Through 18 hours of wind and rain, Ashlee braved live power lines and deep water to help save more than 40 lives. Ashlee, we all thank you. Thank you very much.

We heard about Americans like firefighter David Dahlberg. He's here with us also. David faced down walls of flame to rescue almost 60 children trapped at a California summer camp threatened by those devastating wildfires.

To everyone still recovering in Texas, Florida, Louisiana, Puerto Rico, and the Virgin Islands—everywhere—we are with you, we love you, and we always will pull through together, always.

Thank you to David and the brave people of California. Thank you very much, David. Great job.

Some trials over the past year touched this chamber very personally. With us tonight is one of the toughest people ever to serve in this House—a guy who took a bullet, almost died, and was back to work three and a half months later: the legend from Louisiana, Congressman Steve Scalise. I think they like you, Steve.

We are incredibly grateful for the heroic efforts of the Capitol Police officers, the Alexandria Police, and the doctors, nurses, and paramedics who saved his life and the lives of many others; some in this room. In the aftermath—yes. Yes.

In the aftermath of that terrible shooting, we came together, not as Republicans or Democrats, but as representatives of the people. But it is not enough to come together only in times of tragedy. Tonight, I call upon all of us to set aside our differences, to seek out common ground, and to summon the unity we need to deliver for the people. This is really the key. These are the people we were elected to serve.

Over the last year, the world has seen what we always knew: that no people on Earth are so fearless, or daring, or determined as Americans. If there is a mountain, we climb it. If there is a frontier, we cross it. If there's a challenge, we tame it. If there's an opportunity, we seize it.

So let's begin tonight by recognizing that the state of our Union is strong because our people are strong. And together, we are building a safe, strong, and proud America.

Since the election, we have created 2.4 million new jobs, including—including 200,000 new jobs in manufacturing alone. Tremendous numbers. After years and years of wage stagnation, we are finally seeing rising wages.

Unemployment claims have hit a 45-year low. It's something I'm very proud of. African American unemployment stands at the lowest rate ever recorded. And Hispanic American unemployment has also reached the lowest levels in history.

Small-business confidence is at an all-time high. The stock market has smashed one record after another, gaining $8 trillion, and more, in value in just this short period of time. The great news—the great news for Americans' 401(k), retirement, pension, and college savings accounts have gone through the roof.

And just as I promised the American people from this podium 11 months ago, we enacted the biggest tax cuts and reforms in American history.

Our massive tax cuts provide tremendous relief for the middle class and small business. To lower tax rates for hardworking Americans, we nearly doubled the standard deduction for everyone. Now, the first $24,000 earned by a married couple is completely tax-free. We also doubled the child tax credit. A typical family of four making $75,000 will see their tax bill reduced by $2,000, slashing their tax bill in half.

In April, this will be the last time you will ever file under the old and very broken system, and millions of Americans will have more take-home pay starting next month—a lot more.

We eliminated an especially cruel tax that fell mostly on Americans making less than $50,000 a year, forcing them to pay tremendous penalties simply because they couldn't afford government-ordered health plans. We repealed the core of the disastrous Obamacare. The individual mandate is now gone. Thank heaven.

We slashed the business tax rate from 35 percent all the way down to 21 percent, so American companies can compete and win against anyone else anywhere in the world. These changes alone are estimated to increase average family income by more than $4,000. A lot of money.

Small businesses have also received a massive tax cut, and can now deduct 20 percent of their business income.

Here tonight are Steve Staub and Sandy Keplinger of Staub Manufacturing, a small, beautiful business in Ohio. They've just finished the best year in their 20-year history. Because of tax reform, they are handing out raises, hiring an additional 14 people, and expanding into the building next door. Good feeling.

One of Staub's employees, Corey Adams, is also with us tonight. Corey is an all-American worker. He supported himself through high school, lost his job during the 2008 recession, and was later hired by Staub, where he trained to become a welder. Like many hardworking Americans, Corey plans to invest his tax cut raise into his new home and his two daughters' education. Corey, please stand. And he's a great welder. I was told that by the man that owns that company that's doing so well. So congratulations, Corey.

Since we passed tax cuts, roughly 3 million workers have already gotten tax cut bonuses—many of them thousands and thousands of dollars per worker. And it's getting more every month, every week. Apple has just announced it plans to invest a total of $350 billion in America, and hire another 20,000 workers. And just a little while ago, ExxonMobil announced a $50 billion investment in the United States, just a little while ago.

This, in fact, is our new American moment. There has never been a better time to start living the American Dream.

So to every citizen watching at home tonight, no matter where you've been, or where you've come from, this is your time. If you work hard, if you believe in yourself, if you believe in America, then you can dream anything, you can be anything, and together, we can achieve absolutely anything.

Tonight, I want to talk about what kind of future we are going to have, and what kind of a nation we are going to be. All of us, together, as one team, one people, and one American family can do anything.

We all share the same home, the same heart, the same destiny, and the same great American flag.

Together, we are rediscovering the American way. In America, we know that faith and family, not government and bureaucracy, are the center of American life. The motto is, "In God We Trust."

And we celebrate our police, our military, and our amazing veterans as heroes who deserve our total and unwavering support.

Here tonight is Preston Sharp, a 12-year-old boy from Redding, California, who noticed that veterans' graves were not marked with flags on Veterans Day. He decided all by himself to change that, and started a movement that has now placed 40,000 flags at the graves of our great heroes. Preston, a job well done.

Young patriots, like Preston, teach all of us about our civic duty as Americans. And I met Preston a little while ago, and he is something very special—that I can tell you. Great future. Thank you very much for all you've done, Preston. Thank you very much.

Preston's reverence for those who have served our nation reminds us of why we salute our flag, why we put our hands on our hearts for the Pledge of Allegiance, and why we proudly stand for the National Anthem.

Americans love their country, and they deserve a government that shows them the same love and loyalty in return. For the last year, we have sought to restore the bonds of trust between our citizens and their government.

Working with the Senate, we are appointing judges who will interpret the Constitution as written, including a great new Supreme Court justice, and more circuit court judges than any new administration in the history of our country.

We are totally defending our Second Amendment, and have taken historic actions to protect religious liberty.

And we are serving our brave veterans, including giving our veterans choice in their healthcare decisions. Last year, Congress also passed, and I signed, the landmark VA Accountability Act. Since its passage, my administration has already removed more than 1,500 VA employees who failed to give our veterans the care they deserve. And we are hiring talented people who love our vets as much as we do.

And I will not stop until our veterans are properly taken care of, which has been my promise to them from the very beginning of this great journey.

All Americans deserve accountability and respect, and that's what we are giving to our wonderful heroes, our veterans. Thank you.

So, tonight, I call on Congress to empower every Cabinet Secretary with the authority to reward good workers and to remove federal employees who undermine the public trust or fail the American people.

In our drive to make Washington accountable, we have eliminated more regulations in our first year than any administration in the history of our country.

We have ended the war on American energy, and we have ended the war on beautiful clean coal. We are now very proudly an exporter of energy to the world.

In Detroit, I halted government mandates that crippled America's great, beautiful autoworkers so that we can get Motor City revving its engines again. And that's what's happening. Many car companies are now building and expanding plants in the United States—something we haven't seen for decades. Chrysler is moving a major plant from Mexico to Michigan. Toyota and Mazda are opening up a plant in Alabama—a big one. And we haven't seen this in a long time. It's all coming back.

Very soon, auto plants and other plants will be opening up all over our country. This is all news Americans are totally unaccustomed to hearing. For many years, companies and jobs were only leaving us. But now they are roaring back. They're coming back. They want to be where the action is. They want to be in the United States of America. That's where they want to be.

Exciting progress is happening every single day. To speed access to breakthrough cures and affordable generic drugs, last year the FDA approved more new and generic drugs and medical devices than ever before in our country's history.

We also believe that patients with terminal conditions, and terminal illness, should have access to experimental treatment immediately that could potentially save their lives.

People who are terminally ill should not have to go from country to country to seek a cure. I want to give them a chance right here at home. It's time for Congress to give these wonderful, incredible Americans the right to try.

One of my greatest priorities is to reduce the price of prescription drugs. In many other countries, these drugs cost far less than what we pay in the United States. And it's very, very unfair. That is why I have directed my administration to make fixing the injustice of high drug prices one of my top priorities for the year. And prices will come down substantially. Watch.

America has also finally turned the page on decades of unfair trade deals that sacrificed our prosperity and shipped away our companies, our jobs, and our wealth. Our nation has lost its wealth, but we're getting it back so fast. The era of economic surrender is totally over. From now on, we expect trading relationships to be fair and, very importantly, reciprocal.

We will work to fix bad trade deals and negotiate new ones. And they'll be good ones, but they'll be fair. And we will protect American workers and American intellectual property through strong enforcement of our trade rules.

As we rebuild our industries, it is also time to rebuild our crumbling infrastructure.

America is a nation of builders. We built the Empire State Building in just one year. Isn't it a disgrace that it can now take 10 years just to get a minor permit approved for the building of a simple road? I am asking both parties to come together to give us safe, fast, reliable, and modern infrastructure that our economy needs and our people deserve.

Tonight, I'm calling on Congress to produce a bill that generates at least $1.5 trillion for the new infrastructure investment that our country so desperately needs. Every federal dollar should be leveraged by partnering with state and local governments and, where appropriate, tapping into private sector investment to permanently fix the infrastructure deficit. And we can do it.

Any bill must also streamline the permitting and approval process, getting it down to no more than two years, and perhaps even one. Together, we can reclaim our great building heritage.

We will build gleaming new roads, bridges, highways, railways, and waterways all across our land. And we will do it with American heart, and American hands, and American grit.

We want every American to know the dignity of a hard day's work. We want every child to be safe in their home at night. And we want every citizen to be proud of this land that we all love so much. We can lift our citizens from welfare to work, from dependence to independence, and from poverty to prosperity.

As tax cuts create new jobs, let's invest in workforce development and let's invest in job training, which we need so badly. Let's open great vocational schools so our future workers can learn a craft and realize their full potential. And let's support working families by supporting paid family leave.

As America regains its strength, opportunity must be extended to all citizens. That is why this year we will embark on reforming our prisons to help former inmates who have served their time get a second chance at life.

Struggling communities, especially immigrant communities, will also be helped by immigration policies that focus on the best interests of American workers and American families.

For decades, open borders have allowed drugs and gangs to pour into our most vulnerable communities. They've allowed millions of low-wage workers to compete for jobs and wages against the poorest Americans. Most tragically, they have caused the loss of many innocent lives.

Here tonight are two fathers and two mothers: Evelyn Rodriguez, Freddy Cuevas, Elizabeth Alvarado, and Robert Mickens. Their two teenage daughters—Kayla Cuevas and Nisa Mickens—were close friends on Long Island. But in September 2016, on the eve of Nisa's 16th Birthday—such a happy time it should have been—neither of them came home. These two precious girls were brutally murdered while walking together in their hometown.

Six members of the savage MS-13 gang have been charged with Kayla and Nisa's murders. Many of these gang members took advantage of glaring loopholes in our laws to enter the country as illegal, unaccompanied alien minors, and wound up in Kayla and Nisa's high school.

Evelyn, Elizabeth, Freddy, and Robert: Tonight, everyone in this chamber is praying for you. Everyone in America is grieving for you. Please stand. Thank you very much. I want you to know that 320 million hearts are right now breaking for you. We love you. Thank you.

While we cannot imagine the depths of that kind of sorrow, we can make sure that other families never have to endure this kind of pain.

Tonight, I am calling on Congress to finally close the deadly loopholes that have allowed MS-13, and other criminal gangs, to break into our country. We have proposed new legislation that will fix our immigration laws and support our ICE and Border Patrol agents— these are great people; these are great, great people—that work so hard in the midst of such danger so that this can never happen again.

The United States is a compassionate nation. We are proud that we do more than any other country anywhere in the world to help the needy, the struggling, and the underprivileged all over the world. But as President of the United States, my highest loyalty, my greatest compassion, my constant concern is for America's children, America's struggling workers, and America's forgotten communities. I want our youth to grow up to achieve great things. I want our poor to have their chance to rise.

So, tonight, I am extending an open hand to work with members of both parties, Democrats and Republicans, to protect our citizens of every background, color, religion, and creed. My duty, and the sacred duty of every elected official in this chamber, is to defend Americans, to protect their safety, their families, their communities, and their right to the American Dream. Because Americans are dreamers too.

Here tonight is one leader in the effort to defend our country, Homeland Security Investigations Special Agent Celestino Martinez. He goes by "DJ" and "CJ." He said, "Call me either one." So we'll call you "CJ." Served 15 years in the Air Force before becoming an ICE agent and spending the last 15 years fighting gang violence and getting dangerous criminals off of our streets. Tough job.

At one point, MS-13 leaders ordered CJ's murder. And they wanted it to happen quickly. But he did not cave to threats or to fear.

Last May, he commanded an operation to track down gang members on Long Island. His team has arrested nearly 400, including more than 220 MS-13 gang members.

And I have to tell you, what the Border Patrol and ICE have done—we have sent thousands and thousands and thousands of MS-13 horrible people out of this country or into our prisons.

So I just want to congratulate you, CJ. You're a brave guy. Thank you very much.

And I asked CJ, "What's the secret?" He said, "We're just tougher than they are." And I like that answer. Now let's get Congress to send you—and all of the people in this great chamber have to do it; we have no choice. CJ, we're going to send you reinforcements, and we're going to send them to you quickly. It's what you need.

Over the next few weeks, the House and Senate will be voting on an immigration reform package. In recent months, my administration has met extensively with both Democrats and Republicans to craft a bipartisan approach to immigration reform. Based on these discussions, we presented Congress with a detailed proposal that should be supported by both parties as a fair compromise, one where nobody gets everything they want, but where our country gets the critical reforms it needs and must have.

Here are the four pillars of our plan: The first pillar of our framework generously offers a path to citizenship for 1.8 million illegal immigrants who were brought here by their parents at a young age. That covers almost three times more people than the previous administration covered. Under our plan, those who meet education and work requirements, and show good moral character, will be able to become full citizens of the United States over a 12-year period.

The second pillar fully secures the border. That means building a great wall on the southern border, and it means hiring more heroes, like CJ, to keep our communities safe. Crucially, our plan closes the terrible loopholes exploited by criminals and terrorists to enter our country, and it finally ends the horrible and dangerous practice of catch and release.

The third pillar ends the visa lottery, a program that randomly hands out green cards without any regard for skill, merit, or the safety of American people. It's time to begin moving towards a merit-based immigration system, one that admits people who are skilled, who want to work, who will contribute to our society, and who will love and respect our country.

The fourth and final pillar protects the nuclear family by ending chain migration. Under the current broken system, a single immigrant can bring in virtually unlimited numbers of distant relatives. Under our plan, we focus on the immediate family by limiting sponsorships to spouses and minor children. This vital reform is necessary, not just for our economy, but for our security and for the future of America.

In recent weeks, two terrorist attacks in New York were made possible by the visa lottery and chain migration. In the age of terrorism, these programs present risks we can just no longer afford.

It's time to reform these outdated immigration rules, and finally bring our immigration system into the 21st century.

These four pillars represent a down-the-middle compromise, and one that will create a safe, modern, and lawful immigration system.

For over 30 years, Washington has tried and failed to solve this problem. This Congress can be the one that finally makes it happen.

Most importantly, these four pillars will produce legislation that fulfills my ironclad pledge to sign a bill that puts America first. So let's come together, set politics aside, and finally get the job done.

These reforms will also support our response to the terrible crisis of opioid and drug addiction. Never before has it been like it is now. It is terrible. We have to do something about it. In 2016, we lost 64,000 Americans to drug overdoses—174 deaths per day; 7 per hour. We must get much tougher on drug dealers and pushers if we are going to succeed in stopping this scourge.

My administration is committed to fighting the drug epidemic and helping get treatment for those in need, for those who have been so terribly hurt. The struggle will be long and it will be difficult, but as Americans always do—in the end, we will succeed. We will prevail.

As we have seen tonight, the most difficult challenges bring out the best in America. We see a vivid expression of this truth in the story of the Holets family of New Mexico. Ryan Holets is 27 years old, an officer with the Albuquerque Police Department. He's here tonight with his wife Rebecca. Thank you, Ryan.

Last year, Ryan was on duty when he saw a pregnant, homeless woman preparing to inject heroin. When Ryan told her she was going to harm her unborn child, she began to weep. She told him she didn't know where to turn, but badly wanted a safe home for her baby.

In that moment, Ryan said he felt God speak to him: "You will do it, because you can." He heard those words. He took out a picture of his wife and their four kids. Then, he went home to tell his wife

Rebecca. In an instant, she agreed to adopt. The Holets named their new daughter Hope. Ryan and Rebecca, you embody the goodness of our nation. Thank you. Thank you, Ryan and Rebecca.

As we rebuild America's strength and confidence at home, we are also restoring our strength and standing abroad.

Around the world, we face rogue regimes, terrorist groups, and rivals like China and Russia that challenge our interests, our economy, and our values. In confronting these horrible dangers, we know that weakness is the surest path to conflict, and unmatched power is the surest means to our true and great defense.

For this reason, I am asking Congress to end the dangerous defense sequester and fully fund our great military.

As part of our defense, we must modernize and rebuild our nuclear arsenal, hopefully never having to use it, but making it so strong and so powerful that it will deter any acts of aggression by any other nation or anyone else.

Perhaps someday in the future, there will be a magical moment when the countries of the world will get together to eliminate their nuclear weapons. Unfortunately, we are not there yet, sadly.

Last year, I also pledged that we would work with our allies to extinguish ISIS from the face of the Earth. One year later, I am proud to report that the coalition to defeat ISIS has liberated very close to 100 percent of the territory just recently held by these killers in Iraq and in Syria and in other locations, as well. But there is much more work to be done. We will continue our fight until ISIS is defeated.

Army Staff Sergeant Justin Peck is here tonight. Near Raqqa, last November, Justin and his comrade, Chief Petty Officer Kenton Stacy, were on a mission to clear buildings that ISIS had rigged with explosive so that civilians could return to that city hopefully soon, and hopefully safely.

Clearing the second floor of a vital hospital, Kenton Stacy was severely wounded by an explosion. Immediately, Justin bounded into the booby-trapped and unbelievably dangerous and unsafe building, and found Kenton, but in very, very bad shape. He applied pressure to the wound and inserted a tube to reopen an airway. He then performed CPR for 20 straight minutes during the ground transport, and maintained artificial respiration through two and a half hours and through emergency surgery.

Kenton Stacy would have died if it were not for Justin's selfless love for his fellow warrior. Tonight, Kenton is recovering in Texas.

Raqqa is liberated. And Justin is wearing his new Bronze Star, with a "V" for "valor." Staff Sergeant Peck, all of America salutes you.

Terrorists who do things like place bombs in civilian hospitals are evil. When possible, we have no choice but to annihilate them. When necessary, we must be able to detain and question them. But we must be clear: Terrorists are not merely criminals. They are unlawful enemy combatants. And when captured overseas, they should be treated like the terrorists they are.

In the past, we have foolishly released hundreds and hundreds of dangerous terrorists, only to meet them again on the battlefield—including the ISIS leader, al-Baghdadi, who we captured, who we had, who we released.

So today, I'm keeping another promise. I just signed, prior to walking in, an order directing Secretary Mattis, who is doing a great job, thank you—to reexamine our military detention policy and to keep open the detention facilities in Guantanamo Bay.

I am asking Congress to ensure that, in the fight against ISIS and al Qaeda, we continue to have all necessary power to detain terrorists, wherever we chase them down, wherever we find them. And in many cases, for them, it will now be Guantanamo Bay.

At the same time, as of a few months ago, our warriors in Afghanistan have new rules of engagement.

Along with their heroic Afghan partners, our military is no longer undermined by artificial timelines, and we no longer tell our enemies our plans.

Last month, I also took an action endorsed unanimously by the U.S. Senate just months before. I recognized Jerusalem as the capital of Israel.

Shortly afterwards, dozens of countries voted in the United Nations General Assembly against America's sovereign right to make this decision. In 2016, American taxpayers generously sent those same countries more than $20 billion in aid.

That is why, tonight, I am asking Congress to pass legislation to help ensure American foreign-assistance dollars always serve American interests, and only go to friends of America, not enemies of America.

As we strengthen friendships all around the world, we are also restoring clarity about our adversaries.

When the people of Iran rose up against the crimes of their

corrupt dictatorship, I did not stay silent. America stands with the people of Iran in their courageous struggle for freedom.

I am asking Congress to address the fundamental flaws in the terrible Iran nuclear deal.

My administration has also imposed tough sanctions on the communist and socialist dictatorships in Cuba and Venezuela.

But no regime has oppressed its own citizens more totally or brutally than the cruel dictatorship in North Korea. North Korea's reckless pursuit of nuclear missiles could very soon threaten our homeland. We are waging a campaign of maximum pressure to prevent that from ever happening.

Past experience has taught us that complacency and concessions only invite aggression and provocation. I will not repeat the mistakes of past administrations that got us into this very dangerous position.

We need only look at the depraved character of the North Korean regime to understand the nature of the nuclear threat it could pose to America and to our allies.

Otto Warmbier was a hardworking student at the University of Virginia—and a great student he was. On his way to study abroad in Asia, Otto joined a tour to North Korea. At its conclusion, this wonderful young man was arrested and charged with crimes against the state. After a shameful trial, the dictatorship sentenced Otto to 15 years of hard labor, before returning him to America last June, horribly injured and on the verge of death. He passed away just days after his return.

Otto's wonderful parents, Fred and Cindy Warmbier, are here with us tonight, along with Otto's brother and sister, Austin and Greta. Please. Incredible people. You are powerful witnesses to a menace that threatens our world, and your strength truly inspires us all. Thank you very much. Thank you.

Tonight, we pledge to honor Otto's memory with total American resolve. Thank you.

Finally, we are joined by one more witness to the ominous nature of this regime. His name is Mr. Ji Seong-ho.

In 1996, Seong-ho was a starving boy in North Korea. One day, he tried to steal coal from a railroad car to barter for a few scraps of food, which were very hard to get. In the process, he passed out on the train tracks, exhausted from hunger. He woke up as a train ran over his limbs. He then endured multiple amputations without anything to dull the pain or the hurt. His brother and sister gave what little food they had to help him recover and ate dirt themselves, permanently stunting their own growth.

Later, he was tortured by North Korean authorities after returning from a brief visit to China. His tormentors wanted to know if he'd met any Christians. He had—and he resolved, after that, to be free.

Seong-ho traveled thousands of miles on crutches all across China and Southeast Asia to freedom. Most of his family followed. His father was caught trying to escape and was tortured to death.

Today he lives in Seoul, where he rescues other defectors, and broadcasts into North Korea what the regime fears most: the truth.

Today, he has a new leg. But, Seong-ho, I understand you still keep those old crutches as a reminder of how far you've come. Your great sacrifice is an inspiration to us all. Please. Thank you. Seong-ho's story is a testament to the yearning of every human soul to live in freedom.

It was that same yearning for freedom that nearly 250 years ago gave birth to a special place called America. It was a small cluster of colonies caught between a great ocean and a vast wilderness. It was home to an incredible people with a revolutionary idea: that they could rule themselves; that they could chart their own destiny; and that, together, they could light up the entire world.

That is what our country has always been about. That is what Americans have always stood for, always strived for, and always done.

Atop the dome of this Capitol stands the Statue of Freedom. She stands tall and dignified among the monuments to our ancestors who fought, and lived, and died to protect her. Monuments to Washington, and Jefferson, and Lincoln, and King. Memorials to the heroes of Yorktown and Saratoga; to young Americans who shed their blood on the shores of Normandy and the fields beyond; and others, who went down in the waters of the Pacific and the skies all over Asia.

And freedom stands tall over one more monument: this one. This Capitol—this living monument—this is the monument to the American people.

We're a people whose heroes live not only in the past, but all around us, defending hope, pride, and defending the American way.

They work in every trade. They sacrifice to raise a family. They care for our children at home. They defend our flag abroad. And they are strong moms and brave kids. They are firefighters, and police officers, and border agents, medics, and Marines. But above all else, they are Americans. And this Capitol, this city, this nation, belongs entirely to them.

Our task is to respect them, to listen to them, to serve them, to protect them, and to always be worthy of them.

Americans fill the world with art and music. They push the bounds of science and discovery. And they forever remind us of what we should never, ever forget: The people dreamed this country. The people built this country. And it's the people who are making America great again.

As long as we are proud of who we are and what we are fighting for, there is nothing we cannot achieve. As long as we have confidence in our values, faith in our citizens, and trust in our God, we will never fail.

Our families will thrive. Our people will prosper. And our nation will forever be safe and strong and proud and mighty and free.

Thank you. And God bless America. Goodnight.

Endnotes

Chapter One: The Fight for Trump's America

1. https://www.creators.com/read/jackie-gingrich-cushman/07/09/obamas
   -new-foundation-change-in-what-we-believe

Chapter Two: The Comeback of "One Nation"

1. https://www.theguardian.com/education/2004/nov/19/tefl
2. https://www.whitehouse.gov/articles/democrats-lost-way-immigration/
3. https://www.brookings.edu/blog/jobs/2012/05/04/what-immigration
   -means-for-u-s-employment-and-wages/
4. https://founders.archives.gov/documents/Hamilton/01-25-02-0282
5. http://edfa2402resources.yolasite.com/resources/The%252520disuniting
   %252520of%252520America%252520pdf.pdf
6. https://www.hoover.org/research/americas-problem-assimilation
7. https://www.migrationpolicy.org/programs/data-hub/charts/immigrant
   -population-over-time?width=1000&height=850&iframe=true
8. http://www.nbcnews.com/id/24871558/#.WjL1ZkqnGUk
9. http://www.miamiherald.com/news/local/immigration/article34217652.html
10. https://www.migrationpolicy.org/data/state-profiles/state/demographics/FL
11. https://www.thisamericanlife.org/radio-archives/episode/632/our-town
12. http://minnesota.publicradio.org/projects/ongoing/somali_timeline/
13. https://www.reuters.com/article/us-health-minorities-cpr/language-barriers
    -and-fear-of-police-may-prevent-minority-911-calls-idUSKBN0K414U
    20141226
14. https://www.nytimes.com/2017/06/16/us/evergreen-state-protests.html?_r=0
15. https://www.theatlantic.com/politics/archive/2015/09/color-blindness-is
    -counterproductive/405037/
16. http://www.foxnews.com/us/2017/10/31/having-white-nuclear-family
    -promotes-white-supremacy-says-new-york-professor-report-says.html
17. https://www.npr.org/2017/05/31/530843658/illegal-border-crossings-are
    -down-and-so-is-business-for-smugglers
18. https://www.nytimes.com/2017/12/04/us/politics/trump-travel-ban-supreme
    -court.html?_r=0

Chapter Three: The Comeback of "Under God"

1. https://www.whitehouse.gov/briefings-statements/remarks-president
   -trump-national-prayer-breakfast/
2. https://www.whitehouse.gov/presidential-actions/presidential-executive
   -order-promoting-free-speech-religious-liberty/
3. https://firstliberty.org/wp-content/uploads/2017/05/Undeniable-2017.pdf

4. http://press-pubs.uchicago.edu/founders/documents/v1ch3s5.html
5. http://press-pubs.uchicago.edu/founders/documents/amendIXs3.html
6. https://www.whitehouse.gov/briefings-statements/remarks-president
-trump-66th-annual-national-prayer-breakfast/
7. https://www.congress.gov/resources/display/content/The+Federalist
+Papers#TheFederalistPapers-51
8. http://www.nationalreview.com/article/219047/faith-our-fathers-michael
-novak-jana-novak
9. https://www.loc.gov/loc/lcib/9806/danpre.html
10. https://founders.archives.gov/documents/Adams/99-02-02-567
11. http://www.ourrepubliconline.com/Quote/303
12. http://www.foxnews.com/politics/2011/11/04/obama-administration
-opposes-fdr-prayer-at-wwii-memorial.html
13. https://www.washingtonpost.com/opinions/trump-is-wrong-pulpit-freedom
-already-exists/2016/08/05/77706c10-5815-11e6-9aee-8075993d73a2_story
.html?utm_term=.971ac4fe2435
14. https://www.adflegal.org/detailspages/blog-details/allianceedge/2017/10/18/
how-to-fix-the-johnson-amendment

Chapter Four: The Comeback of Sovereignty, Ending the New World Order

1. http://www.presidency.ucsb.edu/ws/index.php?pid=110448
2. http://www.presidency.ucsb.edu/ws/?pid=19253
3. https://www.cnbc.com/2016/09/20/us-companies-are-hoarding-2-and-a
-half-trillion-dollars-in-cash-overseas.html
4. https://www.census.gov/foreign-trade/balance/c0004.html#2016
5. https://www.census.gov/foreign-trade/balance/c0004.html#2016
6. https://www.whitehouse.gov/briefings-statements/the-inaugural-address/
7. https://www.whitehouse.gov/wp-content/uploads/2017/12/NSS-Final-12-18
-2017-0905.pdf
8. https://www.whitehouse.gov/wp-content/uploads/2017/12/NSS-Final-12-18
-2017-0905.pdf
9. http://www.bbc.com/news/business-32498715
10. http://rooseveltinstitute.org/why-tpp-bad-deal-america-and-american-workers/
11. http://rooseveltinstitute.org/why-tpp-bad-deal-america-and-american
-workers/
12. http://rooseveltinstitute.org/why-tpp-bad-deal-america-and-american
-workers/
13. https://www.nbcnews.com/business/economy/why-trump-killed-tpp-why-it
-matters-you-n710781
14. https://www.usnews.com/opinion/blogs/peter-roff/2014/02/18/john-kerry
-absurdly-calls-global-warming-a-weapon-of-mass-destruction
15. https://www.whitehouse.gov/articles/president-trump-announces-u-s
-withdrawal-paris-climate-accord/
16. http://www.gingrichproductions.com/2017/06/trump-and-paris-let-the
-negotiations-begin/

17. https://www.whitehouse.gov/articles/president-trump-announces-u-s
    -withdrawal-paris-climate-accord/
18. https://www.whitehouse.gov/articles/president-trump-announces-u-s
    -withdrawal-paris-climate-accord/
19. http://www.gingrichproductions.com/2017/06/trump-and-paris-let-the
    -negotiations-begin/
20. https://www.whitehouse.gov/articles/president-trump-announces-u-s
    -withdrawal-paris-climate-accord/
21. https://www.whitehouse.gov/articles/president-trump-announces-u-s
    -withdrawal-paris-climate-accord/
22. http://unfccc.int/resource/docs/2015/cop21/eng/l09r01.pdf
23. http://thefederalist.com/2017/06/01/15-top-reactions-trumps-withdrawal
    -paris-climate-deal/
24. https://www.whitehouse.gov/briefings-statements/statement-president-trump
    -paris-climate-accord/
25. https://data.worldbank.org/indicator/NY.GDP.PCAP.CD?locations=US
26. https://data.worldbank.org/indicator/NY.GDP.PCAP.CD?locations
    =US-CA
27. https://www.news.virginia.edu/content/qa-uva-economists-study-identifies
    -naftas-winners-and-losers?utm_source=DailyReport&utm_medium
    =email&utm_campaign=news
28. https://data.bls.gov/pdq/SurveyOutputServlet
29. https://data.bls.gov/pdq/SurveyOutputServlet
30. https://data.bls.gov/pdq/SurveyOutputServlet
31. https://www.news.virginia.edu/content/qa-uva-economists-study-identifies
    -naftas-winners-and-losers?utm_source=DailyReport&utm_medium
    =email&utm_campaign=news
32. https://www.news.virginia.edu/content/qa-uva-economists-study-identifies
    -naftas-winners-and-losers?utm_source=DailyReport&utm_medium
    =email&utm_campaign=news
33. http://www.cnn.com/2016/08/03/politics/us-sends-plane-iran-400-million
    -cash/index.html
34. https://www.washingtontimes.com/news/2018/feb/7/inside-the-ring-obama
    -era-cash-traced-to-iran-back/
35. https://www.wsj.com/articles/busting-illusions-about-iran-1514940007
36. https://www.washingtontimes.com/news/2018/feb/7/inside-the-ring-obama
    -era-cash-traced-to-iran-back/
37. https://www.nytimes.com/2016/05/08/magazine/the-aspiring-novelist-who
    -became-obamas-foreign-policy-guru.html
38. https://www.politico.com/interactives/2017/obama-hezbollah-drug
    -trafficking-investigation/
39. https://www.congress.gov/114/plaws/publ17/PLAW-114publ17.pdf
40. http://www.foxnews.com/opinion/2017/10/15/newt-gingrich-death-to-america
    -why-trumps-iran-policy-is-right.html
41. https://www.nbcnews.com/politics/white-house/haley-displays-missile
    -evidence-iran-violating-nuclear-deal-n829761
42. https://apnews.com/df9effcf83a441528b845c8dfd426629

43. http://www.foxnews.com/politics/2018/01/12/trump-waives-iran-nuclear-sanctions-keeping-deal-alive-for-now.html
44. http://www.bbc.com/news/world-us-canada-42464311
45. http://www.foxnews.com/politics/2018/01/22/why-trumps-promise-to-move-us-embassy-to-jerusalem-is-so-controversial.html
46. https://www.nytimes.com/2017/12/21/world/middleeast/trump-jerusalem-united-nations.html
47. https://www.nytimes.com/2017/12/21/world/middleeast/trump-jerusalem-united-nations.html
48. https://www.nytimes.com/2017/12/21/world/middleeast/trump-jerusalem-united-nations.html
49. http://www.bbc.com/news/world-us-canada-42464311
50. https://www.nytimes.com/2017/12/21/world/middleeast/trump-jerusalem-united-nations.html
51. https://www.theguardian.com/world/2017/dec/26/us-to-make-at-least-285m-cut-to-un-budget-after-vote-on-jerusalem
52. https://www.theguardian.com/world/2017/dec/26/us-to-make-at-least-285m-cut-to-un-budget-after-vote-on-jerusalem
53. https://usun.state.gov/remarks/8243
54. https://www.cnn.com/2017/12/20/politics/nikki-haley-taking-names-on-jerusalem/index.html
55. https://www.whitehouse.gov/wp-content/uploads/2017/12/NSS-Final-12-18-2017-0905.pdf
56. https://www.washingtonpost.com/news/posteverything/wp/2017/11/24/trump-is-right-to-protect-u-s-manufacturers-heres-how-he-could-help-us/?utm_term=.fe47b6fccbdc
57. https://www.nytimes.com/2017/04/08/business/china-trade-solar-panels.html
58. https://d12v9rtnomnebu.cloudfront.net/paychek/ITC_Report_Suniva.pdf
59. https://www.nytimes.com/2014/05/20/us/us-to-charge-chinese-workers-with-cyberspying.html
60. http://time.com/5113472/donald-trump-solar-panel-tariff/
61. http://www.nationalreview.com/node/455731/print
62. https://www.uschamber.com/sites/default/files/final_made_in_china_2025_report_full.pdf

Chapter Five: The Comeback of Free Speech

1. https://www.thefire.org/resources/disinvitation-database/#home/?view_2_sort=field_6|desc&view_2_page=1&view_2_filters=%7B%22match%22%3A%22and%22%2C%22rules%22%3A%5B%7B%22field%22%3A%22field_13%22%2C%22operator%22%3A%22is%22%2C%22value%22%3A%22From%20the%20Left%22%2C%22field_name%22%3A%22From%20the%20Right%20or%20Left%20of%20Speaker%22%7D%5D%7D
2. https://www.dailywire.com/news/20008/uc-berkeley-charges-young-republicans-15000-emily-zanotti#
3. http://abcnews.go.com/US/story?id=90356&page=1

4. https://www.monmouth.edu/polling-institute/reports/MonmouthPoll_US
   _121417/
5. https://www.nytimes.com/2016/09/19/nyregion/bill-de-blasio-new-york
   -explosion.html?action=click&contentCollection=N.Y.%20%2F%20Region
   &module=RelatedCoverage&region=Marginalia&pgtype=article
6. http://www.baltimoresun.com/news/maryland/education/bs-md-parcc
   -scores-20170821-story.html
7. https://www.cato.org/blog/poll-71-americans-say-political-correctness-has
   -silenced-discussions-society-needs-have-58-have
8. http://programs.clearerthinking.org/trump_clinton/trump_clinton
   _analysis.htm
9. https://founders.archives.gov/documents/Franklin/01-01-02-0015
10. https://www.wsj.com/articles/white-informed-civility-is-the-latest-target
    -in-the-campus-wars-1514938758?mg=prod/accounts-wsj
11. https://www.nyu.edu/about/leadership-university-administration/office
    -of-the-president/office-of-the-provost/arts/ulrich-baer.html
12. https://www.nytimes.com/2017/04/24/opinion/what-liberal-snowflakes-get
    -right-about-free-speech.html?_r=0
13. https://www.thefire.org/resources/disinvitation-database/#home/
    viewdisinvitationattemptdetails/58e25f3789023849cc90ef63/
14. https://www.thenation.com/article/anti-fascist-activists-are-fighting-the
    -alt-right-in-the-streets/
15. https://www.nytimes.com/2017/07/14/opinion/sunday/when-is-speech
    -violence.html
16. https://www.psychologytoday.com/blog/happiness-and-the-pursuit
    -leadership/201708/when-is-speech-violence-and-what-s-the-real-harm
17. https://medium.com/@Cernovich/full-james-damore-memo-uncensored
    -memo-with-charts-and-cites-339f3d2d05f
18. http://blog.samaltman.com/
19. https://www.usnews.com/news/education-news/articles/2017-09-26/sessions
    -calls-for-national-recommitment-to-free-speech-on-campuses
20. https://www.usnews.com/news/articles/2017-02-02/berkeley-protest-trump
    -tweet-highlight-academias-free-speech-tightrope

Chapter Six: The Comeback of the American Economy, Part 1—Cutting Red Tape

1. https://cei.org/10KC/Chapter-2
2. https://www.whitehouse.gov/sites/whitehouse.gov/files/documents/The
   %2520Growth%2520Potential%2520of%2520Deregulation_0.pdf
3. http://thehill.com/blogs/pundits-blog/economy-budget/325652-how-hasty
   -regulations-end-up-doing-more-harm-than-good
4. https://cei.org/10kc2017
5. https://www.whitehouse.gov/sites/whitehouse.gov/files/documents/The%25
   20Growth%2520Potential%2520of%2520Deregulation_0.pdf
6. https://www.whitehouse.gov/the-press-office/2017/01/30/presidential
   -executive-order-reducing-regulation-and-controlling
7. https://www.reginfo.gov/public/do/eAgendaMain

8. https://www.heritage.org/jobs-and-labor/report/oshas-ergonomics-rule
-costly-unfunded-mandate-the-states
9. https://www.americanactionforum.org/insight/15550/
10. https://www.wsj.com/articles/the-myth-of-trumps-do-nothing-presidency
-1501072779
11. https://www.americanactionforum.org/research/phase-1-one-two-order
-final-update/
12. http://www.weeklystandard.com/donald-trump-king-of-deregulation/
article/2010141#!
13. https://www.brookings.edu/interactives/tracking-deregulation-in-the
-trump-era/
14. https://www.americanactionforum.org/insight/epas-sue-settle-directive
-step-toward-transparency/
15. http://www.washingtonexaminer.com/labor-department-rescinds-expanded
-joint-employer-rule/article/2625200
16. https://www.entrepreneur.com/franchises/subway/282839
17. http://www.washingtonexaminer.com/fat-paychecks-for-cfpb-officials
-hundreds-paid-more-than-fed-chairman-congressmen-supreme-court
-justices/article/2533189
18. http://www.cleveland.com/open/index.ssf/2014/04/richard_cordrays
_federal_agenc.html
19. https://www.regulations.gov/

Chapter Seven: The Comeback of the American Economy, Part 2—The Tax Cuts and Jobs Act of 2017

1. http://www.foxnews.com/politics/2017/09/27/republicans-unveil-tax-plan
-call-for-doubling-deduction-and-cutting-rates.html
2. https://waysandmeans.house.gov/wp-content/uploads/2017/12/TCJA
_TaxpayerExamples121817.pdf
3. https://waysandmeans.house.gov/numbers-tax-cuts-jobs-act-delivers-tax
-cuts-families-every-congressional-district-2/
4. https://www.sba.gov/sites/default/files/advocacy/SB-FAQ-2016_WEB.pdf
5. https://www.treasury.gov/resource-center/tax-policy/tax-analysis/Documents
/TP-4.pdf
6. http://www.411sbfacts.com/files/Financial%2520Questions.pdf
7. https://taxfoundation.org/territorial-tax-system-oecd-review/
8. https://www.cnbc.com/2017/04/28/companies-are-holding-trillions-in-cash
-overseas.html
9. https://www.washingtonpost.com/news/fact-checker/wp/2017/11/02/senate
-democrats-falsely-claim-gop-tax-plan-will-raise-taxes-for-most-working
-class-families/?utm_term=.d3f21758b4da
10. https://fred.stlouisfed.org/series/MSPUS
11. https://www.cbsnews.com/news/how-the-tax-bill-will-affect-three-american
-families/
12. https://www.atr.org/list
13. http://www.baltimoresun.com/business/money/bs-bz-bge-tax-savings
-20180105-story.html

14. https://www.opensecrets.org/personal-finances/net-worth/Nancy-Pelosi
?cid=N00007360&year=2016
15. http://www.businessinsider.com/poll-gop-tax-law-favorability-approval
-trump-2018-2
16. https://www.realclearpolitics.com/epolls/other/2018_generic_congressional
_vote-6185.html#polls

Chapter Eight: The Comeback of the Constitutional Judiciary

1. http://www.uscourts.gov/judges-judgeships/judicial-vacancies/archive
-judicial-vacancies/2010/01/confirmations/html
2. https://papers.ssrn.com/sol3/papers.cfm?abstract-id=290186
3. http://www.newsweek.com/trump-first-year-big-win-conservative-judges
-787461

Chapter Nine: The Comeback of American Health Care

1. http://www.nejm.org/doi/full/10.1056/NEJMsa1706475

Chapter Ten: Fighting Fake News

1. https://townhall.com/columnists/stephenmoore/2018/01/03/1-year-in-office
-trump-keeps-defying-his-critics-n2429154
2. https://www.politico.com/story/2016/10/donald-trump-wall-street-effect
-markets-230164
3. https://www.nytimes.com/interactive/projects/cp/opinion/election-night
-2016/paul-krugman-the-economic-fallout
4. http://www.businessinsider.com/paul-krugman-on-trump-stocks-market
-puerto-rico-2017-10
5. https://www.cbsnews.com/news/trumps-budget-is-unrealistic-economists-say/
6. http://finance-commerce.com/2017/05/experts-trump-budget-unlikely-to
-boost-growth/
7. https://www.reuters.com/article/us-usa-economy-gdp/u-s-third-quarter
-economic-growth-fastest-in-three-years-idUSKBN1DT1W7
8. https://blogs.wsj.com/economics/2018/01/26/how-hurricanes-helped-and
-hurt-fourth-quarter-growth/
9. https://www.newsbusters.org/blogs/business/julia-seymour/2018/01/09/
all-three-networks-highlight-lower-december-jobs-report
10. https://www.wsj.com/articles/u-s-gained-200-000-jobs-in-january-as-wages
-picked-up-1517578320
11. http://www.cnn.com/2018/01/13/us/wolff-smerconish-cnntv/index.html
12. http://money.cnn.com/2018/01/05/media/president-trump-michael-wolff
/index.html
13. https://www.newsbusters.org/blogs/nb/geoffrey-dickens/2018/01/10/
networks-stuff-shows-over-2-hours-wolff-gossip-book-insults
14. http://www.foxnews.com/entertainment/2017/12/02/abc-news-suspends
-brian-ross-over-serious-error-in-flynn-report.html
15. https://www.nytimes.com/2018/01/10/opinion/trumps-how-democracies
-die.html?mtrref=www.nytimes.com&assetType=opinion&_r=0

16. http://thehill.com/homenews/media/368458-scarborough-slams-entire
    -mainstream-media-for-being-reflexively-anti-trump
17. http://www.journalism.org/2017/10/02/a-comparison-to-early-coverage-of
    -past-administrations/
18. http://news.gallup.com/poll/207794/six-partisan-bias-news-media.aspx
19. https://www.themaven.net/theresurgent/erick-erickson/the-media-s-own
    -incestuousness-is-causing-it-to-break-down-KOI9w01tUEytko4oPrvLmw
    ?full=1

Chapter Eleven: The Rule of Law versus the Rule of Mueller

1. http://www.nationalreview.com/article/454543/mueller-investigation-too
    -many-anti-trump-coincidences
2. https://www.washingtonpost.com/apps/g/page/politics/read-the-charge
    -against-former-national-security-adviser-michael-flynn/2263/?tid=a_inl
3. https://www.washingtonpost.com/apps/g/page/politics/george-papadopoulos
    -charges-and-plea-deal/2253/?hpid=hp_rhp-top-table-main_papadopouloslink
    -1201pm%253Ahomepage%252Fstory
4. http://www.gingrichproductions.com/2017/04/no-immunity-no-testimony/
5. https://www.washingtonpost.com/graphics/2017/national/robert-mueller
    -special-counsel-indictments-timeline/?utm_term=.7fd4d7e21dd9
6. https://www.politico.com/story/2017/06/08/full-text-james-comey-trump
    -russia-testimony-239295
7. http://thehill.com/homenews/campaign/302817-government-workers-shun
    -trump-give-big-money-to-clinton-campaign
8. https://www.judicialwatch.org/press-room/press-releases/judicial-watch
    -new-documents-show-fbi-deputy-director-mccabe-not-recuse-clinton
    -email-scandal-investigation-week-presidential-election/
9. http://www.businessinsider.com/who-is-andrew-weissman-mueller-trump
    -clinton-russia-investigation-fbi-2017-12
10. http://www.foxnews.com/politics/2018/01/29/strzok-page-and-fbi-texting
    -scandal-explained.html
11. https://www.wsj.com/articles/in-fbi-agents-account-insurance-policy-text
    -referred-to-russia-probe-1513624580?mg=prod/accounts-wsj
12. http://dailycaller.com/2018/01/23/in-jaw-dropping-text-peter-strzok
    -expressed-concern-about-joining-mueller-team/
13. https://www.cnn.com/2018/01/21/politics/second-strzok-text-production
    /index.html
14. https://www.realclearpolitics.com/video/2017/12/04/cnn_fbi_agent_strzok
    _changed_comeys_clinton_language_from_grossly_negligent_to_extremely
    _careless.html
15. http://www.foxnews.com/politics/2018/01/22/questions-grow-over-fbis
    -missing-strzok-page-text-messages.html
16. http://docs.house.gov/meetings/IG/IG00/20180118/106796/HMTG-115
    -IG00-20180118-SD002.pdf
17. https://www.nationalreview.com/2018/02/donald-trump-russia-investigation
    -obstruction-justice-department-justice-office-legal-counsel/

Chapter Twelve: Draining the Swamp

1. https://www.alec.org/app/uploads/2017/03/2017-Center-Point_-21st-Century
-Civil-Service_Final.pdf

2. https://www.washingtonpost.com/opinions/the-rise-of-the-fourth-branch
-of-government/2013/05/24/c7faaad0-c2ed-11e2-9fe2-6ee52d0eb7c1_story
.html?utm_term=.578162fb51bb

3. https://www.alec.org/app/uploads/2017/03/2017-Center-Point_-21st-Century
-Civil-Service_Final.pdf

4. https://supreme.justia.com/cases/federal/us/569/11-1545/dissent5.html

5. http://politicalappointeeproject.org/presidential-appointments-and
-managing-the-executive-branch.html

6. https://supreme.justia.com/cases/federal/us/572/12-1182/dissent4.html

7. https://books.google.com/books?id=vKD8i1-8bgAC&pg=PA112&lpg
=PA112&dq=public+now+relies+more+heavily+on+courts+to+ensure
+the+fairness+and+rationality+of+agency+decisions&source=bl&ots
=Bwx8WWBOiM&sig=TBbVSGwxm8cpio9E-u5nUwr_5PI&hl=en&sa
=X&ved=0ahUKE

8. http://avalon.law.yale.edu/18th_century/fed47.asp

9. https://www.washingtonpost.com/news/the-fix/wp/2014/05/21/a-guide-to
-the-va-and-the-scandals-engulfing-it/?utm_term=.f495b2e4a697

10. http://www.nationalreview.com/article/433760/va-still-unreformed

11. https://www.congress.gov/bill/113th-congress/house-bill/3230

12. https://www.washingtonpost.com/news/federal-eye/wp/2015/10/30/more
-than-2500-va-employees-were-on-paid-leave-last-year-the-va-hasnt-tracked
-why/?utm_term=.293a87c3f8c7

13. https://www.usatoday.com/story/news/nation/2015/05/06/ousted-phoenix
-va-chief-lawsuit/70889960/

14. https://www.azcentral.com/story/news/arizona/investigations/2016/01/08
/suspended-va-bosses-return-phoenix-jobs-january-11/78517854/

15. https://www.azcentral.com/story/news/local/arizona-investigations/2016
/06/08/three-more-phoenix-va-officials-fired-after-wait-time-scandal
/85614056/

16. http://dailycaller.com/2016/04/08/va-candy-man-may-keep-his-job-despite
-no-medical-license/

17. https://www.clarionledger.com/story/news/2016/02/13/taxpayers-pay
-millions-to-keep-questionable-va-doctors-on-leave/79659046/

18. http://www.nextgov.com/cio-briefing/2016/09/report-federal-government
-has-near-monopoly-worst-customer-experience/131260/

19. http://www.people-press.org/2015/11/23/beyond-distrust-how-americans
-view-their-government/

20. https://www.congress.gov/bill/115th-congress/senate-bill/1094

21. http://www.govexec.com/management/2017/06/trump-calls-civil-service
-laws-outdated-signing-va-firing-reform/138936/

22. http://www.govexec.com/management/2017/06/trump-calls-civil-service
-laws-outdated-signing-va-firing-reform/138936/

23. http://thefederalist.com/2018/01/31/trumps-biggest-point-last-night-need
-upend-deep-state/

Chapter Thirteen: Let's Trump Addiction

1. https://www.cdc.gov/drugoverdose/data/prescribing.html
2. https://www.pri.org/stories/2017-10-26/why-opioid-crisis-american -problem
3. https://www.archives.gov/research/military/vietnam-war/casualty-statistics
4. https://www.cdc.gov/drugoverdose/maps/rxrate-maps.html
5. http://www.cbc.ca/news/canada/british-columbia/fentanyl-science-potent -deadly-1.3760244
6. https://www.cdc.gov/drugoverdose/opioids/fentanyl.html
7. http://www.timesgazette.com/news/23584/china-pledges-to-cooperate-on -fentanyl-shipments-as-portman-committee-slams-postal-transports
8. http://www.hsgac.senate.gov/download/majority-report-drugs-for-dollars -how-medicaid-has-helped-fuel-the-opioid-epidemic
9. http://www.samhsa.gov/data/
10. http://www.scientificamerican.com/products/its-chemistry-not-character -transforming-the-treatment-of-opioid-addiction/
11. http://www.bmj.com/content/357/bmj.j1550
12. https://www.healthaffairs.org/do/10.1377/hblog20180104.835958/full/
13. https://psmag.com/social-justice/dea-plan-rural-americans-addiction -treatment-access
14. https://www.samhsa.gov/data/sites/default/files/report_3192/ShortReport -3192.pdf
15. https://www.drugabuse.gov/related-topics/trends-statistics/overdose-death -rates
16. http://www.mentalhealthamerica.net/issues/issue-brief-parity
17. Kantor, E. D., Rehm, C. D., Haas, J. S., Chan, A. T., & Giovannucci, E. L. (2015). *Trends in Prescription Drug Use among Adults in the United States from 1999–2012. JAMA*, 314(17), 1818–1831. http://doi.org/10.1001/jama .2015.13766
18. U.S. Department of Health and Human Services, National Institute on Drug Abuse National Institutes. *Prescription Drug Abuse*. Retrieved from https://www.drugabuse.gov/about-nida/legislative-activities/testimony-to -congress/2010/09/prescription-drug-abuse
19. http://www.milliman.com/NQTLDisparityAnalysis/
20. https://addiction.surgeongeneral.gov/surgeon-generals-report.pdf
21. http://www.myajc.com/news/local/proportion-black-people-sent-state -prison-hits-historic-lows/kSVudQ2MbdLJHu4WUWmtxJ/
22. Page 6: http://www.justicepolicy.org/uploads/justicepolicy/documents/04-01 _rep_mdtreatmentorincarceration_ac-dp.pdf
23. The Surgeon General's addiction report issued last month.

Chapter Fourteen: Helping Americans Return to Work

1. https://www.infrastructurereportcard.org/americas-grades
2. http://money.cnn.com/2018/02/11/news/economy/trump-infrastructure -plan-details/index.html

3. https://www.usnews.com/news/articles/2017-06-15/donald-trump-unveils
-apprenticeship-executive-order

4. https://fns-prod.azureedge.net/sites/default/files/pd/29SNAPcurrPP.pdf

5. https://thefga.org/news/new-report-calls-medicaid-work-requirements
-reduce-dependency/

6. http://www.washingtonpost.com/sf/local/2017/03/30/disabled-or-just
-desperate/?utm_term=.982755d1bc05

7. https://fns-prod.azureedge.net/sites/default/files/datastatistics/keydata-august
-2017.pdf

8. https://www.forbes.com/sites/jaredmeyer/2017/06/01/maine-shows-how-to
-make-welfare-work/#5e3c13955ee1

9. https://www.bls.gov/news.release/archives/empsit_03072014.pdf

10. https://www.prisonpolicy.org/reports/money.html

Chapter Fifteen: Reaching Beyond the Stars

1. https://www.wsj.com/articles/america-will-return-to-the-moonand-go
-beyond-1507158341

About the Author

Newt Gingrich is a former Speaker of the House of Representatives and 2012 presidential candidate. He is a Fox News contributor and the author of 36 books, including 15 *New York Times* bestsellers. Through Gingrich Productions, he has also produced and hosted documentary films. Recent films include *The First American* and *Nine Days that Changed the World*.